Teaching Writing in Middle and Secondary Schools

**TULANE UNIVERSITY
TEACHER PREPARATION &
CERTIFICATION PROGRAM**

JIM BLASINGAME
Arizona State University

JOHN H. BUSHMAN
University of Kansas

D1537415

PEARSON

Merrill
Prentice Hall

Upper Saddle River, New Jersey
Columbus, Ohio

Library of Congress Cataloging in Publication Data
Blasingame, Jim.
    Teaching writing in middle and secondary schools / by Jim Blasingame and John H. Bushman.
        p. cm.
    Includes bibliographical references and index.
    ISBN 0-13-098163-X
        1. English language—Composition and exercises—Study and teaching (Middle school) 2.
    English language—Composition and exercises—Study and teaching (Secondary) I.
    Bushman, John H. II. Title.

    LB1631.B57 2005
    808'.042'0712—dc22

                                                                            2003068890

Vice President and Executive Publisher: Jeffery W. Johnston
Senior Editor: Linda Ashe Montgomery
Associate Editor: Ben M. Stephen
Production Editor: Mary M. Irvin
Production Coordination: Jolynn Feller, Carlisle Publishers Services
Design Coordinator: Diane C. Lorenzo
Cover Designer: Jeff Vanik
Cover Image: Getty Images
Production Manager: Pamela D. Bennett
Director of Marketing: Ann Castel Davis
Marketing Manager: Darcy Betts Prybella
Marketing Coordinator: Tyra Poole

This book was set in Galliard by Carlisle Communications, Ltd., and was printed and bound
by R. R. Donnelley & Sons Company. The cover was printed by Coral Graphic Services, Inc.

Pearson Education Ltd.
Pearson Education Singapore Pte. Ltd.
Pearson Education Canada, Ltd.
Pearson Education—Japan

Pearson Education Australia Pty. Limited
Pearson Education North Asia Ltd.
Pearson Educación de Mexico, S.A. de C.V.
Pearson Education Malaysia Pte. Ltd.

10 9 8 7 6 5 4 3 2 1
ISBN: 0-13-098163-X

To Margaret Blasingame (1928–1986) who believed that all children are special, and that all children can learn

Jim Blasingame

To Jean H. Bushman for her continued support in all that I do

John Bushman

Educator Learning Center: An Invaluable Online Resource

Merrill Education and the Association for Supervision and Curriculum Development (ASCD) invite you to take advantage of a new online resource, one that provides access to the top research and proven strategies associated with ASCD and Merrill—the Educator Learning Center. At www.EducatorLearningCenter.com you will find resources that will enhance your students' understanding of course topics and of current educational issues, in addition to being invaluable for further research.

HOW THE EDUCATOR LEARNING CENTER WILL HELP YOUR STUDENTS BECOME BETTER TEACHERS

With the combined resources of Merrill Education and ASCD, you and your students will find a wealth of tools and materials to better prepare them for the classroom.

Research

- More than 600 articles from the ASCD journal *Educational Leadership* discuss everyday issues faced by practicing teachers.
- A direct link on the site to Research Navigator™ gives students access to many of the leading education journals, as well as extensive content detailing the research process.
- Excerpts from Merrill Education texts give your students insights on important topics of instructional methods, diverse populations, assessment, classroom management, technology, and refining classroom practice.

Classroom Practice

- Hundreds of lesson plans and teaching strategies are categorized by content area and age range.
- Case studies and classroom video footage provide virtual field experience for student reflection.
- Computer simulations and other electronic tools keep your students abreast of today's classrooms and current technologies.

LOOK INTO THE VALUE OF EDUCATOR LEARNING CENTER YOURSELF

A four-month subscription to Educator Learning Center is $25 but is FREE when used in conjunction with this text. To obtain free passcodes for your students, simply contact your local Merrill/Prentice Hall sales representative, and your representative will give you a special ISBN to give to your bookstore when ordering your textbooks. To preview the value of this website to you and your students, please go to www.EducatorLearningCenter.com and click on "Demo."

Preface

Our major reason for creating *Teaching Writing in Middle and Secondary Schools* is because we have found that most of the books available on writing instruction are too narrowly focused. Some books contain theory but no practice (or vice versa). Some are classic but not current. Some contain writing workshop strategies but offer nothing concrete on writing assessment. Still others cover one kind of research paper but no other genres, pure poetry or personal writing without teaching and assessing conventions, ESL strategies but nothing else, and so on. Over the years, classroom teachers and our university colleagues have told us that they often have had to compromise when selecting books on writing pedagogy.

Teaching Writing in Middle and Secondary Schools is a comprehensive work that weaves all topics together in an integrated approach; in fact, it might have been better titled *Everything You Always Wanted to Know About Secondary Writing but Were Afraid to Ask,* because that's what we have attempted to accomplish. Our text provides rudimentary foundations of adolescent psychology as well as writing instruction to help you meet state standards. It shares classroom approaches, including stories of real teachers and what they are doing successfully right now in their classrooms, so that you have an opportunity to learn from those who are successful at teaching writing. Finally, it offers multiple examples of what young people are writing right now and provides you concrete examples of writing rubrics and assessed work.

How Is This Book Organized?

Teaching Writing in Middle and Secondary Schools is organized into three parts: Part 1, Instruction; Part 2, Assessment; and Part 3, Planning for Instruction: A Compendium of Instructional Resources.

Part I starts from scratch, including preparing the physical classroom, conducting the first day of class, and establishing an appropriate environment for the rest of the year. It continues with detailed information from theory to practice, including concrete examples about what to do from day to day in the writing classroom.

Part II provides the means for assessing students' writing performance and growth over time, including not only theory and research but also detailed information on what to do, how to do it, and how to document it.

Part III contains specialized information that a given teacher's situation may call for, such as incorporating service learning into the curriculum, proven methods for proactive and effective communication with parents and school administration, and teaching writing with the English as a Second Language student.

Appendix A, Sample Multi-Genre Paper and Rubric, contains a sample multi-genre paper and a proven sample rubric used by successful English teachers for scoring multi-genre papers.

Appendix B, Resources for Creating and Assessing Portfolios, contains a detailed set of forms, used by teachers in the field, for creating and assessing writing portfolios.

Appendix C, Sample High School Papers and Rating Rationales, contains a full set of anonymous high school papers and provides examples of high-, middle-, and low-scoring papers that cover the Six-Trait Model for writing. Detailed explanations for each paper's ratings are included.

Appendix D, Sample Middle School/Junior High School Papers and Rating Rationales, contains a full set of anonymous middle school papers and provide examples of high-, middle- and low-scoring papers that cover the Six-Trait Model for writing. Detailed explanations for each paper's ratings are included.

We carefully arranged the segments of this book for ease of reading and use, no matter what the reader's purpose or experience level. University professors guiding students through their required methods class can work through the book page by page, covering theory, practice, sample lessons, and sample grading examples. Classroom teachers can easily locate and pull out items that they need right now, such as minilessons, sample papers from actual high school and middle students, writing activities, assessment rubrics, and more. Individual chapters, as well as sections within chapters, can easily stand alone but also integrate well with the whole, so the book can be used in whatever order the user deems most effective.

WHAT SPECIAL FEATURES MAKE THIS BOOK AN INVALUABLE RESOURCE?

- *Quick Tips.* Ideas teachers can take right to the classroom are set aside from the regular text.
- *Quotation boxes.* Striking quotations from authors of young adult literature and writing gurus (Robert Cormier, Karen Hesse, and Lois Duncan, for example)
- Anonymous *sample papers from middle and high school students* with rating explanations for use as grading practice by pre-service teachers or anchor papers for veteran teachers
- URLs to link readers to a wealth of Internet resources
- *Rubrics.* Used by teachers in the field and ready to be taken right to the classroom
- *Writing Activities.* In many genres, accompanied by samples that teachers can show their students
- Materials for *complete portfolio design* and use
- *Complete program for implementing the Six-Trait Model for Writing Instruction and Assessment*

ACKNOWLEDGMENTS

Many individuals contributed in some way to the preparation of this book. Our students, both experienced and prospective classroom teachers, have readily shared their ideas and suggestions about unique and interesting teaching strategies. Certainly, as we discussed these ideas with our students, they became a part of our thinking.

Other contributors influenced us in more specific ways. They need to be thanked directly for their contributions to Chapter 3: Micaela Muñoz, Melissa Reid, Mary Rezak, Beth Cramer, and Dr. Carlos Bejarano (Fees Middle School, Tempe, Arizona); Chapter 4: Brian McGee (Garner-Edgerton High School, Gardner, Kansas), Kelly Pagnac (Ganodo High School, Ganado, Arizona), and Kathi Baron (Flagstaff High School, Flagstaff, Arizona); Chapter 6: Keri Austin-Janousek (West Junior High, Lawrence, Kansas), Elizabeth O'Brien (Prairie Village, Kansas), Kenan Metzger (University of Kansas), Jill Adams (University of Kansas), and Mike Trendel (Wellsville High School, Kansas); Chapter 7: Ruth Culham (The Writing Traits Company, Portland, Oregon), Peter Bellamy (Northwest Regional Educational Laboratory, Portland, Oregon) Laura Sivadge, and Gale Beerman (Norwalk School District, Norwalk, Iowa); Part III: Dr. Janice Kelly and Dr. Gay Brack (Arizona State University), Jan Nawoj and Sue Leece (Williams Bay School System, Williams Bay, Wisconsin), and Dr. Joseph Passantino (Bishop Miege High School, Roeland Park, Kansas). We as authors are grateful for your generous and practical support. The unique value of this text is directly linked to your contributions.

No text is successful without valuable input from peer review. We especially thank our text reviewers for their insight, encouragement, and constructive criticism: Harold Nelson, Minot State University; Patricia P. Kelly, Virginia Tech University; Peggy Albers, Georgia State University; Karen Kusiak, Colby College; and Anna Bolling, California State University; Stanislaus.

Finally, we wish to acknowledge you, our readers. We hope you will find this text a useful resource and we welcome your feedback and suggestions for improving this work in future editions.

Jim Blasingame
John H. Bushman

Contents

PART III
Planning for Instruction: A Compendium of Instructional Resources 145

APPENDIX A

APPENDIX B

APPENDIX C

APPENDIX D

INDEX 247

PART I

Instruction

CHAPTER 1

Establishing a Writing Environment

If he the teacher is indeed wise, he does not bid you
enter the house of his wisdom, but rather leads you to
the threshold of your own mind.

Kahlil Gibran (1962)

ESTABLISHING A COMMUNITY OF WRITERS

A positive classroom climate is a must if young adults are to function in a writing program that involves personal risk. Students, who place their thoughts on paper for all to see, need to be in a supportive environment. Writing, like all other important activities, involves risk if we do it well. Teachers ask students to share on an intimate level when writing about what they know best—themselves. For adolescents to share their innermost thoughts and feelings with others involves courage of the highest sort, and if teachers open the thresholds of their own minds to students, students will be motivated to give no less. For students to put their egos and their self-esteem at risk, they must trust their teachers and their peers, and teachers must provide students with an environment that makes this possible.

Establishing a positive classroom climate is the foundation of a good writing program. If teachers want their students actively involved in the learning process, and if they want to use peer evaluation in the writing process, a nurturing classroom climate is an absolute necessity.

Writing Apprehension

Most, if not all, teachers who have students write know that many students seem to "freeze up" when given that task. Two basic reasons for this seem to prevail: previous experience in writing and the lack of a positive classroom climate.

In early research by Daly and Miller (1975a) that explored writing apprehension, an apprehensive writer was described as "an individual who will avoid communication situations or react in some anxious manner if forced into them because he foresees primarily negative consequences from such engagements" (p. 243). Because their findings indicate writing apprehension is a relatively independent trait—that is, it is not linked to other personality traits (1975b, p. 250)—this apprehension seems to be the result of "previous negative experiences in writing." The specific academic effects, according to Daly and Miller, are that students will not turn work in, that they will be absent for in-class writing, and that they will avoid enrolling in classes that require writing. Further, they will not participate in extracurricular activities associated with writing (1975a).

Other research on writing apprehension involves the effect of anxiety on what is written and on teachers' expectations of student performance. Apprehension has been shown to influence quantitatively "the number of words written, the amount of qualification present in the message, and the intensity of the language chosen" (Daly, 1979, p. 38). In addition, the general quality of writing produced by apprehensives is "significantly lower, . . . [and their writing is] less effective in counter attitudinal attempts than that written by low apprehensives" (p. 38). Moreover, apprehension influences teachers' expectations. Boys are generally more apprehensive than girls, and Daly's study shows that teachers tend to favor girls in high school writing classes. Those students seen as most fearful are also "seen as significantly less likely to do well in regard to success in other subjects as well." Daly concludes that the consequences of these expectations on "actual teacher behavior or student learning" are not yet known, but he thinks both areas may be affected (p. 43).

According to Reeves (1997), individuals experiencing writing apprehension manifest their anxiety through specific behaviors and attitudes that are reflected in their written products.

Apprehensive writers exhibit certain *behaviors*.

They tend to select careers which they perceive to require little or no writing.
They tend to avoid courses and majors which require writing on a daily basis.
They write very little out of class.
They lack role models for writing at home, in school, and in the society at large.
They score lower on tests of verbal ability (SAT), reading comprehension, and standardized tests of writing ability used for college placement.
They do not necessarily lack motivation.

Apprehensive writers also exhibit certain *attitudes*.

Their self-concept is often lower, and they may lack self-confidence.
They report low success in prior experiences with school-related writing.
They have received negative teacher responses to prior writing attempts.

They are more apprehensive when writing personal narratives in which they must express personal feelings, beliefs, and experiences.

They exhibit less apprehension when writing argumentative persuasive essays in which they are told not to inject personal feelings and not to use the first person point of view.

Apprehensive writers exhibit *common characteristics* in their written products.

They have more difficulty with invention—getting ideas of what to write.

They produce shorter pieces of writing, i.e., fewer total words per piece.

Their ideas are not as well developed.

Their writing is judged to be lower quality when holistic scoring is employed.

They score lower on scales of syntactic maturity. T-units are shorter, and there is less right branching (placing of participles to the right of the main clause).

They include less information in each clause or T-unit.

They have more difficulty with usage and mechanics.

They use less variety in sentence patterns. (p. 38)

Since apprehension has such far-reaching effects on students and their writing, teachers must provide a setting for writing in which that apprehension can be reduced. What are the characteristics of such a setting? Certainly it must be intellectually stimulating, but it must also be psychologically secure. Teachers should seek a relaxed, informal atmosphere in the writing classroom, and the climate should be open, supportive, and nurturing. The writing class must be a place where teachers and students respect, care about, and trust each other. It must, in short, be a place where mutuality—"a relationship in which partners depend on each other for the development of their respective strengths"—exists (Erikson, 1964, p. 231).

Wachholz and Etheridge speak to the issue of high- and low-apprehensive writers in their *Journal of Developmental Education* (1996, Spring) article. They studied 43 second-semester freshman writers who were administered the Daly and Miller Writing Apprehension Test and were asked to write about what they perceived to be a good writer. In addition, the authors interviewed five high- and five low-apprehensive writers. The study found that low-apprehensive writers reported more positive and successful experiences with categories of influence, whereas high-apprehensive writers reported more failure and negative experiences. High-apprehensive writers believed that the ability to produce good writing is an innate quality rather than a process, and they did not realize that writers sometimes need to accept less-than-perfect papers. It is important to note that high-apprehensive writers seemed to be teacher dependent, to have a sense of isolation regarding their writing self-efficacy beliefs, and to lack involvement and commitment (pp. 16–18).

A study by Pajares (1996, 2001a, 2001b, in press; Pajares and Johnson, 1994) supports the relationship between confidence in one's writing abilities and subsequent writing performance. Students' beliefs about their own composition skills and the pre-performance measure were the only significant predictors. Writing apprehension was negatively correlated with writing self-confidence but was not predictive of writing performance. Another interesting facet of this study indicated that general self-confidence was correlated with writing self-confidence, expected outcomes, apprehension, and performance, but was not predictive.

Certainly the aforementioned studies, as well as the classroom experiences of teachers, suggest that teachers must do everything possible to make the environment for writers as positive as they can. The report from the U. S. Department of Education (1999), which offers trends in academic progress in writing, would seem to support this need as well. The report shows trends in grades 4, 8, and 11 over the period from 1984 through 1994. In most cases, only half of the students in each grade level indicated that the following statements were true more than half the time.

> Writing helps me think more clearly.
> Writing helps me tell others what I think.
> Writing helps tell others how I feel.
> Writing helps me understand my own feelings.
> People who write well have a better chance of getting good jobs.
> People who write well are more influential.
> I like to write.
> I am a good writer.
> People like what I write.
> I write on my own outside of school.
> I don't like to write things that will be graded.
> If I didn't have to write for school, I wouldn't write anything.

Adjusting Students' Attitudes Toward Writing

Laurence E. Musgrove (2001) presents a rather complex view of attitudes toward writing in his eight-page Internet essay (**www.http://english.sxu.edu/mustrove/jacpl. htm**). Musgrove suggests that writers have "heart-felt stories, narratives of success and failure played out in the English classroom" (p. 1). He goes on to say: "Unfortunately, the most common of these stories are filled with fear and despair—students fearing teachers' comments and peer response, students despairing of success or approval. Repeated again and again over time, these narratives of hurt become internalized and shape students' attitudes toward future writing experiences" (p. 1). Musgrove believes that teachers must provide students with a vocabulary of attitude, to "help them use this terminology to recount and revise their writing experiences, and [to] provide them with short narratives, parables, and poems that exemplify specific pre-dispositional attitudes which contribute to or interfere with their chances of success in the writing class" (p. 1).

Musgrove has an interesting point. If teachers of writing are to create a community of writers in the classroom, it seems that student writers must have a positive attitude toward writing. Our past experiences in teaching students tell us that they don't. Perhaps, then, it would be beneficial to help students reflect on their writing histories, to help them see how these past experiences affect their attitudes toward writing. In many classrooms, students write with very little frequency; therefore, they often have a negative attitude about the process of writing. Students often comment, "I can't write," which is consistent with the U.S. Department of Education report (1999) previously cited. This student response is particularly true when teachers return papers with red marks that make the papers look like road maps. The student comments, "See, I told you. I can't write." If this scenario is repeated often enough year after year, students will no doubt bring to the act of writing a very negative attitude.

If students have these values and attitudes about writing, classroom teachers must ask why and then proceed to help these students develop a different attitude toward writing. We offer the following areas of exploration for classroom teachers.

Room Décor

Both teachers and students are responsible for achieving a physical setting that is conducive to writing. The first task of teachers is to create a physical environment that enables the establishment of a positive classroom climate. Many times, what students see as they enter a classroom forms their first impression and expectations of the curriculum and the teacher. Most would agree that the classroom should be a pleasant place for learning. Tchudi and Tchudi (1999) maintain that industrial psychologists have long recognized that the pleasantness (or unpleasantness) of an environment strongly influences people's motivation and productivity. To encourage learning, then, the classroom should be well lighted and a comfortable temperature should be maintained. Both of these conditions may be outside the scope of what the teacher can provide, but they are nonetheless very important. The classroom should be decorated as attractively as possible with plants, posters, and bulletin boards.

One 9th-grade teacher takes photos of her students when they graduate from high school and places these pictures on a bulletin board. Pictures of her students dressed in their caps and gowns make quite an impression in her classroom. It certainly makes the statement "Students are welcome here."

Many schools are built with so few classroom windows that placement of living plants may be problematic. One creative teacher created a window by drawing it on butcher paper and attaching it to the wall. It included the scenery that would be seen by looking out a window. Below the "window," the teacher placed plants that do well without sunlight.

Having writing tools available in the classroom for students creates the atmosphere of a writing community. Quality paper, art supplies, and computers certainly will enable students to sense that they are part of a community of writers.

Furniture and its arrangement also make statements about the classroom climate. Rows of desks that require students to look constantly at the backs of others' heads do not encourage students to get to know each other or to share ideas in any meaningful way. Students must be able to see each other's faces if successful discussions are to take place. Circles, semicircles, grape clusters, and horseshoes create functional designs for small and large group discussions. The objective for the day should determine how the desks are arranged. At times, it may be quite appropriate for desks to be organized in rows, but that determination should be made because the lesson of the day suggests that arrangement. Other furniture also may be appropriate. Small tables allow groups of students to discuss their writing work most effectively in a writing workshop format. Other work stations around the room create an atmosphere of community.

Many teachers find it advantageous to encourage students to work together to create or change the physical environment of the classroom. We have on occasion stated, "Choice leads to ownership, which leads to success." So it is with a room arrangement, or at least the physical components of a room. When students make choices for "their" writing room, they take ownership of that room. They make a commitment to the room and to the process. Allowing students to participate is also a way for them to get to know each other and thereby to participate in establishing a warm, friendly, and useful climate. What the school doesn't or can't provide may be something students can contribute. In one school, students were instrumental in getting an old-fashioned bathtub for the classroom. It became the center for reading and writing experiences.

The Psychological Environment

The second duty of teachers is to create the psychologically secure atmosphere of honesty and trust alluded to earlier, and this involves a host of complex tasks. Primary among them is cultivation of an attitude of

> *The secret of education lies in respecting the pupil.*
>
> *Ralph Waldo Emerson*

openness to new thoughts, feelings, and insights about their own teaching. This attitude centers on knowing about students' needs and addressing them; moreover, teachers must be flexible enough to allow interruptions, which is indicative of their caring, rather than their being slaves to subject matter. In order to achieve this environment, teachers must become reflective practitioners—that is, they must reflect periodically not only upon what they are doing in the classroom but also upon how they are doing it.

The Reflective Practitioner

To reduce writing apprehension in a writing community, student opinions, beliefs, needs, and personalities are extremely important. It seems then that teachers must consider their teaching modes and skills very carefully so that a positive classroom climate is not damaged. Reflective teaching, with its emphasis on learning to reflect and reflecting to learn, offers students an opportunity to become personally involved in their learning. However, by themselves reflective teaching and learning may not create the desired positive classroom climate. However, once that warm climate is present, employing this strategy strengthens and reinforces this climate.

Characteristics of reflective teaching that reinforce the writing environment to which we all should aspire would include a classroom in which student opinion is cherished. Teachers are eager to give students choice of topics and genres about which to write. An attempt is made to encourage ownership—that is, students choose their writing topics and their genres, and much more ownership of that writing results. In such a writing community, teachers and students together develop goals for the class and for individual writing. As a result, students begin to take full responsibility for their classroom behavior—how they act and what they write. The reflective teacher knows that collaboration between the teacher and learner fosters a greater feeling of camaraderie, which supports a positive classroom climate.

Copeland and Grout (2001) suggest that "a person who thinks reflectively is able to link ideas to previous, current, and predicted experiences. In addition, a reflective thinker can assess the self and the situation. Reflective thinkers can monitor their own learning progress by reflecting on how they used to think about or perform a task and comparing that to how they now think or perform" (p. 19). They also say that "teachers must be willing to leave their 'comfort zones,' use their imaginations to create thought-provoking lessons, and be willing to let students be responsible for their own learning" (p. 19). For this to happen, teachers must be "warm, supportive, and encouraging and at the same time maintain their sense of order, discipline, and high expectations" (p. 21).

The teacher's role in the creation of a beneficial classroom climate is indeed complex, but if mutuality is the most prominent feature of a caring, supportive, and trust-filled learning environment, teachers also must attend to the role of students in this partnership. Students must be willing to listen attentively to others, to participate in the process, to risk sharing themselves, to cooperate with their peers and help them to achieve, and to put forth their own best effort. Teachers aid their students in achieving these goals as they go through the writing process together, but the students' ultimate goal is to become independent learners.

Murray (1968) sees this as redefining the role of the teacher. He writes, "When the teacher can stop teaching . . . then he has succeeded" (p. 133). Without a nurturing, supportive atmosphere, however, the sequential writing process will fail. Students will not achieve their independence, nor will they be led to the threshold of their own minds. The supported writing community is the foundation upon which all is built, and it behooves both teacher and student to see that they build not upon the shifting sands of popularity and ease but upon solid rock—upon mutual respect, genuine caring, and unfailing trust.

QUICK TIPS

MAKING IT HAPPEN IN THE CLASSROOM

Using the Yearbook. Check last year's yearbook for names and faces.

Letter to the Teacher. Ask students to write you a letter telling about themselves.

Backpacking. Facilitate an activity so students learn each other's names.

Time Lines. Explore events that happened in the students' lives

Naming a Character. Consider a well-known person whom students admire.

An Autobiography. Have students write an autobiography as a writer.

Yarn and Stuff. Students share facts about themselves represented by colored yarn

Who am I? Students finish a sentence (I am [. . .]) with five different endings.

All-About-Me Portoflios. Find out who your students are, what they know, and what they are able to do.

Making It Happen in the Classroom

Finding specific activities that foster a nurturing climate for writing is another of the teacher's responsibilities. Following are a few activities designed to establish and maintain a desirable classroom climate.

Using the Yearbook

After you have received your roster of names for the coming year, check the previous year's yearbook. This source will give you names, nicknames, and, perhaps, something about each of your students that will help you to get a head start on knowing the students in your classes. The yearbook is a shortcut to associating faces with names.

Letter to the Teacher

Ask students to write a letter to you about themselves. You can learn a great deal about students by reading these letters, including specific information as well as writing skills. This is a very nonthreatening way to learn about their writing skills and may be considered low in apprehension. It also provides information important to have prior to beginning a writing program. You might choose to get a writing sample in a different way, but this activity elicits two types of information simultaneously.

Backpacking

Put your class in a circle. Have students include their names and something that begins with the same initial sound as their first name in an introduction—for example, "I'm John. I'm going on a backpacking trip, and I am going to take some jellybeans." Teresa, the next student in the circle, introduces herself in a similar way: "My name is Teresa, I'm going on a backpacking trip with John, and I'm going to take a tent." The process continues around the circle with each student introducing himself/herself and renaming all the proceding students. Normally, students only use their first names since it may be too much for them to remember surnames also at this time. Last names will come naturally during the course of the semester. Also, students do not have to repeat what students are taking with them. That item is used for association with each person's name. One variation of this activity includes the following: Halfway around the circle, have those students who have given their names change places with each other, so the order of this list of names changes; the emphasis is thereby placed on names and faces rather than on the memory of a sequence.

Time Lines

Have students create a two-part time line of their lives. The first part should include special events or occurrences that have happened thus far in their lives. These events can be of any nature. For example, the students may list an event that had a particular influence on them, goals that they achieved, or something remembered as being particularly fun, exciting, or sad. The events may be explained in writing or represented by a symbol of some type. When possible, a date should accompany the event.

The second part of the time line consists of the students predicting future events or goals that they either want to happen or that they realistically can see occurring at some time. The future may be represented by symbols or descriptions and should be accompanied by a date, if students can predict a specific time. After time lines have been completed, students share in pairs. After sharing, all students go back to the large group. Each student then introduces his or her partner to the large group on the basis of what he or she has learned from the time line explanation. After introductions, display the time lines around the room for a closer examination by the students.

Naming a Character

Have students consider a character, an idea, or a concept in literature, film, or real life that they admire. Have students share these by either contributing around the circle or responding spontaneously. As a second activity, have students share a dislike.

Yarn and Stuff

Have students cut pieces of yarn as long as they want from a skein. Ask students to tell about themselves as they wrap the yarn around their index fingers—one wrap for each item shared.

Who Am I?

Have students write "I am" on a sheet of paper, followed by five items that accurately complete the statement. For example, a ninth-grader wrote the following:

I Am

Talkative
excited about this English class
worried about the game Friday night
afraid of snakes
concerned that I have to write in this class

An Autobiography

Ask students to write about how they see themselves as writers. Be sure to recommend that students include their experiences as writers, how often they write outside of school, how much they have written in past years in school, what they fear about writing, how they have overcome any or all of those fears, what goals they now have as writers, what previously completed writing is most meaningful to them, and what writing genres they prefer.

All-About-Me Portfolios

Ask students to bring in items to place in their portfolios that represent who they are, what they know, and what they are able to do. These items should in some way relate to how they see themselves as learners, as participants in school, or as individuals in the community. Have students choose one or more items from their portfolios to use as they introduce themselves to the class. As an alternative activity, students may display their items on their desks while working with partners who use the items to introduce each other to the class. It is interesting to explore whether or not the interpretation of the items is the same as what the individual who brought them had in mind. This activity can also be used as an introduction to portfolios if they are to be used in the class.

Immersion in Literature

Atwell (1998) believes writers must constantly read and be exposed to a variety of written material, including prose, poetry, fiction, and nonfiction. Young adults and

> *Writing is recycled literature.*
> *Will Hobbs*

children who are given freedom of choice for their own reading and writing will show the teacher that reading and writing are important to them. It would seem important, then, to help inexperienced writers lower their apprehension about writing by immersing them in quality writing found in the age-appropriate literature they are reading. It is apparent that young adults learn to read from writing. At the same time, it is evident that they learn to write from reading. As a result, this integration of reading and writing must be part of our classroom practices. In the past, these curricula components were considered solitary activities, but more recently "a radical shift in our approaches to both subjects has taken place" (Burkland and Peterson, 1986, p. 190). Bromley (1989) states that "both research and theory support the notion that combining instruction in reading and writing in the classroom enhances children's literacy learning" (p. 122). She suggests three major reasons for making the combination work in the classroom: Both skills are developed at the same time; each reinforces the other; and, through reading and writing, language is used for communication.

Reasons abound for teaching writing and reading together. Students find it very difficult to make connections—to feel personal involvement—when writing is done in isolated assignments. Literature provides the needed context in which students can write and learn about writing. The content of the literature, discussion of that content, and discussion of the style of the writer provide ample information to help students in their writing. The literature helps young writers to make connections with—to respond to—the themes of literature. Literature often helps students to make connections with their own personal experiences.

Perhaps the most important reason for this combination of writing and reading is that students see what authors do. They interact with the published writing of the "real" authors. They experience what authors write about. They experience the techniques that authors use. When student writers realize that authors deliberately choose certain words and that they begin sentences and paragraphs differently depending on the effect they wish to produce, students begin to emulate and experiment, trying to find what is best for them, and thus they become better writers.

More than one classroom teacher we know has used literature effectively in a writing class. In one instance, students were having problems getting started with their writing. They brainstormed about topics and what they wanted to say. They did considerable prewriting and free writing to see where they wanted to go. They had early drafts and wanted to make their beginnings more effective. The teacher helped by bringing to class six or seven young adult novels and reading the first two or three paragraphs of each to her students. Some of the novels began in dialogue, some with an incident, and some with description of a person or event. Students were able to see examples of what authors do when they begin a work. The following are a few examples of opening lines:

> *From* The Rag and Bone Shop, *by Robert Cormier (2001)*
>
> "Feeling better?"
> "I guess so. My headache's gone. Is there a connection?
> "Maybe. They say confession's good for the soul. But I don't know if it eliminates headaches" (p. 3).

> *From* Shattering Glass *by Gail Giles (2002)*
>
> "Simon Glass was easy to hate. I never knew exactly why, there was too much to pick from. . . . but we didn't realize it until the day we killed him" (p. 1).

> *From* Jungle Dogs *by Graham Salisbury (1998)*
>
> "Far out on the ocean a small reef of clouds sat still and silent over a black sea, just above where the sun would rise" (p. 1).

We must not lose sight of the reason for using literature in the writing classroom. We certainly want teachers to use literature to help make better writers, but for our purposes here, we suggest literature because we want to help students feel more comfortable in the writing process. Helping students work simultaneously with writing and reading and encouraging them to talk about what the authors are doing and how they are doing it can only help student writers feel more at ease with the process.

This does bring up the question "What literature do we teach?" This question has been cussed and discussed in the hallowed halls of academia for some time. One argument states that we must teach the canon as it is our duty to teach the cultural and historical heritage of our society. The other argument derives from a different point of view: The canon is certainly great literature, but if students are not developmentally ready to read it, why should they be set up for failure? If we believe that the integrated approach for writing and reading is most beneficial for students as they are beginning and even continuing the writing process, then classroom teachers must be very careful what literature is included. We would find it very difficult to set up a writing/reading workshop approach for ninth-graders and have as the major literature assignment *Great Expectations* by Charles Dickens. While that work may be part of the canon and considered great literature, it is not, in our opinion, appropriate for ninth-graders if, indeed, they are going to use it as a model for writing. We know of no one who believes that ninth-graders ought to write as Dickens did.

A number of researchers/theorists have investigated the relationship of reading and writing. A few are presented in the following paragraphs.

McMahan and Day (1983) argue that using imaginative literature, short stories, and poems has several advantages over using essays. The former genres provide an emotional response often not expressed in essays. "Imaginative literature deals with individual human experiences and . . . it can provide an incentive to students to write out of their own experiences" (pp. 111–112).

Sheley (1983) found that literature could be a model of written language as well as a global view of human experience. "Literature enlarges the student's knowledge and understanding of human behavior for it exhibits thoughts and feelings which are often concealed in real life" (p. 123). An interesting result of Sheley's research is that students realized that writing is not a mysterious event that just happens. As students began to see the choices that authors made, they became better writers.

Wilson (1983) found that literature had a positive effect on the writing style of students who speak nonstandard English. Students who were exposed to interesting literature improved their writing skills, something that did not occur after weeks of red correction marks and extensive grammar exercises.

If, then, a connection exists between the literature that is read and the writing that is written, we return to the question raised earlier: "What literature do we model?" If the intent is to reduce apprehension in writing, it would seem appropriate that we not increase apprehension in reading. Therefore, we believe that age-appropriate literature should be central to the writing curriculum. Students must read literature that speaks to them. It is important that teachers use age-appropriate literature that meets the interests and needs of these young people, who are confronting a range of experiences in physical, social, intellectual, and moral development. The classroom itself ought to contain quality literature that addresses writing concerns. The literature should have complexity of plot, fully developed characters, settings that contribute to the other elements of the work, and a theme that addresses the interests of readers. Students should be able to "read" the work with little help from the teacher. With little guidance, students should be able to see how authors have used humor, personification, symbolism, hyperbole, allusion, metaphor, or flashback. Students should study the author's word choice, sentence beginnings, and other writing devices. We are strongly suggesting that the reading/writing connection is very important to the writing program—so important that the literature must be reader friendly to students.

Reading Aloud

Many benefits are had by reading aloud in the classroom, one of which may be connected to developing a community of writers in an environment conducive to writing. Hall and Moats in their book *Straight Talk About Reading* (1999) list six benefits for reading aloud. The child

1. develops background about a variety of topics.
2. builds his or her vocabulary.
3. becomes familiar with rich language patterns.
4. becomes familiar with story structure and the reading process.
5. identifies reading as a pleasurable activity. (p. 53)

Further, the Creating Writers Institute developed by the Northwest Regional Educational Laboratory (NWREL) suggests ten reasons why young people should be read to. They believe student writers

1. hear new words.
2. develop sentence sense and an ear for rhythm.

3. enjoy and compare diverse writing styles.
4. create common connections to ideas (as a class).
5. use reading as a springboard to discussion and writing.
6. gain new knowledge and understanding.
7. hear standard forms of English.
8. learn about a variety of genres of writing.
9. feel things they've never felt before.
10. share a wonderful time—it's fun. (NWREL, 1999, p. 85)

While most of the benefits mentioned are connected in some way to the act of writing, it would seem that the benefits of "sharing a wonderful time because it is fun" and "reading aloud identifies reading as a pleasurable activity" lead teachers to use reading aloud to develop a comfortable atmosphere in which to write. If the classroom is immersed with age-appropriate literature and if some of that literature is read aloud, students cannot help but feel better about the process of writing. We have heard students say "I can do that." Teachers in our graduate writing classes have commented on how much more at ease their students were when working on a multigenre paper after having heard Sharon Draper's *Tears of a Tiger* (1994) read to them. Not only did the students get a sense of the many genres available to them, but the discussion about these genres with their classmates also gave them a sense of "I can do it" about the project.

Reading aloud creates "teachable moments; sparks of interest in learning about where or when or how an event in the story occurred; moments at which a child practically demands to be taught a piece of geography or history or science. These sparks are not the learnings themselves, but they are the necessary beginnings for all learning. They must be cared for and attended to right away, or else they will likely die" (Russell, 1986, p. 2). Exposing students to all genres of reading materials is important because they will get exposure to items they normally might not have read. "Reading a variety of materials helps children grow in knowledge of the world, language and the multi-dimensionality of books (Jett-Simpson, 1984, p. 5). And of course, it fosters writing. The teacher need only stop at a prearranged point in the story so the students can then write their responses to any number of questions. Among the questions students could respond to are what they are thinking of, if they have had a similar experience, what they are picturing in their heads, what feelings they have about the characters, and what questions they have about the story. Response journals, in which students react to the reading by writing, provide another avenue to promote reflections about the literature being read and to enable student writers to begin the process in comfortable surroundings.

Harnessing Developmental Levels

In the past, teaching writing has not taken into account the developmental process of young writers—that is, time and difficulty of subject matter are related as students learn. Over the years, we have noticed in our visits to schools that many times 7th-graders are asked to complete the same writing tasks that 12th-graders are asked to complete. When this happens, both sets of students have difficulty. The

7th-graders become very frustrated since, in all probability, they are being asked to do something they are not intellectually capable of doing; the 12th-graders are not successful because they discarded the importance of writing long ago, when they, too, were not successful. When this unfortunate situation occurs, it is evident that a writing curriculum based on the developmental stages of student writers does not exist. Students in the early grades are not taught differently from those at the upper levels. A major contributor to this approach was the emphasis given to the knowledge-base philosophy of curriculum development. Subject matter was assigned to certain grade levels and taught at that level regardless of the ability of the students to comprehend it.

Fortunately, in the last few years, schools have been more willing to accept a different view of curriculum design: one based on human growth and development. In this approach, subject matter and skill development are presented consistent with students' abilities to understand them. As a result of this change in attitude and philosophy, educators are more able to provide meaningful experiences for younger students, which provide the foundation for growth as these students move through different grade levels.

The shift in emphasis has challenged teachers in general and writing teachers in particular to provide meaningful experiences based on what young people can learn and are able to do at any given level. Teachers have become more aware of the physical, emotional, and cognitive characteristics of preadolescents and adolescents and how these characteristics affect the classroom curriculum.

THE EMERGING ADOLESCENT

Preadolescents are people in transition. They are no longer children, nor are they adults. They are in the middle. Thornburg (1974) calls this period the "bubble gum years." Because of this fluctuation between childlike and adultlike behavior, we desperately need to understand this age group, not just so that we can get along with our students but also so that we can prepare an educational program that will meet their needs.

Physical Characteristics

The emerging adolescent changes frequently and rapidly between the ages of 9 and 14. Of all the changes that occur, physical growth is the most pronounced. It is during this period that the pituitary gland increases production of two hormones.

One hormone stimulates growth of bones and tissues, causing tremendous growth spurts. This rapid change in growth causes a drastic change in the preadolescent: Height often increases 25 percent and many times weight doubles. Young people in this stage experience a craving for food and frequent periods of fatigue.

The second hormone influences sexual development and is responsible for the appearance of secondary sexual characteristics, such as change of voice, appearance of the beard in males, and breast growth in females. Educators must be sensitive to how their students perceive themselves as different and how they become self-conscious of their behavior. The school, teacher, and curriculum must attempt to meet the needs of these young people in this unsettled time.

Emotional Characteristics

To say the least, the emotions of emerging adolescents are unstable. These young people shift their emotional behavior from one extreme to another, exhibiting both extremes almost at the same time. They are up, then down; they are creative, then dull; they are cooperative, then obnoxious; they are energetic, then lifeless; they are child-like, then adult.

Peer group pressure is a major concern for 9- to 14-year-olds. They look to the group for stability in their unstable world. The conflict between establishing standards for themselves and going along with the crowd offers additional struggles. Conflicts between parents and young adults often embody this influence. For example, a teenager wearing non-matching socks is ready to leave for school when the parent questions the decision to wear unmatched socks. The young adult argues, "I want to be myself; I want to be different; besides, everyone is wearing them like this!" Preadolescents, while continuing to rely on the social structure of the group, begin to acknowledge the importance of adults even though the adults may not be their parents, thus creating internal conflict.

As a result of these inconsistent conditions, it is imperative that preadolescents feel that the people working with them are aware of these emotional instabilities and that they are concerned for their well-being. Acceptance, communication, and encouragement are all necessary for preadolescents to feel good about themselves and to attain emotional growth.

Cognitive Characteristics

Middle-level students have interests in many areas. They enjoy exploring a variety of subjects. Their concern is for the real, the concrete; they may reject the abstract. They are active but often have short attention spans.

Piaget and Cognitive Development

Jean Piaget, perhaps more than any other person, made a substantial contribution to our understanding of cognitive development. It is through his works that we come a little closer to understanding how people think, especially young people 9 to 14 years old. While it is important for educators to know and to understand this research as it applies to the younger child, it seems as important, if not more important—at least for our understanding of the writing process in grades 5 through 12—for the emphasis to be placed on the emerging adolescent and the adolescent. A very brief summary of Piaget's theory (Piaget and Inhelder, 1969) is presented here and is used as part of the foundation for teaching writing.

Piaget states that cognitive changes from infancy to adulthood are the result of a developmental process. He suggests that this process occurs in four stages: the sensorimotor period (birth to 2 years), the preoperational period (2 to 7 years), the concrete operational period (7 to 12 years), and the formal operational period (12 years to adulthood). While these stages may appear to be start-and-stop operations, they are not. Piaget's theory suggests a gradual movement from any one period to another. Certainly the age classification is not etched in stone. These categories are meant only as general time frames for the stages.

These stages have other characteristics as well:

1. Different reasoning takes place at different stages, with the reasoning occurring at later stages being superior to the reasoning in the previous stages.
2. The reasoning in each stage is inclusive rather than particular.
3. What has been learned in a previous stage is incorporated into new knowledge at a later stage.
4. Each operational level is developed from the previous state; that is, formal reasoning cannot develop before concrete reasoning is developed.

Since this book deals primarily with the writing process as it relates to the preadolescent and adolescent, the periods of concrete and formal operations are emphasized. During the concrete operational stage, children become a bit more independent in their thinking. They can think logically, they can classify, and they can show relationships. The real world (experience) is extremely important to these young people whose thinking revolves around immediate and concrete objects rather than concepts and abstractions. The research indicates that the preadolescent is able to think backward as well as forward in time.

As preadolescents move out of the concrete operational level, they develop more formal operations, which they retain throughout their adulthood. Adolescents are able to apply logical operations to all classes of problems. During this final stage, abstract thinking prevails, with adolescents being able to reason about abstract propositions, objects, and concepts that they have not directly experienced. At this stage, young people also are able to hypothesize and use deductive and inductive reasoning.

While Piaget did not apply his theories to education, many have made that relationship. Furth (1970), Elkind (1981), Wadsworth (1978), and Thornburg (1970, 1981) suggest interpretations of Piaget's theories and offer application to teaching. All emphasize the importance of thinking, the development of learning capacities, the relationship of reasoning, and the active involvement of students in their learning at various levels. Elkind (1981) makes the case for the Piagetian theories in building curriculum. He says, "Each stage of cognitive development has its own set of mental operations and these provide the analytical tools for that stage. If curriculum materials for children at that stage are consistent with mental operations of that stage, then they are appropriate. If they are too simple or too complex, then they are not appropriate" (p. 227).

Vygotsky (1978) writes about the issue of cognitive development and social interaction. He believes that social interaction—that is, what happens in a classroom with a strong classroom climate—plays a fundamental role in the development of cognition. Vygotsky states, "Every function in the child's cultural development appears twice: first, on the social level, and later, on the individual level; first between people (interpsychological) and then inside the child (intrapsychological). This applies equally to voluntary attention, to logical memory, and to the formation of concepts. All the higher functions originate as actual relationships between individuals" (p. 57).

It would seem that Vygotsky's theory is appropriate to our discussion of the social interaction (classroom climate) that occurs in a writing program. For classroom teachers of writing, the importance lies, it seems to us, in the development of this social interaction so that students may indeed develop. It is up to the writing teacher to provide sufficient structure to keep students productive without confining them to straight jackets that destroy initiative, motivation, and resourcefulness.

APPLICATION TO THE WRITING PROCESS

It would seem that with what we know and what we think we know about the preadolescent and the adolescent, we would structure our writing programs so that they offer different experiences for young people in grades 6, 7, and 8 than in grades 11 and 12. As suggested previously, this is not always so. Writing assignments that call for sophisticated, abstract reasoning are frequently found in the lower grades. These experiences are often included because "they will need it when they get to high school." We have often wondered why the teachers who make these statements do not think that it will be taught when it is needed!

More often than not, this reasoning does not hold forth. If we believe that those students who are still at the concrete operational level use thinking processes that involve mostly categorizing and labeling—and depend greatly on direct observation for the generation of ideas—we must provide a program of writing strategies that meet the needs of these young people. These writing strategies are quite different from those given to upper-level students who have moved through the transitional period into formal functioning. For example, requiring an 8th-grader who is probably still thinking in concrete terms to write a structured persuasive essay with all of its components would probably be an unsuccessful venture. In fact, we question the writing assessments in several states that require all students in the same grade to write in the same mode and on the same topic under a time requirement that is not consistent with how writing is taught in schools.

Implementation of a writing program that allows for individual student abilities and that fosters personal, expressive, and expository writing should be one of the goals of English teachers. The following may be helpful as we examine what might be appropriate for the middle and upper grades.

Middle Grades

Establishing a classroom climate in which students feel good about themselves and about what they are doing is very important for students in grades 6 through 8. While this climate must continue through the 12th grade, it is very important for the preadolescents who are struggling with physical, emotional, and cognitive changes. Therefore, before any part of the writing sequence is included, the classroom must be comfortable, emotionally and physically.

In the middle grades, writing begins with an emphasis on prewriting, for the negative attitude toward writing must be dissolved in these students. Students spend substantial amounts of time collecting effective uses of language from a variety of sources and attempting to create their own effective language. Word games, word puzzles, bumper stickers, book titles, license plates, and "hink pinks" can all be used to encourage students to have fun with language as they make it fresh and alive (see Figure 2–1 on p. 28 for specific examples). Teachers should encourage experimentation with words as well. Emphasis is on what is right with the language and what is exciting about the language, not what is wrong with it.

A great deal of time is spent in oral activities as well. Talk is important for the writing process. This talk generates ideas that will be useful as students begin to write. They talk of concepts that do not exist (What if clouds had strings running to Earth?), they share their worst-and best-sounding words (dinky vs. draconian), they create new expressions for previously undescribed stimuli (How would you describe the color of excitement?), and they play with their language to create new possibilities of expression.

As these middle-school students create new and explore old language expressions, they also are writing. They must have the opportunity to communicate about self in an atmosphere that is built around respect for each other's ideas, support for individual contributions, and acceptance of a positive attitude toward learning. Some time should be given to students to write without concern for structure. This writing is personal and usually is based on real experiences. The writing flows without regard to structure or form. Students are free to express themselves in any way that seems appropriate to them at the time. They explore their feelings and emotions through their writing. Most agree that preadolescents are primarily interested in themselves and that this egocentrism should be explored in classroom activities. One effective tool for tapping this egocentric behavior is use of a journal. The journal encourages fluency in writing, emphasizes nonevaluative writing, and offers a place to experiment with—and perhaps share—ideas and language. At the same time, it offers students a place to record their likes and dislikes and concerns. The journal frequently becomes an important part of the middle-level writing program. It may be used daily, perhaps at the beginning of class, or it may be used periodically throughout the year. However it is used, it is an effective teaching tool to help achieve fluency in writing. One caution that must be suggested: The journal may be used too much. Students sometimes see journal writing as repetitive with little meaning. Teachers must be aware of student attitudes about journal writing.

In addition, some structure occurs in student writing at this age. The narrative is most often the genre of choice for the middle-level program. The narrative is often more personal and usually incorporates the experiences of the writer. The middle-grade student can more easily tell stories and as a result can operate more easily in the narrative mode. The expository mode provides a great deal of trouble for middle-school students. In most cases, they have not moved into the formal operational stage and find it difficult to hypothesize and to work with abstractions. The more formal writing—expository—usually draws on these elements. The narrative enables students to be successful when working with real-life situations as they tell their "truth" through the narrative form. "By telling stories," states O'Brien (1990), "you objectify your own experience. You separate it from yourself" (p. 179). Romano (1995) suggests that narrative thinking is rendering experience as opposed to explaining it, abstracting it, or summing it up (p. 3).

Upper Grades

The research of Piaget and others seems to indicate that most of the adolescents found in the upper grades, or what we commonly call "high school," are able to reason at the formal operational level. In general, these students have reached intellectual maturity, and most are able to think in a systematic manner, to reason by implication at the abstract level, and to synthesize variables.

It would seem, then, that emphasis on the revision component of the writing process should be later rather than sooner. While many of the revisions that students make can be made as they move through the middle grades, the bulk of the revisions—the more serious revisions—ought to take place with older students. Some of the concrete-level editing that may occur with middle-level students includes capitalization, terminal punctuation, commas in a series, use of the hyphen, use of italics, and use of quotation marks. Writing concepts that are addressed through revision for older students include effective use of phrases, the concept of subordination, fragments and run-ons, sentence variety, consistency of verb tense, parallel construction, paragraph development, use of transitions, patterns of organization, paraphrasing, and research skills.

It would seem that middle-level students have had the opportunity to build basic writing skills through more informal writing activities. As students' developmental levels rise, the writing tasks appropriately become more formal and more structured. Students who are more developmentally and intellectually ready confront exposition, a much more difficult genre of writing. Exposition is taught when and only when the intellectual level of students has readied them for formal writing. (The hypothetical reasoning that is the major difference between concrete and formal operations is one of the foundations for this more formal writing.) Therefore, students who have not reached this intellectual level may be frustrated and, thus, unsuccessful in any attempts to write in this mode. Concrete thinkers may be able to initiate a pattern in expository writing and to complete the writing assignment, but they will struggle with it and certainly will not produce adequate samples of their abilities.

Even for upper-grade students, a range of difficulty may be needed to meet the intellectual levels of all students. Just because students have reached high school does not mean that they have reached the higher developmental level; in fact, many adults have not reached that level. Through their writing programs, teachers must provide a variety of writing experiences to meet all their students' needs and abilities.

BIBLIOGRAPHY

Atwell, N. (1998). *In the middle: Writing, reading, and learning with adolescents* (2nd ed.). Portsmouth, NH: Heinemann.

Bromley, K. D. (1989). Buddy journals make the reading-writing connection. *Reading Teacher, 43,* 122–129.

Burkland, J. N., & Peterson, B. T. (1986). An integrative approach to research: Theory and practice. In B. T. Peterson (Ed.), *Convergences: Transactions in Reading and Writing* (pp. 189–203). Urbana, IL: National Council of Teachers of English.

Copeland, M., and Grout, M. (2001). *At the Crossroads: Learning to Reflect and Reflecting to Learn.* Ottawa, KS: The Writing Conference, Inc.

Cormier, R. (2001). *The rag and bone shop.* New York: Delacorte Press.

Daly, J. A. (1979). Writing apprehension in the classroom: Teacher role expectancies of the apprehensive writer. *Research in the English Classroom, 13*(1), 37–44.

Daly, J. A., & Miller, M. D. (1975a). The empirical development of an instrument to measure writing apprehension. *Research in the Teaching of English, 9*(3), 242–249.

Daly, J. A., & Miller, M. D. (1975b). Further studies on writing apprehension: SAT scores, success expectancies, willingness to take advanced courses and sex differences. *Research in the Teaching of English, 9*(3), 250–256.

Draper, S. (1994). *Tears of a tiger.* New York: Simon & Schuster.

Elkind, D. (1981). *Children and adolescents.* New York: Oxford University Press.

Erikson, E. H. (1964). *Insight and responsibility.* New York: Norton.

Furth, H. G. (1970). *Piaget for teachers.* Englewood Cliffs, NJ: Prentice Hall.

Gibran, K. (1962). On teaching. In K. Gibran, *The prophet.* New York: Alfred A. Knopf.

Giles, G. (2002). *Shattering glass.* Brookfield, CT: Roaring Brook Press.

Hall, S., & Moats, L. C. (1999). *Straight talk about reading.* Chicago: Illinois Contemporary Publishing Co.

Jett-Simpson, M. (1984). *Parents and beginning reading.* Atlanta, GA: Humanities Limited.

McMahan, E., & Day, S. (1983). Integrating literature into the composition classroom. *Writing Instructor, 2,*115–121.

Murray, D. (1968) *A writer teaches writing: A practical method of teaching composition.* Boston: Houghton Mifflin.

Musgrove, L. (2001). *Attitudes toward writing.* Accessed November 13, 2002, from **http:// english.sxu.edu/mustrove/jaepl.htm.**

Northwest Regional Educational Laboratory. (1999). *A Writing Teacher's Action Handbook.* Portland: NWREL

O'Brien, T. (1990). *The things they carried.* New York: Penguin Books.

Pajares, F. (1996). *Assessing self-efficacy beliefs and academic outcomes: The case for specificity and correspondence.* Paper presented at the 1966 Annual Meeting of the American Educational Research Association (AERA). Retrieved January 8, 2002, from **http://www.emory.edu/EDUCATION/ mfp/aera2.html**

Pajares, F. (2001a). Overview of self-efficacy. Retrieved December 23, 2001, from Emory University, Web site, **http://www.emory.edu/ EDUCATION/mfp/eff.html**

Pajares, F. (2001b). Self-efficacy beliefs in academic contexts. Retrieved December 23, 2001, from Emory University Web site, **http://emory.edu/ EDUCATION/mfp/eff.html**

Pajares, F. (in press). Self-efficacy beliefs, motivation, and achievement in writing: A review of the literature. *Reading and Writing Quarterly.* Retrieved December 23, 2001, from Emory University Web site, **http://emory.edu/ EDUCATION/ mfp/effpage.html**

Pajares, F., & Johnson, M. (1994). Confidence and competence in writing: The role of self-efficacy, outcome expectancy, and apprehension. *Research in the Teaching of English, 28* (October), 313–315.

Piaget, J., & Inhelder, B. (1969). *The psychology of the child*. New York: Basic Books.

Reeves, L. L. (1997). Minimizing writing apprehension in the learner centered classroom. *English Journal, 86*(6), (October), 38–45.

Romano, T. (1995). *Writing with passion*. Portsmouth, NH: Heinemann.

Russell, W. F. (1986). *More classics to read aloud to your children*. New York: Crown Publishers.

Salisbury, G. (1998). *Jungle dogs*. New York: Delacorte Press.

Sheley, C. (1983). Active learning: Writing from literature. *Writing instructor, 2,* 123–128.

Tchudi, S., & Tchudi, S. (1999) *The English language arts handbook* (2nd ed.). Portsmouth, NH: Heinemann.

Thornburg, H. D. (1970). Learning and maturation in middle school age youth. *Clearing House, 45* (November) 150–155.

Thornburg, H. D. (1974) *Preadolescent development*. Tucson: University of Arizona Press.

Thornburg, H. D. (1981). Developmental characteristics of middle schoolers and middle school organization. *Contemporary Education, 52* (Spring), 134–137.

U.S. Department of Education (1999). *Trends in academic progress, NAEP,* 1992, 1994. Washington, D.C.

Vygotsky, L. S. (1978). *Mind in society.* Cambridge, MA: Harvard University Press.

Wachholz, P. B. & Etheridge, C. (1996). Writing self-efficacy beliefs of high- and low-apprehensive writers. *Journal of Developmental Education, 19* (Spring), 16–18.

Wadsworth, B. (1978). *Piaget for the classroom teacher.* New York: Longman.

Wilson, A. (1983). The study of literature and the development of standard English proficiency. *Writing Instructor, 2,* 115–121.

CHAPTER 2

The Composing Process

Literacy is not an elective. To succeed in any field, you
have to be able to read skeptically, write persuasively,
speak logically, and listen creatively. And of these, the
most important talent is listening.

Richard Peck

ADVICE FROM THE EXPERTS

Many well-known young adult authors provide writing teachers with important food for thought as we examine how writing is or should be taught in the classroom. Richard Peck suggests that in order to do well in society we must, among other things, write persuasively. Karen Hesse would have would-be writers write and read every day, and, she says, "Don't be afraid to revise." Robert Cormier suggests that since revision is a privilege, writers should take advantage of it. Lois Duncan seems to support Hesse's view that writers need to write often. Duncan also indicates that writers should consider writing in many genres.

> *Reading and writing muscles need daily exercise. You should read every day. You should write every day. You don't have to write a book or a story . . . you can write a poem or a letter or an entry in your diary. All writing counts. All writing flexes the writing muscle. Don't be afraid to revise. The first draft is always a miracle. How we get an idea in our minds translated into words on a page that someone else will read and experience inside their minds is simply extraordinary. But if you discover ways to communicate your idea more clearly, embrace the opportunity to do so.*
>
> *Karen Hesse*

Now, can we take what professional writers say about writing and incorporate those ideas in the writing methodology that we suggest for the classroom? We believe we can and should.

> *Revision is a writer's privilege—one that a brain surgeon doesn't have.*
>
> Robert Cormier

> *The only way to become a writer is by writing. I spent my childhood filling notebooks with poems, making entries in diaries, and writing articles for the school paper, and by age thirteen I was selling stories to magazines. All that effort paid off, because as an adult I have been able to earn a living doing the thing I love best.*
>
> Lois Duncan

> *Stay open. That is keep your eyes open and your ears open to observe everything around you. An open heart doesn't hurt, either. Ask questions, but only accept answers that lead to more questions. Read. Write. Above all, allow your mind to be open to all possibilities.*
>
> Lois Ruby

> *I get my ideas from the world around me. A newspaper headline can work its way into a story on any given day. People taking on tough challenges is always fertile ground for a story. When I see what I perceive as injustice, I can't get to my word processor fast enough.*
>
> Chris Crutcher

Taking advice from published professional writers has not always been part of the writing curriculum in middle and high schools. Assigning the essay at 10:00 and having it due at 10:50 does not seem to be what published writers do. It would be difficult to imagine any of the authors of the short stories found in Duncan's *On the Edge: Stories at the Brink* (2000) spending an hour or less creating any one of those stories.

Scenarios that find students being asked to write this way occur too often in schools. Teachers ask students to write about topics they don't care about and of which they have little, if any, experience. Also, little in the way of preparation occurs to help them get started. Often students are told to write on a given topic—for example, to write on the symbolism found in *The Scarlet Letter*—and they are given a fixed amount of time in which to complete the task. Most often in these scenarios, students are set up for failure. They are given assignments that test their inherent writing abilities rather than given experiences in which they can move through the process of writing. Students generally avoid writing because writing usually is separated from any experiences the students have had.

School writing, then, becomes very product oriented. The assignment is made, the writing occurs, and a finished project is created. Most writing serves as a test, emphasizing subject matter that has been read. The writing, therefore, is a means for finding out if the students have the knowledge of specific content rather than for encouraging them to write as a meaningful experience in which they can explore their understanding of content. It seems to us that teachers are giving students a false sense of what writing is all about. Students may come from these experiences thinking they can write a polished piece of writing in a very short period of time. Professional writers know how false that is. Effective writing takes time and patience.

THE WRITING PROCESS

First of all, let us be clear: We use a number of terms or phrases that describe how one writes—the writing process, process writing, sequencing writing, and such. While we may use the term "writing process," we do not want to give the impression that there is only one process that all writers use. Quite the contrary. There are many processes. Some writers start in one place; others start in another. Some revise as they go along; others wait until a segment of the writing is completed before they take a look at revision. Some writers do a lot of thinking before writing; others do their thinking as they write. For our purposes, we take all those processes and put them together in the term "writing process."

Janet Emig (1971), one of the early investigators of the process of writing, enlightens writers through her study of 12th-grade writers. After having her students compose aloud, she deduced that two major modes of writing exist: extensive and reflexive. Emig found that extensive writing (school writing, to test content knowledge, for example, such as that described previously in this chapter) occurs simply to communicate with another person. This communication usually occurs in schools and has little emotional attachment to it. The topics are based on literature or some abstract idea, and the audience is the teacher. Students do very little, if any, prewriting and are not open to revision. As a result, student writers see themselves as putting together a product to be handed in to the teacher, and the writing is sterile with no personal feelings attached to it. The writing usually takes place in a short, controlled amount of time.

Reflexive writing is quite different. Emig found that students become much more attached to this type of writing by focusing on their thoughts and feelings concerning their experiences. They write for their peers, and there is much more self in their writing; the message is more personal. The writing, too, comes about in stages: Students think before they write, make notations about their topic, write, interrupt their writing to make additional notations, and then rewrite.

In another early study, Stallard (1974) contributed to the research of process writing. He found that better writers emphasize a process ranging from prewriting to revision. He also found that his students contemplate their writing before revising it. Stallard concluded, as did Emig, that this is a recognizable process that students can learn and that by using it they can improve their writing.

Paulis (1992) also makes the case for the process approach to writing. He believes that "writing is thinking made visible. It is the messy business of listening for, exploring, and discovering what we know or mean . . . or thought we meant when we started. It involves rehearsing, mapping, discarding, revising, shaping, weighing, and negotiating with meaning" (p. 335).

In *Write to Learn* (1990), Murray suggests that students move through a series of steps: collecting, focusing, ordering, developing, and clarifying (p. 9). Murray also says that when students are involved in the process of writing, they do not go through these steps sequentially but follow a format similar to what Emig described as recursive. Writers may move from collecting to focusing to developing, and then, as they move toward the end of that piece of writing, they may find that they have to move back to collecting and refocusing. Spandel (2001) suggests steps similar to Murray's but adds editing and publishing (p. 133).

Tchudi and Tchudi (1999) highlight the experiential approach that seems to them "takes neither a rigid product stance nor a process stance, but rather focuses on the experience of composing text about the experiences one has in real life. In real life students need to put their writing into 'grammatically correct' or simply 'appropriate' language. Our real life observations also teach us that real writers sometimes agonize over what they write, often doing multiple drafts and revisions, but sometimes bang out a polished piece and get it right the first time" (p. 138).

Those teachers who have changed their practice of teaching writing from the more traditional knowledge-based approach to the process approach have found that student writers seem to have a clearer purpose in their writing with fewer errors. They believe that students have a much more caring attitude about the writing that they do. Teachers realize that in process writing, students start, stop, and start again; and they write about what interests them. These inexperienced writers have trouble relating to school-sponsored topics but can share much more easily experiences they have had. The writing that comes from this process is much more likely to be writing that will be read, but the process includes more than just the sequence of its individual components. It also includes attention to the importance of experience.

We have thought for many years that experience (ownership) is one of the key factors in good writing. Students must write about what they know or what they have learned through research. The evidence is quite clear that when writers write about their personal experiences, or at least about knowledge they have secured, their writing is much better. Richard Peck has said on many occasions that student writers need to do more than just write about what they know; they need to find out what they need to know and then, through the imaginative process, to bring that to the printed page. Peck was asked in a question-and-answer setting if he had a grandmother like Grandma Dowdel *(A Long Way from Chicago* [1998] and *A Year Down Yonder* [2000]). His response was classic: "Give the writer some credit for imagination! The writer creates characters based on many factors—personal experience may be one of them but certainly not the only one."

Coupled with the component of ownership is choice. Students must have some say in what they want to write about. Topic of choice as well as genre of choice lead to stronger ownership of the writing that is to be done. The expression "Choice leads to ownership, which leads to success" was mentioned previously and bears repeating here.

What we are saying, then, as we think of encouraging students to write, is that while we want to offer students a variety of writing modes, the important consideration must be the students' ability to bring experience or knowledge to that writing. It is important not only for teachers to encourage students to write from their own knowledge base but also, if the situation demands it, to provide that knowledge vicariously. Through discussion, role-playing, improvisation, interviewing, and Internet and library research, students may come to understand the subject matter to the extent that they can write about it with some degree of honesty. Without this personal confrontation with the content, the students will more than likely have a failing experience.

Prewriting

We believe that teachers need to help inexperienced writers move beyond the blank page. Certainly the most common way for that to happen is to provide students with activities that they can use just prior to the act of writing. We also believe that there may be some time spent in the beginning of the year prior to the introduction of the writing program in which activities can be introduced to help students move through their apprehension about the writing process. We address writing apprehension in more detail in Chapter 1; however, we do believe that students can participate in activities that will help them ease into the process that will soon start.

Students can begin by collecting creative and effective uses of language. They can share these with their peers. They can experiment with words and language patterns before starting to write extended discourse. They can see how published writers make effective use of fresh and exciting language and, in turn, can experiment with their choice of words and sentence patterns. For example, student writers may examine Will Hobbs's (1996) *Far North* to see how he uses repetition effectively. One message in the novel is the importance of the environment. Hobbs says it well: "Take care of the land, take care of yourself, take care of each other" (p. 223). Writers might look at Lois Lowry's use of vivid word choice and imagery in *The Giver*, to fully describe Jonas's first experience sledding down a snowy hill: "pinpricks," "featherlike," "peppered," "whirling torrent of crystals," "propelled," and "glee" (1993, pp. 80–81).

Teachers may direct students to newspapers to see how language is used effectively or perhaps not so effectively. Sports pages are good sources. Royals Blast Cubs, Red Sox Squeak by Yankees, White Sox Succumb to Rangers in the 9th: How many ways can one say that one team beats another? Figure 2–1 provides examples of other creative word usage.

Students do a great deal of talking, too. Time is set aside for the continued sharing of ideas. Frequently, students complain of nothing to write about as they stare at a blank piece of paper. This frequent exchange of ideas floods the classroom with potential writing topics. Students are sharing their experiences and are relating to the experiences of others, and so this interaction becomes the source for writing.

The use of computers in the writing process provides yet another source for prewriting. Students may do many of the prewriting activities suggested here on the computer and then pass their results on to other students for their additions and comments. Students may be writing about similar topics and can help each other generate ideas and specific language.

All this experimentation with and sharing of ideas allows students to become more at ease with language and their understanding of concepts before they attempt to focus their thoughts and to structure their writing.

Many times students bring to the writing process a negative attitude, almost a fear of writing. The prewriting component seems to help students understand the process and to ease their fears and frustrations about writing. During this time, students begin to realize that while writing may be hard work, it can be fun. A comparison to the game of tennis may help to clarify. To complete a tennis set is often very strenuous and may be quite exhausting, but that doesn't mean that those who play do not enjoy themselves and do not have fun. So it is with writing. It may be difficult at times, but students are involved in a process, and they can succeed and can find the experience enjoyable.

Figure 2–1 Effective uses of language

Bumper Stickers
    Illiterate? Write Now for Help
    If you think education is expensive, try ignorance.
    If you can read this, thank a teacher.

License Plates
    Dr. 2th (Dentist)
    ICNCNC (Optometrist)

Book Titles
    Meet You Later by Ron D. Voo
    To Be on Top of Things by C. Ling

Hink Pinks
    Barber's furniture—hair chair
    Nervous picket—tense fence

Hinky Pinkies
    Oily dance floor—Crisco Disco
    Dislike fishing—hating baiting

Hinketty Pinketties
    Frozen two-wheeler—icicle bicycle

As teachers introduce the writing program, it is important to foster a sense of experimentation—encouraging students to use language that is fresh, alive, and workable to express their ideas. This is a time to take chances with words and phrases. It may be a new way of looking at ideas for students. They can play with word choices; they can investigate how other writers have made similar choices. Reading aloud to them can provide quality writing for students to hear. In addition, students can work with abstractions, clichés, twisted phrases, and graffiti boards. They can collect examples of effective use of language from billboards, bumper stickers, signs, comic strips, and newspaper, magazine, television, and Internet advertisements.

The second and more common type of prewriting occurs as students begin the act of creating a particular piece of writing, although student writers may do prewriting activities while they write, too, as they need to find new information or think of new directions. In either case, writers attempt to generate additional ideas. Students may work in large or small groups, with partners, or by themselves. The idea is to flesh out a topic or get help in deciding what genre best suits the topic. It is a time for getting ready. It is similar to the readiness found in other performances: sports, music, reading, and so on. Before athletic contests, participants spend ample time warming up. Any student who has played a musical instrument or sung knows the importance of getting ready mentally as well as physically before giving a performance. Actors and actresses spend a liberal amount of time warming up before a performance. In writing, readiness time is when students think about what they want to say—perhaps they jot down notes about material they want to include—and, for some, it is when they secure information about their topic. Brainstorming, interviewing, clustering, webbing, and discussing are good examples of prewriting activities used in the readiness time.

Brainstorming is an excellent activity for individuals, as well as groups of students, to jot down ideas for possible use in writing. Teachers may wish to use the following guidelines when asking students to brainstorm:

1. Set a time limit of 3 to 7 minutes for brainstorming.
2. Record all suggestions.
3. Encourage far-out, zany ideas.
4. Encourage piggybacking on ideas.
5. Stipulate no negative comments to the suggestions made.
6. Help students to group ideas generated into categories.

After brainstorming, teachers help students to put generated ideas into groups or categories so that students may find a more focused idea on which to write.

Melissa (not her real name) was a student in a writing camp. She came to the camp hesitant about writing, not having had great success; however, she was willing to give it a try. Having been asked by her camp facilitator to create a cluster on a topic using as the core the five senses, Melissa created the cluster shown in Figure 2–2.

Figure 2–2 Melissa's cluster

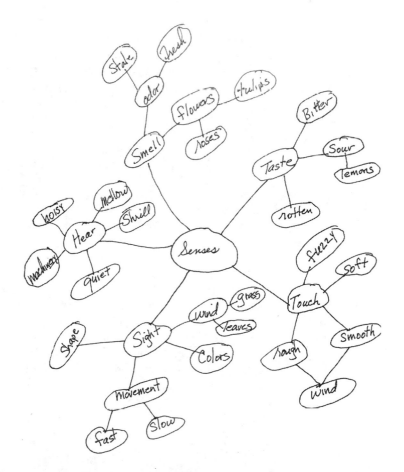

Prewriting on the topic of the five senses, as shown in Figure 2–2, allowed Melissa to generate as many ideas as she could. Perhaps more importantly, the process enabled her to be more selective in what she wrote about. Inexperienced writers often will choose a topic like the five senses, will try to tell everything they know about it, and will do it poorly. This clustering technique shows students an organizational layout and may, in and of itself, suggest one area instead of the entire topic on which to write. Students then may choose to write a narrative or a poem about an experience that comes out of the cluster.

We are often asked, especially by our preservice teachers, how much time we spend on prewriting. A first response, probably not very useful, is "As long as it takes." Seriously, teachers need to gauge how well students are doing with prewriting as they adjust their attitude and prepare for success in writing. Of course, teachers cannot spend an entire semester or year doing only prewriting activities. We make this suggestion: Spend the first couple of weeks of a writing project on prewriting to help students get started. Students need to get their juices flowing and to get focused on the writing that is to be done. As the semester or project proceeds, a return now and then to prewriting activities may provide appropriate refreshers.

Drafting

Drafting takes many forms. Some teachers have a more liberal point of view and consider any extended discourse as a draft whether it be in the form of a journal entry or a piece of free or experimental writing. Others argue that drafting is more narrowly defined, and they suggest that the draft is an organized piece on its way to becoming a product. We consider drafting to be any form of writing with some extended discourse. We suggest, in a sense, that a sequence of writing takes place in drafting from the very unstructured journal entry through the experimental/stream-of-consciousness piece to the organized draft. Each, it seems to us, provides additional help for the student writer. Journaling and experimental writing enable students to establish fluency in writing; the more formal draft helps students with organization and other facets of writing.

Journaling

Journal writing facilitates an increase in fluency in student writing and thus is an integral part of the writing process. The student who has never written and has publicly stated, "I hate to write. I ain't got nothing to say," often gets hooked as he begins to write in a journal.

Teachers use many different kinds of journals. Kirby and Liner (1981) suggest four: the writer's notebook, the class journal, the project journal, and the diary. It seems to us that having students keep a journal in school offers many advantages. The journal is a place where students can share their ideas. We also offer a caution: Writing in a journal in school must be a public process or at least have the potential of being so. Students should be told not to write anything that can't be read in class. Of course, not every entry will be read in class, but from time to time it is good to have journal entries shared in groups. For those who wish to write more intimate, personal entries, the diary that is kept at home may be just the answer. Teachers who suggest both the journal and the diary are emphasizing writing both at school and at home.

It would seem appropriate to hold this view concerning public journals and private diaries because teachers may not have the patient/doctor or client/lawyer relationship that is found in those professions. We know of one school district that requires teachers to read students' journals word by word and act immediately on any issues that suggest abuse, suicide, or threats of violence against anyone. Many problems with confidentiality of content that might arise simply do not occur with the two-journal approach. In addition, many teachers indicate that private diaries in schools have a way of getting lost and then found by the wrong people. In a sense, it is for the teacher's protection as well as for the welfare of the students that a private diary be kept at home. It also seems apparent that the motivation for keeping a diary is not the same as the one for keeping a writer's journal. While the former emphasizes personal, intimate ideas primarily related to self, the latter emphasizes ideas of a more general nature, and these ideas, as well as the writing techniques used to convey them, are what really are important in teaching writing.

Certainly, much could be said in support of the more liberal point of view concerning journaling. Proponents argue for allowing students to see their journals as their friends and as places for them to share the more intimate details of their lives. The argument goes that this is an important way to help establish fluency. Indeed, it does. If the other dangers expressed concerning journals are not of concern to teachers, then that type of journaling would be appropriate.

The school journal is much like a financial institution. From time to time, students make deposits. These deposits grow as students think about what they have written and return to that particular entry to add more to it. The journal is a place in which withdrawals are made as well, for students may take an entry from the journal for a classroom writing activity. While the analogy may fall apart in places, it is evident that the journal is a vehicle for writing, a place in which students can test out their writing strategies and ideas continually. It is a place to help with fluency—to practice writing and to test ideas.

Burnout arises quickly when journals are used often. This burnout is true for both students and teachers. If the journal becomes "old hat" and is not taken seriously by students, it is time to stop the activity. While it may be beneficial to have students write in the journal daily during the first part of the school year, it may be that students would benefit more from periodic writing as the year moves on. Again, if the journal is used to practice writing strategies and to test ideas for writing and not just for a place to share intimate thoughts, the chance for overuse is minimized.

Experimenting

The unrestricted flow of words on paper characterizes experimental writing or free writing. Students are given the freedom to write whatever is important to them at the time without concern for grammatical correctness. While the writing that occurs does not stand by itself as a written product, it does give students the opportunity to write freely about their feelings and ideas. Students see a chance to personalize their writing; they begin to see that they do have something to say. It is a time to experiment with structure as well as content. Also, perhaps most important of all, it enables students to write frequently, a necessity if fluency is to be achieved.

We think this writing is much like the process the children go through as they begin to use language orally. From the time children first begin to speak, they experiment with the sounds they hear until they stumble onto the right combination to make themselves understood. Most parents react excitedly, praising their children and encouraging them to repeat that success. Thus, children learn to speak in an atmosphere of encouraged experimentation that leads to successful building of meaningful language through positive reinforcement.

So it should be when working with young people in the writing process. Students need this time for experimentation without the fear of penalty. They should be encouraged to build on their successes, gradually leaving behind the awkward broken phrases that parallel their vocal baby talk. Those around them must encourage their written successes through positive reinforcement just as their parents did when they were children learning to talk.

The writing becomes a "random rehearsal" (Macrorie, 1968) for what is to come. The writing is tentative; it may serve as a source for future writing. In any event, students writing in this way are not concerned with how they write but rather with what they write. For example, in a stream-of-consciousness activity, teachers ask student writers to write for 7 to 10 minutes without stopping. Writers simply put pencil to paper and begin when the teacher says "Go" and they continue until the teacher says "Stop." They can turn their attention to ideas that they want to communicate. Since there is no correct or incorrect form at this time, students find themselves much more interested in writing something meaningful.

Many times, teachers will have students write for 6 or 7 minutes, filling a page with thoughts about something that they really care about, something that is especially meaningful to them. This something may be a particular person with whom they have a special relationship, or it may be an issue that is important to them. The idea behind this activity, as well as similar activities, is to see what is generated from this unstructured format. Perhaps nothing will come of it; on the other hand, perhaps an idea that the student wishes to develop further will be generated.

The nature of this writing serves as an early step in completing a particular piece of writing. In many cases, it serves as a very rough draft. Just as a journalist sketches an outline of ideas before submitting the final article or as a politician creates several drafts before settling on the best prepared speech, students must see the need to write frequently before they can expect to compose the best expression of ideas. More importantly, they must feel confident that their experimentation, their journaling, their rough drafts will not be judged as finished products but will be appreciated as steps in the development of projects.

Figure 2–3 shows Melissa's first attempt to do something in poetic form from her cluster on the five senses. Readers can see that she is playing with some of the words—making statements, asking questions, simply experimenting with language at this point.

Figure 2–3 Melissa's first poetry attempt

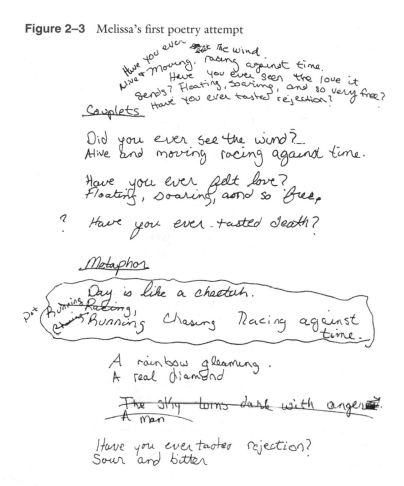

After spending time journaling and free writing, students move on to a more sophisticated writing task—a more focused piece of writing. As in the previous writing, students continue to retain their freshness and honesty in writing but now focus on specific ideas they wish to express. Students are encouraged to write with excitement, to continue to experiment with language, and to develop their authentic voices, but to do so while focusing on a specific idea. While the previous emphases have employed creative uses of language, meaningful and relevant content, and honest writing, and while teachers will want to continue to encourage these elements of good writing, the emphasis now is on helping students in the selection, organization, and presentation of their ideas.

Frequently, students tell "all they know" when they write about something meaningful to them. They tend to ramble on and on. The emphasis now must be on helping them to be more selective in what they write, to determine the hook or angle they wish to use to organize their ideas, and to suggest alternatives for effective presentations. To do this, teachers may want to suggest to students the Secret of Once activity suggested by Macrorie (1976). Since students tend to ramble, the Secret of Once focuses their thinking on one or two items rather than on many. For example, students may write about going to the beach for an annual vacation. They may write about all they did during that week-long experience. In this activity, students begin their writing by stating that they went on this vacation as they do each year but that it was different this time. It is not a collection of all the experiences. It is a focused description of one of the events that occurred during the vacation.

As in other parts of this student writing sequence, sharing and criticizing play important roles. Positive comments from peers in small groups and/or partners about the quality of writing are continued with this more focused writing. However, after a few writing experiences, students begin to receive suggestions as to what strategies might be used to improve their writing. Rubrics can be used to help students better understand their writing and that of others. We recommend the use of the Six-Trait Analytic Model as described in Chapter 7.

Because a positive classroom climate (see Chapter 1) has been established and because students feel comfortable sharing their writing in groups, suggestions about the improvement of writing are accepted easily. The successes in writing that students have already attained through positive reinforcement make the suggested changes even more meaningful. After spending some time in a writing group, Melissa made some elementary changes in her poem (See Figure 2–4).

Revising

A most crucial step in the writing sequence is the second or third look that writers take when moving toward a finished product. It is that privilege that Robert Cormier speaks of (see the beginning of this chapter). Teachers frequently tell students to look over their writing before handing it in, and that is about the extent of revision for some students. They attempt to clean up spelling mistakes, sentence

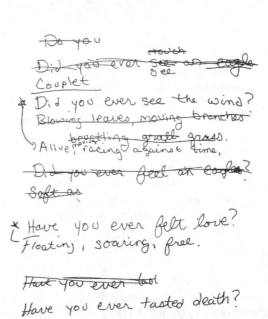

Figure 2–4 Melissa's first rough draft

fragments, and run-ons, but many times the process simply means recopying a piece of writing in pencil into the same piece of writing in ink. Certainly proofreading and editing are important, but reviewing and "reseeing" a piece of writing have greater priority. Helping students see the need for taking another look is quite a challenge, but an important one, for it is at this time that all that has gone before in prewriting, journaling, and drafting comes together in one finished, polished product. The practice writing that has preceded is now refined so that it can be submitted for final assessment. The process of revision means writers must see their ideas again and again until they perfect what they want to say and how they want to say it.

It is through this process that students acquire improved writing skills. Students think through a piece of writing in order to revise the original into something better and thus become better writers. During the process, students work with a piece that has been discussed in a group or with a partner. They weigh the suggestions that they have received. Do they need to make the changes? Would these make the piece more effective? Not all suggestions are used. We caution against having the draft given to the teacher for correction. When this occurs, the draft and then the final paper often become the teacher's paper.

In addition to suggestions from others, students consider how they have used elements of good writing that have been discussed in class. Teachers may want to isolate particular elements for emphasis in the revision process. Students may be instructed to emphasize repetition, beginnings and endings, detail, imagery, or types of verbs, for example. Certainly, as the writing sequence continues through the year, the writing will be evaluated more and more as a total, well-written piece of writing. Once students have reworked their writing to their satisfaction, they can then submit it for publication (assessment) as a finished product. Readers will note the sequence in Melissa's writing as she moves through the revision process to the finished product (Figures 2–5 through 2–9).

The major goal of any writing program is to develop within the student lifelong skills to expand ideas and to write them effectively to others. Certainly this also is true for any one of the parts of the process. If students can see the need for and can practice revising their writing, especially within a classroom setting in which help is available, we are convinced that students will carry a positive attitude toward revision outside the classroom. Teachers will have achieved great success if they can instill in students the desire to rework, to revise, their writing before allowing others to read it as if it were a finished product. Perhaps one way to do that is to emphasize to students that writing is an art form, something of beauty, something worthy of admiration. Teachers must convey to students that writing is worth the time it takes to do it well. The underlying assumption here is that if students care about their subjects and audiences—if they make their own choices and achieve ownership—they will care about writing and, subsequently, about revising.

Publishing

Certainly one way to help students see the importance of their writing is to publish it in some form. Many avenues are open to the classroom teacher for this. On one level, teachers may collect student writing in a "published" classroom collection. At another level, teachers may encourage students to submit their writing to national publications.

Figure 2–5 Melissa's second rough draft

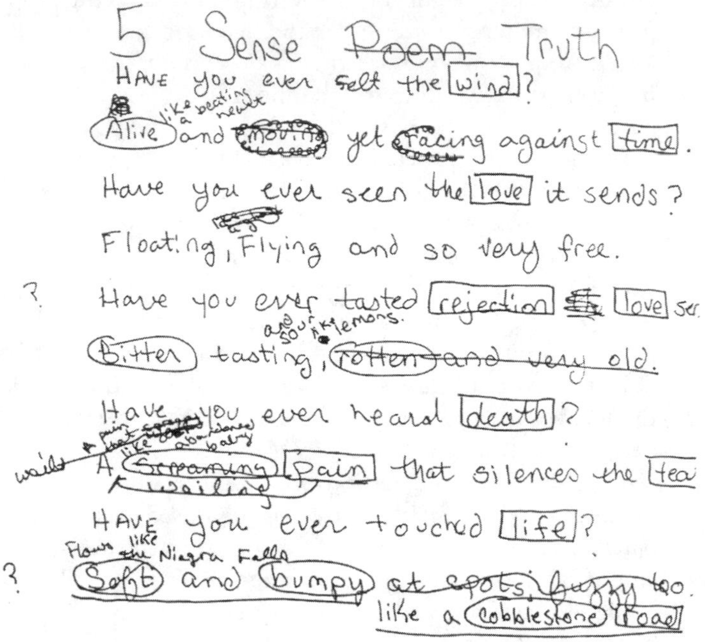

5 Sense ~~Poem~~ Truth
HAVE you ever felt the [wind]?
like a beating heart
(Alive) and ~~moving~~ yet (racing) against [time].

Have you ever seen the [love] it sends?
Floating, Flying and so very free.

? Have you ever tasted [rejection] ~~&~~ [love] se
a sour lemons.
(Bitter) tasting, ~~rotten and~~ very old.

Have you ever heard [death]?
wails A (screaming) [pain] that silences the [tea
wailing

HAVE you ever touched [life]?
Flows like the Niagra Falls
? (Soft) and (bumpy) at spots, ~~fuzzy~~ too.
like a (cobblestone) [road]

Figure 2–6
Melissa's third
rough draft

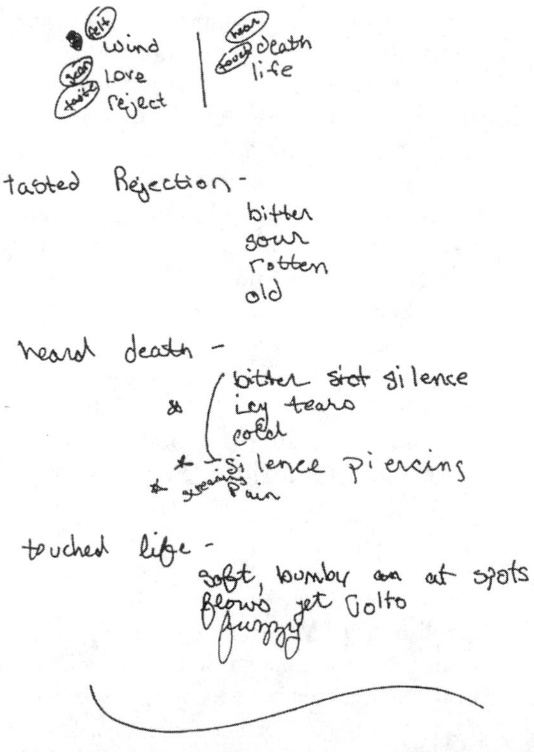

wind   death
Love   life
reject

tasted Rejection –
                   bitter
                   sour
                   rotten
                   old

heard death –
        & (bitter sot silence
           (icy tears
           (cold
        * –silence piercing
        * Pain

touched life –
        soft, bumpy an at spots
        flows yet Jolto
        fuzzy

36

Figure 2–7 Melissa's fourth rough draft

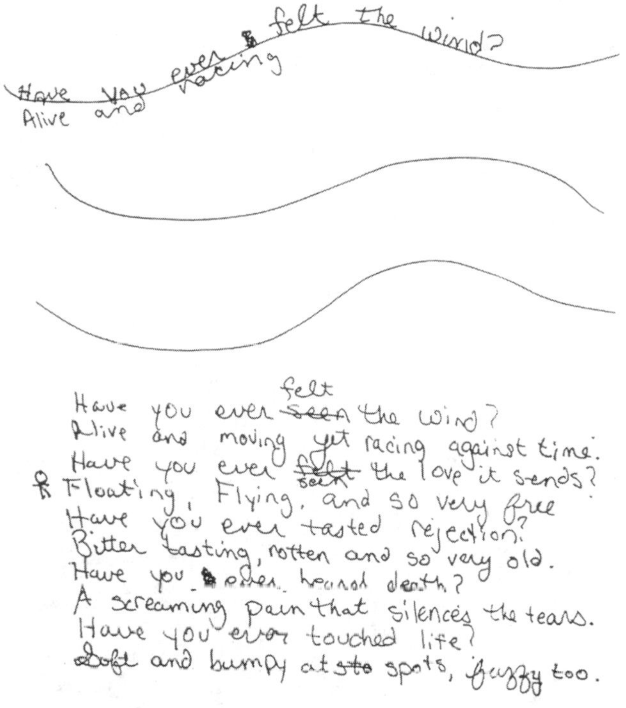

Have you ever felt the wind?
Alive and racing

Have you ever felt the wind?
Alive and moving yet racing against time.
Have you ever felt the love it sends?
Floating, Flying, and so very free
Have you ever tasted rejection?
Bitter tasting, rotten and so very old.
Have you ever heard death?
A screaming pain that silences the tears.
Have you ever touched life?
Soft and bumpy at spots, fuzzy too.

Whatever the source, it is important for writers to see their writing in print and to have it read by others. The following are a few of the sources for student publication.

In-Class Collections

The most nonthreatening way of publishing student writing is in in-class collections. Throughout the semester or year, teachers simply collect writing periodically from everyone in the class and place it in a collection. No selection process is needed as each student submits one piece for the collection. The collection is given to each student and it remains in the class—that is, it is not formally distributed to other people to read. Students may take the collection home for others to read if they so choose.

Collection Exchanges

Teachers collect writing as indicated above but exchange the class collections with other teachers in other classes. By doing this, teachers may be encouraging other teachers to help in the effort to publish student work.

School Publications

A specific change occurs in this category of publication. Teachers and students move beyond the collection procedures in which everyone participates to a selective process in which selected pieces of writing are included in the publication. Teachers and/or students may comprise a panel created to make the decisions about what pieces will be

Figure 2–8   Melissa's fifth rough draft

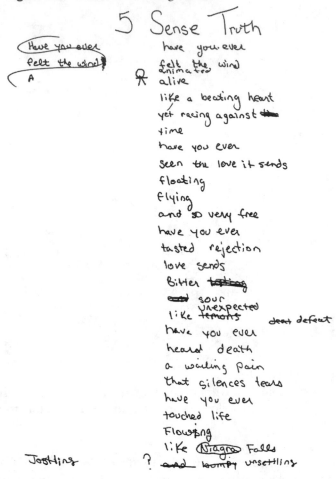

included. Such publications are often called literary journals. These are often submitted to contests in which awards are given to quality literary journals.

District Publications
The process used in school publications can also be used at the district level if the district is large enough that many schools can participate. Students from across the district submit writing to a panel comprised of students and teachers. This panel selects quality writing for a district publication.

State Publications
English organizations at the state level, many of which are affiliated with the National Council of Teachers of English (NCTE), publish student writing. Inquiries to state organizations (addresses may be secured from NCTE) should provide information about the writing that is published if, indeed, publication does occur.

Figure 2–9 Melissa's final poem

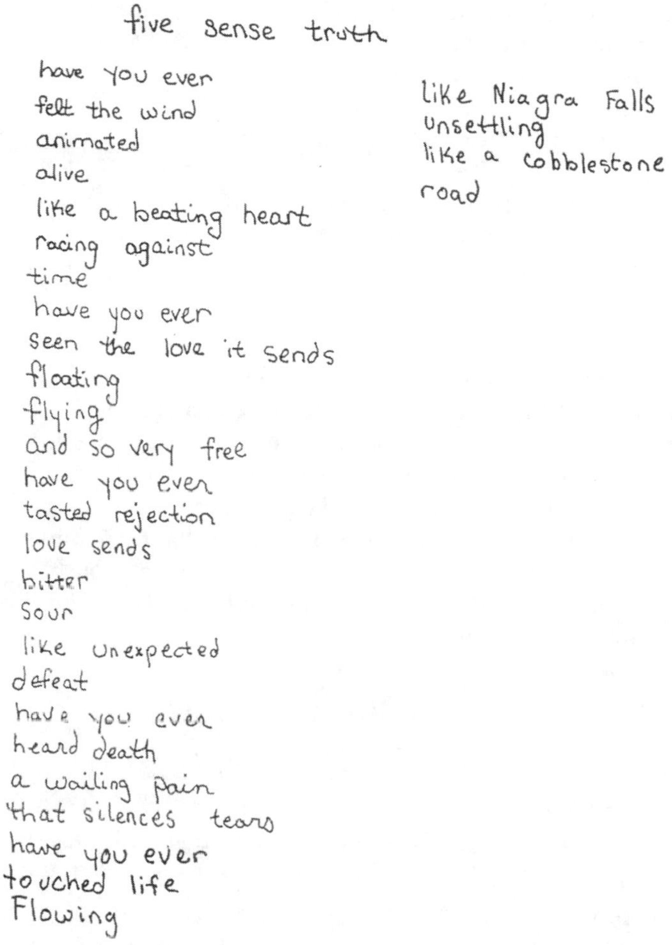

five sense truth

have you ever
felt the wind
animated
alive
like a beating heart
racing against
time
have you ever
seen the love it sends
floating
flying
and so very free
have you ever
tasted rejection
love sends
bitter
sour
like unexpected
defeat
have you ever
heard death
a wailing pain
that silences tears
have you ever
touched life
Flowing

like Niagra Falls
unsettling
like a cobblestone
road

National Publications

If at all possible, teachers should encourage student writers to submit writing to national publications. The joy that arises in adolescents when they receive a complimentary copy of the journal containing their essay, short story, or poem cannot be matched. Competition is keen in these publications since the number of journals is limited and publishers can publish only a limited amount of student writing. A leader in the field of national publications is *Merlyn's Pen.* The organization publishes one issue a year. The address for information is PO Box 1058, East Greenwich, RI 02818. Those interested can also find information at the Web site: **www.merlynspen.com.** A second journal with national distribution is *The Writers' Slate.* It publishes student writing from grades K through 12 in three issues per year. Writers and teachers may obtain information by writing PO Box 664, Ottawa, Kansas 66067 or visiting the Web site: **www.writingconference.com** Other sources include *Scholastic Voice,* 730 Broadway, New York, NY 10003; *Stone Soup,* PO Box 83, Santa Cruz, CA 95063; *The 21st Century,*

PO Box 30, Newton, MA 02161; *Writes of Passage,* 817 Broadway, 6th Fl, New York, NY 10003 *YO! Youth Outlook,* 450 Mission St, Suite 204, San Francisco, CA 94105; and *Potato Hill Poetry* (limited to poetry), 81 Speen St, Natick, MA 01760. In addition, the following Web site address will connect young writers with authors and additional ways to publish their writing: **www.usawrites4kids.cjb.net.** Student writers may also want to investigate Landmark Editions, Inc, PO Box 4469, Kansas City, MO 64127. That organization publishes *Books for Students by Students* and *The Emotional Impact Series.* Its Web address is **www.landmarkeditions.com.** Two additional sources for publications for young writers are *Children's Writer's & Illustrator's Market* and *The Market Guide for Young Writers.* Both are published by Writer's Digest, 1507 Dana Ave, Cincinnati, OH 45207.

Internet Publications

Many teachers and schools have developed their own Web sites. Schools do this to provide information about the district to patrons and visitors to the Web site: faculty information, curriculum matters, dates of special meetings, and such. Teachers often create Web sites to promote what they are doing in the classroom. They include syllabi for the courses they are teaching, recommendations for outside reading, and information about special programs or projects that their students are developing. It is one way for teachers to keep in touch with the parents of their students.

Both types of Web sites—teacher and school—can be effective resources for student writing.

BIBLIOGRAPHY

Cormier, R. Mini Poster, Ottawa, KS: The Writing Conference, Inc.

Crutcher, C. Mini Poster, Ottawa, KS: The Wiring Conference, Inc.

Duncan, L. Mini Poster, Ottawa, KS: The Writing Conference, Inc.

Emig, J. (1971). *The composing process of twelfth graders.* Urbana, IL: National Council of Teachers of English.

Hesse, K. Mini Poster, Ottawa, KS: The Writing Conference, Inc.

Hobbs, Will. (1996). *Far north.* New York: William Marrow.

Kirby, D., & Liner, T. (1981). *Inside out: Developmental strategies for teaching writing.* Montclair, NJ: Boynton/Cook Publishers.

Lowry, Lois. (1993). *The giver.* New York: Houghton Mifflin Walter Lorraine Books

Macrorie, K. (1968). *Writing to be read.* (3rd ed.) Portsmouth, NH: Boynton/Cook.

Macrorie, K. (1976). *Writing to be read.* New York: Hayden Book Company.

Murray, D. (1990). *Write to learn* (3rd ed.). Fort Worth, TX: Holt, Rinehart and Winston.

Paulis, C. (1992). A Christmas carol of writing. *The Clearing House.* 65(6) (July–August), 353–357.

Peck, R. (1998). *A long way from Chicago.* New York: Dial Books.

Peck, R. (2000). *A Year down yonder.* New York: Dial Books.

Ruby, L. Mini Poster, Ottawa, KS: The Writing Conference, Inc.

Spandel, V. (2001). *Creating writers* (3rd ed.). New York: Addison Wesley/Longman.

Stallard, C. K. (1974). An analysis of the writing behavior of good student writers. *Research in the Teaching of English, 8*(Fall), 206–207.

Tchudi, S., & Tchudi, S. (1999). *The English language arts handbook* (2nd ed.). Portsmouth, NH: Boynton/Cook.

C H A P T E R   3

The Writing Workshop

But the core of a workshop—the heart, the marrow—is
kids putting words on paper.

Ralph Fletcher and JoAnn Portalupi (2001, p. 3)

WRITING IN THE REAL WORLD

In much the same way a pottery, jewelry, or furniture workshop operates, a writing
workshop attempts to provide all the tools, materials, and resources that will help an
artisan to create a desired product—in this
case, a piece of quality writing. Unlike a furniture, jewelry, or pottery workshop, however, the workers in the writing workshop
are all apprentices and the workshop super-
visor, the teacher, is more concerned with
the growth of the artisans in their craft than

> *"We found out that in-school writing
> could actually be good for something—
> that it could serve kids as a way to solve
> problems and see the world."*
>
> *Nancie Atwell (1998, p. 14)*

in the polished quality of each individual work produced. The writing workshop
teacher creates the physical, operational, and psychological environment that will most
effectively foster this growth in writing skills, as well as an understanding and appreciation of quality writing, both in their own work and in the work of others. Also as
in all workshops, the work progresses through a number of well-reasoned steps in a
process, moving from a very crude form of the creation to a final, polished form.
Evaluation and improvement of the product are planned into process and take place
at the most beneficial points.

The writing workshop may be modified to fit the specific needs of students and
the various considerations of an individual classroom, but most writing workshops

41

share a number of characteristics. Students are given all the tools they need to create a variety of written products, tools that include physical resources such as a myriad of reference materials, Internet access, word processing equipment, and an environment and schedule conducive to writing and conferencing, as well as instructional resources such as mini-lessons about writing conventions and techniques that students will be able to employ immediately in the work they are doing. Students also receive individual attention tailored to suit their instructional needs at the moment as they create a written work.

In the typical writing workshop, students work independently as they make their way through specific steps in the writing process. Often they are expected to choose their own writing topics, genres, and audience, which may mean that every student is not working on exactly the same piece of writing at the same time. Although students may not be working on identical pieces of writing simultaneously and may not be working at the same step in the writing process, they still receive guidance and instruction on genres and process steps during the course of the workshop.

Since many writing activities may be happening simultaneously, the classroom could seem a little chaotic to the uninformed observer. Some students may be reading their writing out loud, others may be peer conferencing, one student or group could be conferencing with the teacher, some might be consulting reference works in another part of the room, using a computer for word processing or investigating on the Internet, or doing any one of many other activities needed to create a written product. Students are free to operate on their own as they move individual writing projects through the process from start to finish. No students are held back or rushed forward, but rather each one moves according to his or her needs at any given point. All of the writing workshop time is not devoted to individual work, however, since many days will have brief, regularly scheduled mini-lessons, literature readings, and sharing.

To appreciate how closely the writing workshop reflects real world writing practices, imagine a vast newsroom at a major newspaper. What comes to mind is most likely a swarm of journalists noisily hurrying through a variety of individual tasks, sometimes alone, sometimes in pairs or groups, sometimes with an editor, and sometimes on the phone or computer, as they attempt to put out a quality product. The opposite, a vast room full of reporters all sitting quietly at their desks, moving in virtual lockstep through the writing process as they approach their publication seems highly unlikely. A survey of real newspaper newsrooms would most likely yield the image of subdued chaos.

ORGANIZING THE CLASSROOM

What arrangement of materials and desks would best facilitate the workshop approach so that student writers would get the resources they need easily and quickly, merge into and out of cooperative groups, and transition from activity to activity, all with the least amount of distraction and wasted time? What could be in view from their desks? What could be at their desks? How could their desks be arranged? Where should word processors be placed? Where should quiet places be designated? Where should reference works and other resources be placed?

PLANNING THE WRITING WORKSHOP

Although it may look like chaos at times, teachers who successfully employ this instructional approach actually have to be more organized than teachers who don't. Time needs to be carefully planned out, both for the short and long term. Educational objectives do not fly out the window during a writing workshop, nor does accountability for meeting those objectives. The writing workshop teacher still needs to do short-range and long-range planning and to keep careful tabs on where every student is on each day, especially given that they are not all at the same point at the same time.

PLANNING FOR THE LONG RANGE

Long-range planning for the writing workshop will still require attention to educational goals, their sequence, and how and in what depth learning activities will address them. When first designing a curriculum to include a writing workshop, teachers may choose to review the Standards for the English Language Arts developed by the National Council of Teachers of English (NCTE) and the International Reading Association (IRA) for general goals, and then focus more specifically by looking at their state standards, as well as district and school English curriculum objectives for writing. The following are the basic elements for writing workshop long-range planning, along with one or two examples of what specifics would fit in each category. A complete long-range plan would have many more specifics than just these examples:

1. Curriculum goals/standards/objectives to be addressed
   Example: One of the Arizona Department of Education Standards for Writing (2003) for grades 6 to 8 is "W–E2: Write a personal experience narrative or creative story that includes a plot and show the reader what happens through well-developed characters, setting, dialogue, and themes and uses figurative language, descriptive words, and phrases."
2. Genres or modes of writing to be included
   a. What types of papers will students learn to write?
      Example: Personal narratives
   b. What specific products will they create?
      Example: Complete narratives about significant events from the students' pasts, including descriptions of what took place, who was involved, and what it means now to the student.
3. Specific writing skills to be included
   Example: Using words of transition
   Example: Writing an engaging opening
   Example: Developing a main idea
4. Conventions to be covered
   Example: Grammatically correct use of transitions and their punctuation
   Example: Punctuation of dialogue
   Example: Misplaced modifiers

5. Literature to be integrated
   Example: Sandra Cisneros's short story "Eleven"
6. Portfolio requirements
   Example: Students will choose three entries from their journals for the showcase portfolio.
   Example: Students will include one book review.
   Example: Students will include two personal narratives and all the steps included in the process of writing each.
   Example: Students will include a personalized spelling list generated and maintained as they progressed through the writing workshop.
7. Assessment
   Example: Of the total points for the quarter, 40 percent will come from the rubric score on the writing portfolio.
8. Other language arts to be integrated
   Example: Listening and speaking (Students will perform book talks in small groups and participate in discussions of similarities and differences.)
9. Learning activities to meet objectives
   Example: Daily mini-lessons on writing skills, process, conventions, literature analysis
   Example: Student/teacher conferences at midpoint in each major writing project
   Example: Book talks
   Example: Daily literature discussions
   Example: Guided steps in the writing process
   Example: Class reading for Desert Vista Retirement Community
10. Productive sequencing of activities

This might take the form of a calendar or a chronological listing of events by day (see Figure 3–1).

1. Opening activity
   a. Literature selection
   b. Writing activity
2. Mini-lesson
3. Steps in the writing process
   a. prewriting
   b. drafting
   c. conferencing
   d. revising
   e. editing
   f. publishing
4. Sharing

Figure 3–1 An average day in a writing workshop

Sequencing is vital to effective long-range planning; knowing *what* the plan will include and *why* are the most beneficial if that information is employed in determining *when* each learning activity would be best scheduled. The plan should give students instruction in the skills that are used in the writing product they are creating at the time when they can use it most. In the past, writing skills and use of conventions such as punctuation and grammar have often been taught in isolation from their useful employment in writing. In other words, students were taught these things en masse and writing was done at a different time and place in the schedule for instruction. The writing workshop does just the opposite by teaching the individual conventions and techniques of writing as near the moment students will be using them as possible; for example, a mini-lesson about punctuating dialogue would be taught during those days when students are writing narratives that include conversations between characters. Students' learning will be at a higher cognitive level and will have greater retention if they learn the various aspects of writing while employing them. In addition, since certain skills build upon others, planning should take this into consideration; for example, a lesson on choosing words with strong sensory imagery should not come after students have written a descriptive paper but rather before or during that time. A lesson on various ways to open a paper should come early in the writing workshop time line rather than after students have been asked to take several modes of writing all the way to completion. At the very beginning of the writing workshop, the long-range plan should include activities to teach students about steps in the writing process, options for employing them, and ways to adapt them to suit personal writing strengths.

Teachers engaged in long-range planning may benefit from filling out a full semester of daily class topics in the form of a calendar so that they can get a feel for how things fit together and then can experiment with arranging and rearranging them until they find the sequence that seems most logical. This long-range plan can be changed as needed or after implementation in the classroom suggests a better sequence.

PLANNING FOR THE SHORT RANGE

In general, short-range planning for a writing workshop—planning for individual days—benefits from the same steps or elements used to guide short-range planning for any other daily lesson plan. Many of the steps in a traditional model such as Madeline Hunter's from the 1970s—stating objectives, establishing anticipatory set, guided practice, and independent practice and closure—still deserve attention (Pushkin, 2001). The learning objectives, for example, are still the focus of the lesson and need to be in alignment with learning activities. Also, assessment, diverse cultural background, learning styles, and abilities still need to be considered, and students' progress still must be monitored and addressed.

An effective opening, referred to as an *anticipatory set* in the Madeline Hunter model (Pushkin, 2001, p. 41), is no less important in a writing workshop than in any other class. As any veteran teacher can attest to, simply saying "Go to work" is a poor means of getting students off to a productive start. A good opening is designed to do a number of things, including (1) grab the students' attention, (2) pique their curiosity and interest about the day's learning, (3) tie in to what they already know, and (4) introduce new

---

QUICK TIPS

LITERATURE TO OPEN WRITING WORKSHOP: A FEW MORE SUGGESTIONS

"Anthem," Buck Ramsey

Bless Me, Ultima, Rudolfo Anaya

Captain Abdul's Pirate School, Colin McNaughton

The Chocolate War, Robert Cormier

Dogteam, Gary Paulson

"Dream Deferred," Langston Hughes

Fallen Angels, Walter Dean Myers

The Ghost Dance, Alice McLerran

The Giver, Lois Lowry

Holes, Louis Sachar

The House on Mango Street, Sandra Cisneros

Ironman, Chris Crutcher

Lord of the Flies, William Golding

Meanwhile Back at the Ranch, Trinka Hakes Noble

Many Stones, Carolyn Coman

Math Curse, John Sciezska

The Mysteries of Harris Burdick, Chris Van Allsburg

"On the Pulse of Morning," Maya Angelou

Out of the Dust, Karen Hesse

The Outsiders, S. E. Hinton

The Paper Bag Princess, Robert N. Munsch

The Smallest Muscle in the Human Body, Alberto Rios

Sonnet 18, William Shakespeare

"Staircase," Paul Zarzyski

Storm on the Desert, Carolyn Lesser

Stuck in Neutral, Terry Trueman

The Teacher from the Black Lagoon, Mike Thaler

Tears of a Tiger, Sharon Draper

"The Telltale Heart," Edgar Allan Poe

"Whales Weep Not," D. H. Lawrence

Where the Sidewalk Ends, Shel Silverstein

White Socks Only, Evelyn Coleman

Also include other kinds of writing that might provoke a response from students, such as greeting cards, personal ads, letters to the editor, contracts, service manuals, pharmaceutical catalogs, and so on.

---

material that will be covered in class that day. A short interaction with literature is one possible opening activity that will heighten students' sense of audience and purpose.

Atwell (1998), author of the quintessential writing workshop resource, *In the Middle*, suggests starting class with the reading and discussion of a poem (pp. 140–141). In addition to poems, short passages of literature—or any other written pieces regardless of genre—that read well aloud can have a dramatic impact on the students and create a fertile environment as class begins. A poem or passage that deals in some way with the session's topic will help to transition students' attention to the task at hand. The passage should be one that will provoke a response from the students. A response of passionate agreement and identification is good, but a response of passionate disagreement or disbelief may be just as good. Since writing workshop students are writers, or becoming writers, passages that remind them that writing is for an audience will help them recognize the potential power in their own writing.

Quick Tips

A Few Good Openers

Slogan Writing

The teacher brings products of some kind (consumer items like candy, shampoo, or makeup work well) to class—one for every student in the class, or students can be instructed to each bring in one. Begin with one product on each student's desk. Give students 2 minutes to come up with an advertising slogan for the product. This could be a word, a phrase, or one or two sentences. At the end of 2 minutes, rotate the products to the next student for a fresh slogan. This works well in groups of three to five (writing groups would work well). When the products have all rotated to every member of the group, each group member shares all or some of his or her slogans

Examples:
1. A chewy, fruit-flavored candy/"Juice me!"
2. A chocolate candy bar/"Can't wait for heaven? Have a little heaven on Earth."
3. Underarm deodorant/"Because you never know when someone might ask you to salsa (dance)."

CIA Training

This opener is inspired by "Garbology" from the Northwest Regional Educational Laboratories Six Traits of Writing focus lessons. Students can work in groups or separately, depending on how much preparation the teacher wants to do. Each student is given a bag with various items in it and told the following: "As part of your CIA training, you are coached to develop your powers of deductive reasoning. This bag contains evidence taken from the motel room of a suspect by search warrant. Create a quick profile of this person and explain the significance of these objects in leading you to your conclusions."

_____ Don't Get Me Started!

This is another title for the old "pet peeves" activity. Students fill in the blank with something like "cheap dates" and then continue with a creation of their imagination or events from real life. "My boyfriend is so cheap, we went to the Wal-Mart lunch counter for prom dinner."

EFFECTIVE OPENINGS

An effective opener will not only provoke a response from the students but will also provide a means for them to make connections between literature, their own lives, and their own writing. For example, if middle school students are writing personal narratives and/or poetry about their life experiences, the writing workshop might start each day with any one of the following:

1. Any one of the many poems about the psychological and emotional uncertainty of life from Sara Holbrook's (1995) collection *Walking on the Boundaries of Change*.
2. A short passage from Jerry Renault's point of view in Robert Cormier's (2001) *The Chocolate War*.
3. A short passage from Pony Boy's point of view from S. E. Hinton's (1967) *The Outsiders*.
4. If high school students are writing memoirs, a moving passage from Luis Rodriguez's (1993) *Always Running, La Vida Loca: Gang Days in L.A.*
5. If high school students are writing about life's choices, Robert Frost's (1920) "The Road Not Taken."
6. If students of any age are writing allegories, Dr. Seuss's (1971) *The Lorax*.

Teachers can have fun being creative in choosing opening literature and using a variety of genres from the literary canon to popular culture to picture books to birthday cards: any written piece that will act as a good opening for a writing workshop.

The opening literature selection might even connect to the mini-lesson. For example, if the mini-lesson is about writing descriptions that show rather than tell, the opening literature passage might be one of these:

1. Chapter 1 from Christopher Paul Curtis's (1995) *The Watsons Go to Birmingham—1963*, in which the author describes the cold Michigan winter.
2. Dr. Seuss's (1937) *And to Think That I Saw It on Mulberry Street*, which piles description upon description.

Additional Openers

A different, but equally effective, kind of opening comes from Alan Ziegler, one of the pioneers of the writing workshop and author of volumes one and two of *The Writing Workshop* (1981, 1984). Ziegler suggests starting the workshop with brief thinking/writing activities that "are geared for quick success to help the workshop get off the ground in a non-threatening way . . . [which can be] especially useful if some students have a negative attitude toward writing or an insecurity about their ability to write" (p. 3). These are short, creative pieces that don't require a sustained effort and are fairly entertaining, such as finishing a sentence that begins "I wish I (or someone else) weren't (or wasn't) so . . . " and writing a paragraph or poem to flesh out the idea (which students often use ironically). A hypothetical creation might read something like this:

> I wish I weren't so smart. Those headlines and reporters can get on your nerves. It's "local student breaks IQ record" this and "14-year-old becomes first brain surgeon" that until I just can't find the time to revise Einstein's Theory of Relativity any more.

Some other openers we have had success with include slogan writing, CIA training, and "Don't get me started" (see Quick Tips: "A Few Good Openers," p. 47).

THE MINI-LESSON

Another regular event in the writing workshop schedule is the mini-lesson, which could be daily but would more likely be used on alternate days or twice weekly. Mini-lessons are short bursts of instruction designed to provide students with tools to help them become better writers. They deal with a variety of topics from conventions such as punctuation, grammar, and usage to elements of the writer's craft such as choosing

Quick Tips

A FEW SUGGESTED MINI-LESSON TOPICS

1. "What do I write about?"
2. Showing rather than telling.
3. Using concrete descriptions.
4. Figurative language.
5. Sensory imagery.
6. Avoiding tired adjectives and adverbs.
7. Using precise verbs.
8. Punctuating dialogue.
9. Using and documenting sources
10. Avoiding forms of *to be.*
11. Active and passive voice.
12. Effective characterization.
13. Building suspense.
14. Grammar and usage
15. Address specific problems as they arise.
16. Attention-grabbing openings.
17. Satisfying conclusions.
18. Misplaced modifiers.
19. Creating a character sketch.
20. Improving in the Six Traits.
21. Methods of revision.
22. Citing sources in MLA or APA.

a story's point of view, using flashbacks, or choosing words for their effect on the reader. Mini-lessons should come early in the period and before students turn to their own writing since strategically placed mini-lessons provide information relevant to the students' work on a given day.

Unlike the instructional practice of putting multiple lessons together in one unit, mini-lessons provide instruction in digestible chunks. They are short, usually 5 to 15 minutes, certainly no longer than the students' attention spans. Mini-lessons also supply information at the point where it is useful, during the writing process when students actually use the knowledge or skill acquired from the mini-lesson, rather than weeks later. Part of long-range planning is the placement of mini-lessons at the point where they will do the most good. In addition, teachers should take a year-long look at all the learning objectives that could be addressed through mini-lessons and should spread them out over the course of writing work-shop days when possible.

Mini-Lesson Topics

"What do I write about?" is a good mini-lesson to use in the very beginning so that students can generate a list of subjects to write about that will give them many choices and a high probability of success. We know that young writers write much more and at a higher level of sophistication when they have topics of personal interest to them (Perl, 1979). One of the earliest activities in the writing workshop plan should be generating a list of topics. To generate lists of potential topics, Atwell (1998) has her students "identify and lay claim to their own interests, concerns and areas of expertise," which she calls their "writing territories" (p. 120). Atwell's writing territories include topics, genres, and audiences (pp. 121–122), and she generates her own list to share with students, a sharing intended to help them come up with ideas for their own lists of territories.

Following are a few generic topics to suggest (also see Figure 3–2):

1. Relatives
2. Family stories
3. Pets
4. Favorite pastimes
5. Special talents
6. Childhood memories
7. Jobs
8. Accidents/injuries
9. Successes/failures
10. Embarrassing but funny experiences
11. Stories from school

Students will discover that they have a wealth of topics to write about, especially after they share with each other and add more ideas to their lists.

Students should have two portfolios, a working portfolio that contains everything they have done and a showcase or performance portfolio that contains only

Figure 3–2 A hypothetical student's list of writing topics

1. My Grandma Mae
2. My Uncle John, the actor
3. My mom and dad's funny habits
4. Life with five sisters
5. Hiawatha, Iowa, my hometown
6. Our crazy cousins, the Delcortes
7. Pushkin, our golden retriever
8. The lives and times of our six cats
9. My favorite game: hockey
10. The day I fell off the roof
11. While my sister was a missionary in China
12. My favorite movies (*Alien, Aliens, Aliens 3, Aliens 4*)
13. My favorite band, Nirvana
14. How I broke my leg at camp
15. Fishing with Grandpa Jack
16. Working at McDonald's
17. The day the rattlesnake came in our garage
18. Sailing
19. How I failed gym class in the seventh grade
20. My math teacher's embarrassing pants rip
21. The story of my grandmother and grandfather's romance
22. The best way to cook wild duck

pieces chosen for sharing (see Chapter 6 for additional information on portfolios). Within the portfolio system, students must keep a list of topics that they find interesting or personally relevant enough to write about.

Strategies other than writing territories also can help students find good topics to write about. Gantos, (1994) a prominent author of young adult literature, proposes the use of a neighborhood map complete with sketches of memorable events from growing up. Nelson (1994)—author of *Writing and Being,* Greater Phoenix Area Writing Project Director, and Arizona State University associate professor of English—suggests creating personal biographical time lines (p. 137) to find meaningful events for personal narratives, as well as exploring the history behind scars on the body (p. 109) and scars on the heart (p. 112).

Teachers should also build up a library of provocative prompts designed to generate a high level of interest and/or to stimulate the memory. Lists of prompts can be found already prepared, and teachers will find it does not take long to generate several. The important thing is to accumulate good prompts over time. Following are a few for starters:

1. A time when someone helped you
2. A memorable surprise
3. Being lost
4. Being scared
5. A humorous childhood misconception

6. Who you would like to be other than yourself
7. An old wrong you would like to right
8. Someone whom you would like to thank
9. Hopes for 10 years from now
10. One thing you would change about your life if you could
11. What you fear most

MODES AND GENRES IN WRITING WORKSHOPS

The basic modes and genres of writing most commonly addressed in state and national standards include various forms of narrative, exposition, persuasion, description, various types of research, literary analysis/reader response, and poetry. Following are a few ideas for specific writing tasks students might use to accomplish competency in those modes:

1. Announcements (company, school, city, various departments of government)
2. Autobiographies
3. Billboards
4. Biographies
5. Book reviews
6. Bumper stickers
7. Cards (birthday, sympathy, holiday, congratulations, baby, wedding, friendship, other)
8. Case studies
9. CD reviews
10. Cereal box (or other product container) texts
11. Computer game reviews
12. Descriptions of . . . (my room, our house, my car, my wardrobe, etc.)
13. Descriptions of a favorite: place, activity, person, restaurant, etc.
14. E-mail
15. Essays (compare and contrast, cause and effect, analogy, classification, process analysis, inductive, deductive)
16. Fictitious interviews (with George Washington, Holden Caulfield, etc.)
17. Historical fiction
18. Instructions for operating a device or equipment
19. I-search paper
20. Last will and testaments (serious or comical: I leave my sense of humor to the school's Dean of Discipline, etc.)
21. Letters of complaint
22. Letters of inquiry
23. Letters of introduction (introducing self or a friend to someone)
24. Letters of philanthropic request
25. Letters of romance
26. Letters to friends or pen pals
27. Letters to the editor

28. Letters to the future (to general population in the distant future; to the writer, to the writer's friends or progeny in the not-so-distant future)
29. Letters to the past (to general population of the distant past; to friends or family in the not-so-distant past)
30. Literary interpretations/analyses/responses
31. Memoirs
32. Movie and television program reviews
33. Multi-genre papers
34. News articles (straight news reporting or feature)
35. Novels
36. Park (theme park or national, state, county park) reviews
37. Personal narratives
38. Personal reflections
39. Plays
40. Poems of any form (ballad, blank verse, sonnet, elegy, epic, free verse, haiku, hymn, limerick, sestina, villanelle, slam, etc.)
41. Political speeches
42. Posters
43. Product slogans or jingles
44. Restaurant reviews
45. Short stories (mysteries, adventures, fantasies, science fiction, historical fiction, fairy tales, picture books/children's stories, sports, crime, war, espionage, occult, westerns, romance)
46. Summaries (book or movie plots, news stories, textbook passages, etc.)
47. Thank you notes
48. Travel brochures
49. TV or radio commercial scripts
50. Vanity automobile license plates
51. Weather reports
52. Web sites
53. Word studies

PROGRESS CHART

The writing workshop teacher typically keeps a chart showing students' names, current projects, exactly what step in the writing process each student is now in, and scheduled conferences. The teacher can use this chart to make a regularly scheduled check of every student's progress, to monitor individual students at any time during the workshop, and to guide planning that takes place outside of class time. The chart can be easily constructed using graph paper or, more commonly, by creating a table/template of the kind commonly used computer software such as Microsoft Excel will generate. Such a computer-generated chart can have additional features as sophisticated or basic as the computer skills of the teacher, from a simple chart to a spreadsheet that gives a running tally of points and percentages.

Regardless of its complexity or simplicity, the writing workshop progress chart will allow the teacher to keep abreast of every writer's progress and will allow for a nearly instantaneous appraisal of any workshop participant.

WRITING CONFERENCES

Writing conferences can take place between the writer and anyone who is ready to respond to the writer's work. Most commonly, writers confer with one other person, with a small group, or with the teacher or other writing mentor. Since the teacher-to-pupil ratio in most classrooms puts the teacher's time at a premium, teachers will want to have a strategy for conferencing that provides the writer with the kind of help he or she can use at the time it will be most helpful and from the person most qualified to help at that time. During the drafting process, the teacher is continuously meeting with students to address specific problems or needs, but when the first draft is finished, the conferencing can best be done with peers and will prove a learning experience for both parties if students are taught how to conduct the conference and how to use the feedback.

Conferencing not only provides the resources for improving the quality of a paper but also for the improvement of the writer's skill, provided that the responders give concrete, usable feedback and provided that the writer makes a sincere attempt to use the feedback. Strategies exist (See Chapter 7: The Six-Trait Model) for providing feedback that will help the writer both to improve the paper and to improve his or her writing skills. Teachers must remember that the latter goal is actually more important; any attention to the paper that does not affect a change in the writer is wasted effort.

Teachers and peers will help the writer to identify strengths and weaknesses of the paper and will explore ways to improve it, but the changes must be of the writer's own creation. Responders must not tell the writer what words they would use but must let the writer find his or her own. For example, the writer might be told that the description of the food at a professional baseball game needs to be improved and should appeal to the senses, but the responders should not give specific wording or phrasing such as "Tart, crisp sauerkraut and spicy horseradish erupted inside my mouth" because those would be the responder's words, not the writer's.

A more beneficial approach is to ask questions that help the writer to examine the experience about which he or she is writing and to develop it so that the reader will know and experience what the writer now knows or experienced. Reexamining the example of the weak description of food at a baseball game, we might expect the responders to ask questions such as these: What did you have to eat at the ballpark? What was on that hotdog? Can you describe the first bite? Student writers usually know far more about their topic than their first draft indicates, and questioning designed to help them relive the experience will elicit this knowledge.

Changes to the paper should be made only if the writer wants to make them. Although responders may suggest that a passage needs improvement, and may point out specific weaknesses and engage in questioning that provides the writer with raw material to improve the passage, the writer owns the paper and must have the final say on revision. Only by engaging in the high cognitive process of evaluation of his or her own work and synthesis of a better passage, word, or phrase will the student writer improve skills—and not by mindlessly making any and all changes that a peer or teacher suggests.

Until the publishing step in the writing process, conferences are for the purpose of revision feedback, and that is not the same thing as editing. Editing is synonymous with proofreading, a task that is pointless until the written product has been revised to its nearly final form. Editing at the conference phase is analogous to sanding and polishing wood before it is made into furniture: Much of it will end up as scrap, so the effort is largely wasted. Until the final step, conventions should not get much attention.

PEER CONFERENCING

Ironically, peer conferencing has proven to be both boon and bane in taking students through the writing process. Effective peer conferencing can only take place if students have the skills to analyze a peer's work and to give meaningful feedback, that will tell the writer what is written well and what needs improvement. Feedback must be specific and expressed in terminology familiar to both reader and writer. If students have not learned how to analyze a paper and how to give usable feedback, teachers find that students most often make only superficial suggestions to the writer about conventions, such as spelling and punctuation. Analytical comments about the quality of the writing are often restricted to whether or not the reader liked the paper, and they fail to provide specific details about the author's craft, details that would enable the writer to improve the paper.

Mini-lessons on peer conferencing should do the following:

1. Help students to recognize the characteristics of good writing
2. Provide students with a terminology for discussing writing
3. Give students guided practice in analyzing written work appropriate to their age group

Students will be more open to feedback about their writing if the writing workshop atmosphere and operation have built trust among the members, especially the members of the writing/conferencing groups. One commonly used method to superimpose over the process of talking about writing is the Praise, Question, Polish (PQP) process.

1. *Praise* (What did the writer do well?)
2. *Question* (What questions come to the reader's mind?)
3. *Polish* (What improvements could be made?)

To open the conference, the writer should read his or her paper out loud at least once and twice if time allows. Student responders must know that their first responses should be to *what* the student writer had to say and not *how* it was said. The purpose of writing is to communicate to the reader some idea or experience that is close to the writer's heart, so responders should speak to that first.

When Albert Einstein unveiled the theory of relativity, for example, we can safely guess that those in attendance were awed by the brilliance of his idea and the implications that it held for the commonly held view of reality and that they did not point out his mistakes in homonym use as their first reaction. A personal narrative about the loss of a loved one, for another example, should provoke an emotional response from the reader first, one in which the responder reacts personally to the writer. The appropriate response to such a paper might be "I can tell that you really loved your uncle." The PQP process facilitates that by first affirming the writer in his or her attempt to express this important message and then proceeding to help him or her to do it as well as possible.

A student writer can accommodate a limited amount of feedback at a time. For this reason, the conference must be limited to a certain number of minutes or a certain amount of feedback. Teachers participating in a one-year study of writing instruction reported that beginning writers especially will cease to benefit from feedback when it starts to address too many issues (Blasingame, 2000, p. 287).

As students get into the nuts and bolts of the peer conference, we suggest they use a conferencing sheet that will help them consistently think of concrete characteristics of the writing to evaluate and discuss and that they record what topics the conference addressed, as well as feedback to refer to later in the revision process. We have had success with a conferencing worksheet at our experimental writing center at Fees Middle School in Tempe, Arizona (see Figure 3–3). The worksheet is adapted from the Six-Trait Model Writing materials provided by the Northwest Regional Educational Laboratory. Please refer to Chapter 7 for more information on this model and our recommendation for steps in its implementation, including peer conferencing.

TEACHER CONFERENCING

Students benefit from short conferences with the writing workshop teacher while they are in the writing process, although these will not be comprehensive conferences but rather interactions designed to address problems or obstacles the student writer is faced with mid-process and must resolve or overcome in order to move forward in the writing process.

Atwell (1998) suggests that the teacher move from student to student using a stool or chair to facilitate interaction when engaging in these mid-process conferences (pp. 220–221). Because they feel they know the moment in which the conference has accomplished its goal and the time has come to move on to another student, teachers in the field report to us that they prefer to move from student to student rather than to have students come to their desks. Teachers in the field also report that the use of a chair is dependent on the physical limits of the classroom; they prefer being at eye level with students, but narrow aisles and irregular table or desk shapes can make moving a chair through the classroom too disruptive.

Figure 3–3 Conferencing worksheet

Write specific words, phrases, or line numbers from the paper in the space under a statement.

Ideas

_____ The topic has been narrowed to one main idea.

_____ The paper sticks to the main idea.

_____ This paper has plenty of details.

_____ The writer knows about this topic.

_____ The writer chose information that would answer the readers' questions.

_____ (Advanced) The writer used evidence and examples to support each point.

Organization

_____ An interesting opening grabs the reader's attention.

_____ The paper goes from one point to the next without getting lost or sidetracked.

_____ Every sentence relates in some way to the main idea.

_____ The ending is satisfying (feels like the end).

_____ (Advanced) The ending reinforces and supports the main idea.

Voice

_____ The paper sounds like the person who wrote it.

_____ The writer obviously likes this topic.

_____ After reading this paper, the reader is likely to want to know more about the topic.

_____ The writer had an audience in mind and tried to speak to it.

_____ (Advanced) The voice is strong but under control and does not get too funny, sarcastic, nostalgic, etc.

Word Choice

_____ The writer does not use vague language (*stuff, big, trouble*).

_____ Nouns and their modifiers are concrete. *A 150-pound German shepherd*, not "a dog." *The smell of burning rubber*, not "a bad smell".

_____ Verbs are precise (*strutted* rather than *walked*).

_____ Words appeal to the senses of smell, taste, sight, and touch.

_____ The language sounds natural for the writer (no big words just to impress the reader, etc.).

Sentence Fluency

_____ The paper reads nicely out loud, and the reader does not stumble.

_____ Sentence types and lengths vary.

_____ Sentences begin in a variety of ways.

_____ Sentences are concise (no dead wood).

_____ Sentences are grammatically correct.

_____ (Advanced) Linking words are used often to show how ideas connect.

Conventions

_____ Mechanics are correct:

_____ Spelling

_____ Grammar

_____ Punctuation

_____ Capitalization

_____ If a formal style was needed (a research paper), the paper follows that style's rules.

BIBLIOGRAPHY

Arizona Department of Education. (July 20, 2002). *Academic standards and accountability.* Retrieved January 20, 2003, from http://www.ade.state.az.us/standards.

Atwell, N. (1998) *In the middle: New understandings about writing, reading and learning* (2nd ed.). Portsmouth, NH: Boynton/Cook Heinemann.

Blasingame, J. (2000). Six case studies of first year implementation of the six-trait model for writing instruction and assessment. (Doctoral dissertation, University of Kansas). *Dissertation Abstract International, 61–12A,* 4705.

Cormier, Robert. (2001). *Rag and bone shop.* New York: Delacorte.

Curtis, Christopher Paul. (1995). *The Watsons go to Birmingham—1963.* New York: Delacorte.

Fletcher R., and Portalupi, J. (2001). *Writing workshop: The essential guide.* Portsmouth, NH: Boynton/Cook Heinemann.

Frost, Robert. (1920). *The road not taken. Mountain Interval.* New York: Henry Holt.

Gantos, Jack. (1994). *Heads or tails: Stories for the sixth grade.* New York: Farvar, Straus, & Giroux.

Hinton, S.E. (1967). *The outsiders.* New York: Puffin.

Holbrook, Sara. (1995). *Walking on the boundaries of change.* Cleveland: Kid Poems.

Muschla, G. R. (1993). *Writing workshop survival kit.* West Nyack, NY: The Center for Applied Research in Education, a Simon and Schuster Company.

National Council of Teachers of English and the International Reading Association. (1996). *Standards for the English language arts.* Urbana, IL: NCTE.

Nelson, Lynn. (1994). *Writing and being.* Philadelphia: Innisfree Press.

Perl, S. (1979). The composing processes of unskilled college writers. *Research in the Teaching of English, 13.4,* 324–325.

Pushkin, D. (2001). *Teacher training* (pp. 40–41). Santa Barbara, CA: ABC-CLIO.

Rodriquez, Luis. (1993). *Always running, la vida loca: Gang days in L.A.* Willimantic, CT: Curbstone Press.

Seuss, Dr. (1937). *And to think. . . .* New York: Vanguard.

Seuss, Dr. (1971). *The lorax.* New York: Random House.

Spandel, V. (2001*). Creating writers through six-trait writing assessment and instruction* (3rd ed.). New York: Addison-Wesley Longman, Inc.

Tines, K. (1997). *Using reading and writing workshop in the real classroom.* Ottawa, KS: The Writing Conference, Inc.

Ziegler, A. (1981). *The writing workshop* (vol. 1). New York: Teachers and Writers Collaborative.

Ziegler, A. (1984). *The writing workshop* (vol. 2). New York: Teachers and Writers Collaborative.

CHAPTER 4

The Multi-Genre
Approach in Writing

A multigenre paper arises from research, experience,
and imagination.

Tom Romano (2000)

PAST PROBLEMS

Traditionally, students' research writing has consisted primarily of reports at the lower
grades and term papers, sometimes called library research papers, at the upper grades
and maybe an author report or book review that requires some reading, quoting, and
citing of sources. Report writing has usually involved creating a paper centered on a
topic and made up of information gleaned from reference works. The information may
or may not have been integrated, interpreted, or even reworded, and the topic may or
may not have been of interest to the student. For most students, this began in elementary school with the profile of a state, such as Alabama, or country, such as Brazil,
copied nearly verbatim from the encyclopedia and complete with maps, also copied
from the encyclopedia and colored in by the student. The sophistication of the
research papers increased through the students' education to some point in high
school, when the students did library research centered on a topic about which they
stated an opinion, found pro and con arguments, and used appropriate documentation to cite sources. The writing in these papers, whether it was the elementary school
report or the high school research paper, was all of one mode or genre, usually expository, persuasive, or a combination of the two.

For most high school students, the research paper was the most arduous task of their language arts studies. Although the experience of writing these papers taught students the conventions of citing and using sources (and sometimes the perils of plagiarism), the idea that they provided growth in writing proficiency commensurate with the hours of work that went into them may have been mistaken. If, as Emig (1977) says, writing is the highest cognitive activity in which human beings engage (p. 125), then reports and traditional research papers are at the lower end of the cognitive scale in Bloom's taxonomy.

In comparison to the other types of writing in which students make meaning out of their experience and attempt to express it to other people, traditional reports and research papers are high on clerical effort but low on mental exertion. These papers are just the neatly summarized and documented words of others taken in and spat out again in exposition or persuasion or a combination of the two.

Most state standards, as well as district and school goals and objectives, make some mention of research writing, and that is as it should be. Students must learn to gather and process information, to interpret it, to evaluate it, and to synthesize a written piece that expresses their conclusions.

The same standards, goals, and objectives, however, can be accomplished through the use of a writing project very different from the traditional research paper or report. This alternative writing project integrates a multiplicity of genres in an attempt to examine its topic from many angles rather than from only one. This multiple-genre paper, or multi-genre paper, encourages students to investigate, read, and write in several genres or modes. The multi-genre paper has become a viable alternative to the traditional research paper or report in elementary and secondary schools across the nation. It not only can help students learn to research a topic, process information, and learn the conventions of research writing, but it also can provide a vehicle for meeting many more state and local requirements for language arts, such as media literacy and the reading, interpretation, and writing of modes and genres other than exposition and persuasion.

THE MULTI-GENRE PAPER

Simply put, the multi-genre paper is a writing product that includes many different types of writing, all revolving around a main topic. Students are limited only by their imaginations as to the types of writings they might include and by their abilities to make logical connections and transitions among genres. Multiple genres can refer not only to the student's paper but also to the sources of investigation, as well, sources from which the writer may quote in the final work. A sample multi-genre paper can be found in Appendix A.

A multi-genre paper is usually a research paper, but it may also be an alternative means for a student to write about a topic other than the one-genre paper (and not to include research). Teachers may choose to use a multi-genre approach in lieu of the traditional research paper, in lieu of other papers, or both.

In *Writing with Passion*, Romano (1995) first defines the multi-genre paper by entitling the seventh chapter as "The Multigenre Research Paper[:] Melding Fact, Interpretation and Imagination" (p. 109). He says that the world reveals itself in a multiplicity of genres and each of those genres gives us its own special insight into the world: "Each genre gives me ways of seeing and understanding the world that others do not. I perceive the world through multiple genres. They shape my seeing" (p. 109).

Romano's reasoning seems accurate given the multiple texts with which students are constantly bombarded. From the product information on a microwavable burrito, to the predigested news and high-tech ads on Channel One, to the lyrics of rap and slam poetry, to the hybridized auditory and visual creations that make surfing the Web so engaging, information comes at us in rapid-fire and ever-evolving formats. For students to develop critical literacy in the vast number of genres they experience on a daily basis, they need to work in those genres.

As Allen (2001) points out, "One of the most powerful reasons to have students do multigenre research papers and presentations is that the process allows students to learn skills in context" (p. 9).

The multi-genre approach to creating a research paper addresses not only multiple educational objectives but also multiple intelligences as proposed by Gardner (1983, p. 8) and diverse learning styles. In addition to the traditional use of library research, the multi-genre process will empower student writers to choose ways of learning and accessing information that they prefer and will facilitate their critical literacy within these forms. It will enable not only a larger scope of investigative means but also a much greater scope of means to communicate the findings than the traditional library research paper does.

For example, a student with a burning desire to learn about horses and deliver the truth to a readership will find the multi-genre paper the ideal means for doing so. Beginning with the investigation of horses, in addition to researching nonfiction reference works in the library, the student can explore many more avenues. The writer might read cowboy poetry, listen to western songs, interview rodeo and pleasure riders, read a classic western novel, view a few classic movies about horses, read some veterinarian journals and medical books, research the horse's physiology, attend a rodeo, and ride a horse.

Since different genres depict different aspects of reality, all of which together will help create the mosaic of the writer's experience, the multi-genre format empowers the writer to give the reader a truer feel for what was discovered about horses. The writer must learn to negotiate among the various genres skillfully and with purpose as he or she blends together material from sources and material he or she has created.

Students will choose which sources to quote from and will select which genres to write in and how to put everything together for the most powerful effect on the reader. A writer might use pieces he or she has written from any number of forms (multiple genres) such as journal entries, poems, summaries of news articles, short stories, personal narratives, descriptions, letters, dialogues, and more.

SCHEDULING THE MULTI-GENRE PROJECT

Just as teachers using the traditional research paper have acknowledged a need to set a calendar of research activities, tasks, or checkpoints for their students, so have teachers using the multi-genre paper. When students are first introduced to this approach, a chronology of tasks is especially important given the innovative and open approach this project uses. After students have created their first multi-genre paper, they will not need as much direction—but the first time through, a calendar of activities, tasks, and deadlines will be a welcome guide for them. Just how detailed and specific the calendar should be is up to individual teachers, but we suggest some general ideas for the calendar in the following pages.

Step 1: Introducing the Concept

Multi-genre is nothing new to fiction writers, and many students will have already read novels that make use of many forms of writing to tell a story. Teachers can make use of popular fiction to initiate students into the concept by reading from a multi-genre novel appropriate to the students' grade level, such as Draper's (1994) *Tears of a Tiger* for students in grades 8 through 10.

Nothing can illustrate the multi-genre concept for students better than actual examples of papers written by students from past classes or other schools. Once students have reviewed papers done by others, they will have a flood of ideas about creating papers of their own. After teachers have used the multi-genre paper in class for a few years, they will have no shortage of good sample papers to share with their students— papers on a variety of topics that will both illustrate the project's basic concept and help spark ideas for successful topics. Until that time, however, excellent samples of papers done by lower middle school students can be found in Allen's (2001) *The Multigenre Research Paper: Voice, Passion and Discovery in Grades 4–6*. Samples of papers from middle and high school students are available in Romano's (2000) *Blending Genre, Altering Style*. Our own sample multi-genre paper is found in Appendix A. As the title suggests, "One 24-Hour Unit of Time During the Life Cycle Process of an Adolescent Male Human or a Day in the Life of Chester Funderburk" is on the topic of doublespeak.

Step 2: Choosing a Topic

All successful writing begins with a topic that is close to the writer's heart, something that he or she cares about. Otherwise, the writing will be weak in ideas and voice and the writer will not connect with the reader. In his book *Writing and Being*, Nelson (1994), Arizona State University professor and director of the Greater Phoenix Area Writing Project, says, "Our words must be born in our hearts and find their way to our heads. . . . Without feeling, without the heart, our writing and our being too easily turn into artifice, image, pretense, games" (p. 37). To put in the amount of time and effort that this paper will require, far more than a traditional research paper, the writer must truly want to know more about the topic and have a need to share that newfound knowledge. The student might start by trying to answer this question: What would I really enjoy spending the next two months investigating and writing about? This suggests a topic that the writer knows something about already—and might even be knowledgeable about—but a topic that he or she would like to know much more about. It suggests a topic that the writer could somehow experience, perhaps even directly (see Figure 4–1 for examples).

1. People
   a. Colin Farrell
   b. Norah Jones
   c. Frida Kahlo
   d. LeBron James
   e. Sitting Bull
   f. 9/11 New York firemen
   g. Curt Cobain
   h. Lance Armstrong
2. Places
   a. Hiawatha, Iowa
   b. Nome, Alaska
   c. Peculiar, Missouri
   d. Wyoming
   e. Idaho
   f. Crater Lake National Park
   g. Everglades National Park
   h. Buffalo River NWSR
   i. Dallas Book Depository
   j. Rodeo Drive, Beverly Hills, CA
3. Living things
   a. German shepherd dogs
   b. Grizzly bears
   c. Velociraptors
4. Products
   a. Home teeth whitening
      kits
   b. Mac vs. PC
   c. Sony Playstation
   d. Violent video games
   e. Compact SUV's
   f. The best downhill ski equipment
   g. Oversized drivers (golf)
   h. Prestige/clothing brands
   i. Basketball shoes: fashion
      or function?
5. Important events
   a. Presidential election
   b. World Series
6. Careers
   a. Underwater demolition
   b. Air Force pilot
7. Medical
   a. Modern cosmetic surgery
   b. Laser eye surgery

Figure 4–1 A hypothetical student's list of topics for a multi-genre paper

A good place to start looking for topic ideas is in the list of possible topics created in the writing workshop (p. 51). Some of the topics might be ready to use as they are, and some might be useful only as springboards for other ideas. For example, a student might not write a multi-genre paper about her grandfather specifically, but she might write it about men who fought in tanks in World War II and include interviews with her grandfather. Another student might not write a paper specifically about his German shepherd, Moz, but he might write about that breed and include narratives and observations about Moz. Another student might write not only about her family's encounter with a grizzly bear in Alaska but might include a narrative of what happened in a paper about hiking or grizzly bears or grizzly bear encounters.

For some topics, the writer might narrow down from the personal writing topics list rather than broaden out. For example, a paper on hockey would be too broad, but a paper on playing goalie could work nicely. A paper about movies might also be too broad, but a paper investigating horror movies could be better and one about vampire movies over the decades might be even better.

A few generic categories for topics that might help students generate specific ideas might include the following:

1. People
    a. actors/actresses
    b. artists
    c. authors
    d. athletes
    e. historical figures
    f. heroes
    g. musical performers
    h. politicians
2. Places
    a. cities
    b. states
    c. vacation spots
    d. geological rarities
    e. national parks or wilderness areas
    f. recreational locations
3. Living things
    a. particular animals
    b. creatures from the past
    c. particular plants
    d. pathogenic organisms
    e. record-holding plants and/or animals
4. Products
    a. grooming products
    b. foods
    c. technology
        i. computers
        ii. computer games

              iii. CD players
              iv. DVD players
               v. software
       d. cars
       e. sporting goods
               i. roller blades
              ii. ski equipment
              iii. outdoor equipment
              iv. golfing equipment
       f. clothing
       g. footwear
   5. Important events
   6. Careers
   7. Medical topics
       a. specific maladies
       b. new medical procedures

Step 3: Recording the Experience

Beginning on day one of their multi-genre projects, students should keep records of their experiences. This should not be a record of their research findings but rather a narrative of what happened as they investigated and what their thoughts and feelings were about each event. Students will choose parts of this record to include in the finished product, both written and for presentation. Allen (2001) recommends a "response journal" in which students respond in writing to what they read (p. 23) and a "process journal" in which they record the story of their investigation (p. 24). It is perhaps simplest to ask that they keep a journal of their experiences, thoughts, and feelings as they go through the multi-genre process, with the ultimate purpose of telling parts of the story of their research in the finished product or presentation that they believe will enhance the reader's understanding of the topic.

Step 4: Investigating

Each student should make a list of potential sources for investigating his or her specific topic. Chances are good that they all will have two very good sources in common: (1) a general Internet search (remind them to use a variety of descriptors in naming the subject of their search and not to stop with one search engine if they are dissatisfied with the results) and (2) a search of the library's online catalog and various indices.

    In order to expand their thinking beyond the more obvious resources, take students back to the sample projects that were used to introduce the multi-genre concept and, as a class, create a list illustrating the variety of genres in which those writers researched and wrote. For example, perhaps the writer of a paper on the career of cetology (the study of whales) read D. H. Lawrence's poem "Whales Weep Not," included the first few lines of the poem, and then wrote a poem of her own inspired by an underwater dive she made. Perhaps a paper on finding the perfect mate included a personal ad from a singles newspaper—something like "50-ish, full figured DWNSF in search of SNSM, 40–60, professional. . . . "—and an ad the student wrote as if she were attempting to use that format. A project on a classic car such as the Jaguar XKE might include an interview with an insurance adjuster giving figures on how often that model is stolen and what insurance premiums will cost and a personal budget the student created showing how much of her annual income would have to go into financing ownership of that car. A project on professional wrestling might quote from the pharmaceutical catalog warnings regarding adverse side effects of an anabolic steroid and a similar but fictitious page that includes the potential lifelong consequences of each adverse side effect.

As the list of sources grows, students will see that some of the best sources may not appear in a library catalog search and may depend more upon their creative thinking. As they research their topics, other sources will reveal themselves, but students should not make final topic selections until they have created adequate lists of sources to investigate. Such lists will prevent students from wasting time on topics that seemed good but didn't really provide any means to investigate, in which case another, possibly more fruitful, topic should be chosen.

Following are a few ideas adapted from Chapter 3, the Writing Workshop, for sources of information, as well as forms in which students might read and write:

> Announcements (public—such as company, school, city, or various departments and branches of government; private—such as wedding, graduation, or anniversary)
> Autobiographies
> Billboards
> Biographies
> Book reviews
> Bumper stickers
> Cards (birthday, sympathy, holiday, congratulations, baby, wedding, friendship, other)
> Case studies
> CD reviews
> Cereal box texts (or other product container)
> Computer game reviews
> Descriptions of . . . (my room, our house, my car, my wardrobe, etc.)
> Descriptions of my favorite . . . (place, activity, person, restaurant, etc.)
> E-mail
> Essays (compare and contrast, cause and effect, analogy, classification, process analysis, inductive, deductive)
> Fictitious interviews (with George Washington, Holden Caulfield, etc.)
> Historical fiction
> Instructions for operating a device or equipment
> Interviews
> I-search papers
> Last will and testaments (serious or comical: I leave my sense of humor to the school's Dean of Discipline, etc.)

Letters of complaint

Letters of inquiry

Letters of introduction (introducing yourself or a friend to someone)

Letters of philanthropic request

Letters of romance

Letters to friends or pen pals

Letters to the editor

Letters to the future (to general population in the distant future; to the writer; to the writer's friends or progeny in the not-so-distant future)

Letters to the past (to general population of the distant past; to friends or family in the not-so-distant past)

Literary interpretations/analyses/responses

Memoirs

Movie and television program reviews

Newspaper pieces of all types

Novels

Pamphlets (philanthropic campaigns, information from government agencies or corporations, recreational information such as travel and resort brochures, etc.)

Park reviews (theme park or national, state, or county park)

Personal narratives

Personal reflections

Plays

Poems of any form (ballad, blank verse, sonnet, elegy, epic, free verse, haiku, hymn, limerick, sestina, villanelle, slam, etc.)

Political speeches

Posters

Product slogans or jingles

Restaurant reviews

Short stories (mysteries, adventures, fantasies, science fiction, historical fiction, fairy tales, picture books/children's stories, sports, crime, war, espionage, occult, westerns, romances)

Summaries (book or movie plots, news stories, textbook passage, etc.)

Thank you notes

Travel brochures

TV or radio commercial scripts

Vanity automobile license plates

Weather reports

Web sites

Word studies

Primary sources lend themselves especially well to multi-genre research. Students need to ask themselves what they can actually experience about their topics, where they can go, and whom they can talk to. A student writing about cattle ranching might actually go to a livestock auction or hang out at a veterinarian's large animal facility for a day. A student writing about a professional athlete might actually go to a game. When students write the actual paper, that experience can become a straight news article, a poem, a dialog, a narrative, a police report, an autobiographical or biographical sketch, or any other genre the student thinks will best represent the experience.

Step 5: Writing and Making the Reading/Writing Connection

As students research print material, they need to be encouraged and facilitated to make the reading and writing connection. Too often students see no relationship between the writing products that they read—such as poems, narratives, short stories, novels, plays, essays, and various forms of nonfiction—and the writing products that they create. They fail to think of themselves as writers faced with the same writing tasks—replete with the same challenges inherent in each genre—that the writers of the works they read faced. Hopefully, the multi-genre project will help them to begin to read as writers, as critical thinkers who see beyond just the service of a written piece and can analyze the writer's craft.

Romano (2000) recommends having students read and write in the same genres at the same time:

> In my ideal English/language arts classroom students are both consumers and producers of all kinds of literature and media. As they read free-verse poetry, they write free-verse poetry. As they read fiction, they write scenes themselves. As they read plays, they render their own dramatic scenes through dialog. I want students to see themselves as writers just as they see themselves as readers. (p. 44)

Then not only may students read any genre conceivable as they investigate their topics, but they also may write in any genre conceivable, provided that it suits the purpose of informing the audience about the topic.

Some genres will accomplish this informing in ways that others cannot. An obituary for a drug addict, real or fictitious, for example, might drive home the tragedy of drug abuse in a way reprinted national statistics could never do. Students are only limited by their imaginations.

Perhaps the form of writing that will prove most unnerving at first for teachers who until now have taught only the traditional research paper are the various forms of fiction that are likely to be included. Students should go beyond strictly nonfiction pieces, both in their research and in their own writing. The skillful selection and combining of these can have a powerful effect on the audience and underscore the differences of form and purpose among the various genres for the student writer. (See Figure 4–2 for examples.)

DAILY WORKSHOP

We recommend that the multi-genre paper be written in a workshop setting. (See Chapter 3 for more information on writing workshops.) In a project of this size and complexity, carefully guiding students through steps in the writing process will be essential to break the paper into manageable chunks. Students need to be guided through prewriting, drafting, sharing, responding, revising, and editing especially carefully, and their progress must be assessed daily. Teachers can tailor a workshop to

Figure 4–2 Weaving it all together

How does the multi-genre paper writer decide when and where to insert a given genre? Students are free to exercise their creativity for this purpose. Following are two illustrations of mixing up genres for effect:

1. In a paper on professional rodeo
   a. A real newspaper for-sale ad for an old cowpony and saddle

   immediately following

   b. The fictional obituary of the world's oldest saddle bronc rider

   just after

   c. A poem about the death of a rodeo rider

   followed by

   d. a real or fictitious doctor's report detailing the broken ribs and crushed pelvis suffered by a bull rider at the National Finals Pro Rodeo competition

   followed by

   e. A real magazine ad by one of the rodeo sponsors inviting fans to come and experience the excitement of the National Finals Pro Rodeo in Las Vegas.

2. In a paper on responsible dog ownership
   a. The lyrics to the song "How Much Is That Doggy in the Window?"

   directly after

   b. A few quotations from the National Humane Society on how many dogs are destroyed each year

   followed by

   c. The newspaper photo of a puppy mill owner being arrested for cruelty to animals

   followed by

   d. A summary of the physical needs of a growing puppy, with a citation from an American Kennel Club publication

   after

   e. A summary of the stories of dogs who received the Heinz Reward Dog Hero of the Year Award for saving their masters' lives

fit the specific needs of the students for a particular paper. For example, teachers might consider some of the following:

1. Mini-lessons on:
   a. conducting interviews
   b. evaluating the authenticity of online sources
   c. effective transitions
      i. from idea to idea
      ii. from genre to genre
   d. finding the poetry within prose
   e. punctuating dialog

      f. using quotations
      g. citing sources
      h. traits of individual genres

2. Peer conferencing scheduled at major checkpoints in the project
3. Teacher's progress chart (see p. 53) adapted to fit specific steps in the multi-genre process
4. Access to equipment and resources specific to multi-genre research and writing, such as tape players and transcription devices, Internet, collections of print materials in multiple genres (not just reference books), and so on.

EVALUATION

We recommend that the multi-genre paper be graded using a detailed rubric that includes not only a rating of the quality of each part in the product but also a portion of the total credit given to steps in the process. Evaluation must not be left for the very end but rather should take place at regular intervals over the course of the creation of the paper. In this way, students will know where they stand, and teachers can monitor student progress and can address problems as they arise in the process.

Allen (2001) and Romano (1995, 2000) include means for evaluation in their books on the subject. Allen, whose work deals with upper elementary and lower middle school, has both an extensive self-checklist (p. 116) and a rubric for the teacher to use in determining and explaining a grade (p. 117), both of which she brought in from teachers in the field. Romano has several guides for scoring the paper that have also been shared by teachers in the field (pp. 166–167).

We suggest a fairly simple rubric that lets students know the emphasis given to each category of their work in the total points/grade. Remember that you will be giving points as the project unfolds, in addition to points for the final product. The number of potential points is left to the teacher's discretion and arrived at prior to starting the project. A rubric used successfully by Kathi Baron, Flagstaff High School, Flagstaff, Arizona, and Kelly Pagnac, Ganado High School, Ganado, Arizona, can be found in Appendix A.

BIBLIOGRAPHY

Allen, C. A. (2001). *The multigenre research paper: Voice, passion and discovery in grades 4–6.* Portsmouth, New Hampshire: Boynton/Cook Heinemann.

Draper, S. (1994). *Tears of a tiger.* New York: Aladdin Books, an imprint of Simon and Schuster.

Emig, J. (1977). Writing as a mode of learning. *College Composition and Communication*, 28.2, 122–28.

Gardner, H. (1983). *Frames of mind.* New York: Basic Books, an imprint of HarperCollins.

Nelson, L. (1994). *Writing and being.* Philadelphia: Innisfree Press.

Romano, T. (1995). *Writing with passion.* Portsmouth, New Hampshire: Boynton/Cook Heinemann.

Romano, T. (2000). *Blending genre, altering style.* Portsmouth, New Hampshire: Boynton/Cook Heinemann.

CHAPTER 5

Teaching Modes

The most fundamental mode of human communication
is telling stories.

Ken Macrorie

A TOOL FOR TEACHING WRITING

Why separate writing into modes in the first place? Doesn't good writing have the same qualities regardless of what mode it might be categorized as, and aren't the categories or modes artificial anyway? Hasn't the teaching or focus on modes been done most often to fit neatly within a district's writing curriculum outline or for purposes of preparing students for district, state and national tests, tests used to decide which students are succeeding, which are failing, which will be admitted to prestigious universities, and which will be denied admission?

The answers are yes and no. To say that the average piece of writing in the real world falls into one of the categories of expository, narrative, descriptive, persuasive, poetic, or other literary forms is like saying that the average U.S. family has three and one-half children. The concept of average only works in arithmetic. While real-world writing products may sometimes fit very neatly within the exact definition of one of the modes, and in certain professions written work may most often fall into a specific category, real-world writing products, and hence the writing skills we must teach, more often fall somewhere on a continuum or blend multiple modes.

A single mode may dominate an entire writing product, or different modes may take over at different points as the writer's needs change in progression through a sequence of ideas to be expressed. At one point, a narrative may need to be told, at another point a description may be necessary, and at yet another point the reader may need to be persuaded, and so on. Each mode has its own set of problems to solve or purposes to accomplish. As Kinneavy (1971) points out, "Each of the modes has its own peculiar logic. It also has its own organizational patterns, and to some extent, its own stylistic characteristics" (p. 37).

For these reasons, students must learn about modes and understand that the differences among them are constructs created and used as tools by writers to help create the most effective written pieces. Teachers may be most helpful when getting student writers to consider two questions at some early point in the writing process: (1) Who is my audience? and (2) What is my purpose? These are questions that will have a noticeable influence over qualities of the piece such as its voice, its form, and its language.

In addition, student writers learning about modes can better understand the writing goals of the authors, known or unknown, who construct the written pieces they will read in the course of their careers and everyday lives, including contracts, novels, editorials, credit card solicitations, political appeals, neighborhood petitions, directives handed down from the head office, directions on a prescription bottle, and countless other written products that demand attention every day.

Selecting the Appropriate Mode

In teaching the modes, then, teachers must help students learn to select the best mode(s) for a written work's intended audience and purpose, as well as when to switch from one mode to another (and when to switch back). They then must put the student writers into situations that best facilitate certain modes. This last responsibility—giving students the most effective writing task—is tremendously important, especially considering Hillocks's (1995) assertion that while students may learn to identify quality writing of a certain type, this learned ability does not correlate with an ability to create similar quality writing products (p. 122). To actually create quality writing of a learned form, students need an "explanation [that] is clear and specific and concurrent or nearly concurrent with the learner's attempts to do it" (p. 122). In fact, as Hillocks puts it, "Explicitness is not worth a dead cow in a dairy farm if it is removed from actually using the procedure at some level of sophistication" (p. 123).

We apply Hillocks's contention to the teaching of modes by suggesting that giving students excellent examples of writing that clearly illustrates each mode and having them memorize the characteristics of each will not help improve their writing skills unless everything happens concurrently with their actual writing. A teacher might be tempted to separate teaching the modes as literature from teaching them as applied practice ("Now that we've learned all the modes and their traits, let's try a writing assignment"), a practice that we discourage.

A better practice focuses on the characteristics of a specific mode of writing within a writing workshop mini-lesson on a day when students can immediately apply to their own writing what they have learned. Learning to differentiate an expository paper from a narrative may be valuable for standardized test-taking purposes, but it will not make students better writers. Models may be great to help students understand the characteristics of good writing and identify the specific hall-marks of the different modes, but to create their own writing, they have to write, write, write.

We believe that students have a wealth of ideas and the language to explore them if we'll just set them up for success with the right writing tasks. In Willis's (1984) metaphor for the writing teacher and her pupils, the students are:

> barely contained [nuclear] chain reactions already in progress . . . , just waiting to inundate the room (the world!) with their energy. My job in this situation is to set up power lines and give direction to their energy flow. The direction of the flow is pro-vided by the assignments. (p. 3)

We agree with Willis's sentiment and believe that, given the correct writing task and taken judiciously through a well-developed writing process, students will produce quality written work.

With those caveats, let's take a look at each mode. Because we believe that narra-tive, especially personal narrative, is the most productive means for improving students' writing skills—skills that have substantial transfer to other modes—and because we believe young writers have high intrinsic motivation for writing the narrative, we dis-cuss the narrative mode in greater detail than the others.

> *We've all heard someone say, "Man, it was so great. . . . I just can't describe it!" If you want to be a successful writer, you must be able to describe it, and in a way that will make your readers prickle with recognition.*
>
> Stephen King

NARRATIVE

The purpose of narrative writing is to tell a story: a true story told from the writer's memory, a possible story created from facts about an event, a fantasy story originating completely in the writer's imagination. The Bible is a narrative and so is *The Wonderful Wizard of Oz,* as are *Huckleberry Finn* and *The Autobiography of Malcolm X;* they are very different in content, but they all tell a story.

Narratives are students' earliest and most common experience with the written and spoken word. From a parent's extemporaneous rendition of Goldilocks and the Three Bears to repeated reading of *The Polar Express,* on to *Spiderman,* the movie, and the entire *Harry Potter* book series, and eventually on to John Irving, Toni Morrison, or even personal authorship, human beings grow up with stories.

A 4-year-old playing alone with a teddy bear will create a story through which the two of them weave their way through imagined perils in much the same way that a 14-year-old writes the story of her most memorable life event or a World War II vet-eran writes down his memories of Guadalcanal. Story is one of the most common ways in which people record and express the human experience.

In some respects, literacy itself might be defined not merely as the ability to code and decode graphic symbols but as the ability to create, remember, tell, and analyze stories. Such an ability is one of the most highly respected literacies in human society, as Tapahonso (1998) points out in *Sáanii Dahataall: The Women Are Singing:*

> Once my brother said about my nálí, my paternal grandmother, who died decades ago: "She was a walking storybook. She was full of wisdom." Like many other relatives she had a profound understanding of the function of language. (pp. xi–xii)

To enhance students' chances of success, we recommend starting with personal narratives. Each summer we direct a summer writing camp for students aged 10 through 18 at Drury University in Springfield, Missouri, that is sponsored by the Writing Conference Inc., the Writers Hall of Fame of America, and Drury University. During the first couple of camp writing sessions, many of the new campers/writers often will make their first efforts at writing stories center on the topics of aliens, drug busts, or serial killers (sounds a little like what they see on TV and in the movies, doesn't it?). The narratives they produce are mediocre at best and sound much like someone summarizing bad television from the night before.

As the professional authors who staff the writing camp bring their expertise to bear on the young writers, however, the new authors are gradually convinced that they will have a much greater wealth of interesting details from which to draw if they will write from their own experience. Writing stories grounded in the worlds familiar to them does not necessarily mean writing nonfiction or autobiography; it simply means writing about people and places like the ones they experience every day or have experienced at some time.

Sharon Draper, 1997 National Teacher of the Year, whose novels for young adults have won numerous awards, including the Coretta Scott King Award and Best of the Best by the American Library Association, advises young writers:

> to write about what they know. They've never been to Mars, so don't write about Mars unless you have read enough to know something about what Mars is really like. . . . If you live in Kansas, write about Kansas. Let it take place in Kansas. I tell kids this regardless of where they're from, and they say, "Well nothing ever happens where I live." And I say, "Yes it does. You have to observe what it is that is happening. You have tornadoes in Kansas. Write about that. You have thunder and lightning. . . . Have you ever lived through a thunder and lightning storm? Have you ever been scared? Write about that. (Blasingame 2000, p. 5)

A lifetime of experiences, even one that is only 13 or 14 years long, can provide young writers with a great wealth of information and fascinating details. Personal narrative, or narratives based on fictitious persons very near the author's life experience, will yield the best work the most quickly.

If students still want to write about life on Mars, it's still no problem. Teachers can suggest that students take what they know about life and place it on Mars. Take Paula Danziger's (1986) young adult novel *This Place Has No Atmosphere,* set in the year 2057 on the moon; the setting (time, place, and conditions) and problems arising out of it are beyond the author's knowledge, but the characters' personal problems are not. Growing up on the moon has most of the same problems (and admittedly some additional ones) that growing up in Kansas does.

King (2000) makes this point about John Grisham's first novel, *The Firm*, a runaway success, in which a young lawyer takes his first job out of law school working for a Memphis law firm that turns out to be a front for the mob: "Although I don't know for sure, I will bet my dog and lot that John Grisham never worked for the mob. All of that is total fabrication. . . . He *was* once a lawyer, though, and he has clearly forgotten none of that struggle. Nor has he forgotten the location of the various financial pitfalls and honeytraps that make the field of corporate law so difficult" (p. 162). King says in order to write about the unknown topics that fascinate the writer but draw upon the strength of experience, "Write what you like, then imbue it with life and make it unique by blending in your own personal knowledge of life, friendship, relationships, sex and work" (p. 161).

How can teachers take advantage of Stephen King's advice in order to elicit good personal narratives from their students? We suggest a number of strategies. Begin small and focus on the skills of a good narrative. In addition, collect good writing tasks, and/or prompts, especially ones that help students learn to mine the material for story that lies beneath the surface of their daily lives.

Several authors model this technique, including Jack Gantos, whose books about a young man named Jack Henry are fictionalized autobiographies of certain periods in his own life. Many of Gantos's books, such as *Heads or Tails: Stories for the Sixth Grade (1995), Jack's Black Book (1999b)*, and *Jack on the Tracks (1999a)*, are all based in his experiences within a few blocks or so of his family home. Gantos often includes cartoonlike doodles in his books, actually annotated maps, of places and events from his life. The maps are starting places for stories, a way of brainstorming possible topics in a visible form.

This story mapping, as it might be called, has proven to be a good technique for eliciting good narratives from student writers. In our experimental middle school writing center in Tempe, Arizona, we have our students create maps of their neighborhoods and draw on memory for funny or interesting events that have happened there. Even students who don't believe anything ever happened in their lives that would be worth writing about discover a treasure chest of good material. The maps stir memories waiting just beneath the surface. One student, for example, in going over his map section by section, remembered the time a car jumped the curb and crashed into his house. Another student remembered how a broken arm happened. Both of these students soon found themselves pages into a personal narrative.

We have had repeated success by reading a story from one of the previously mentioned Gantos books to open a writing workshop session on narrative, followed by showing Gantos's own story mapping and then having our students create their own maps. Although *Jack's Black Book* and *Heads or Tails* are about younger children, we have found that several of the stories are popular with high school students when employed in certain ways. "My Brother's Arm" (*Heads or Tails,* p. 107), in which some zany antics lead to a broken arm (the same arm twice) has worked especially well for grades 5 to 12, but any good narrative with lots of details by a popular author will work.

Speaking of broken arms, injuries are good sources of narrative topics for young writers. Not only are they vivid memories, rich in detail, but they also are often told unabashedly. Nelson explains in *Writing and Being* (1994), "Scar stories come easily to us—from childhood to old age, people like to tell stories about their wounds, their operations, their accidents" (p. 109). To elicit material for good narratives, Nelson suggests having young writers draw a rough outline of a human figure on which they mark the locations of various injuries and scars. We have success at all grade levels from 2 through 12 with this technique; apparently, children are never too young to have had stitches, cuts, broken and sprained limbs, and a variety of encounters with broken glass, tree houses, bike accidents, and other hazards that provide a cache of stories.

What makes a good narrative, a good story?

Concrete details help a narrative—or any writing, for that matter. As Fletcher (1993) points out in *What A Writer Needs,* small details affect the reader in a way that larger ones cannot: "Concrete details allow the writer to *understate* an important truth rather than clubbing the reader over the head with it. Such details have an almost magical way of getting to the heart of complex issues, making explanations unnecessary" (pp. 49–51). He cites the example given in a writing class he took from Richard Price (author of the novel *Clockers* and the screenplay for the movie the *Color of Money*): "'The bigger the issue, the smaller you write,' he said. 'Remember that. You don't write about the horrors of war. No. You write about a kid's burnt socks lying on the road'" (p. 49).

Such details can be used to accomplish much in the narrative, including characterization and setting. Details make it true to life. The reader experiences what the writer is describing only if the details of the experience, especially those that appeal to the senses, are rich.

Characters are important to the narrative, whether drawn from life experience or created from imagination. Some authors believe this is best accomplished by creating a well-developed character before actually employing him, her, or it in the narrative. Atwell (1998) recommends a character questionnaire: "The second document I developed is a questionnaire to help writers invent, develop, and reinvent their characters. Even with all the information we generated about fiction, too many students still jumped into their stories first by spinning plot" (p. 403). Atwell's character questionnaire contains 16 questions that read like an interview conducted to find out both the biographical facts and the psychological makeup of the character, including questions like "What do you look like?" "Where do you live?" "What is different about you?" "What are your dreams?" (p. 404).

Draper also emphasizes the importance of a strong connection between author and character (Blasingame, 2000): "Once they [the characters] start to develop, they take on personalities of their own. I hate to get to the end of a book because I like the characters so much I don't want to leave them. I like kind of quirky characters. . . . The characters that kind of go beyond their expectations are the ones I like" (p. 2). Memorable characters help with all other aspects of a narrative, including the plot, and serve as an effective delivery vehicle for gritty details of the kind that help a reader identify with the protagonist.

The "Show, don't tell" maxim enters in with characters, as well. The writer should not describe the character as "mean" but rather should put him or her into action doing something mean, such as stealing candy from babies, as the cliché goes. As Lamott (1994) says in *Bird by Bird,* "You can't write down your intellectual understanding of a hero or villain and expect us to be engaged" (p. 69). Lamott then goes into how Thomas Harris developed the character of Hannibal (the Cannibal) Lector in *Silence of the Lambs,* a reprisal of the sociopathic antagonist from his earlier book

The Red Dragon. Both books have been made into movies, and whether on the screen or on the page, Harris has Lector committing the acts that earned him his nickname—acts (not descriptions) that scare the living daylights out of readers and viewers.

Part of character development is also dialogue, and creating dialogue is not easy. A conversation must sound natural. A character's voice must sound authentic. How would a 15-year-old boy getting out of juvenile detention on a weekend pass ask for directions? How would a 75-year-old grandmother ask for directions?

Dialogue needs to stand on its own, too. Overnarration can remind the reader that it's all made up. King (2000) compares two ways to narrate a line of dialogue: "'Put it down,' she shouted" (p. 125) compared to "'Put it down,' she shouted menacingly" (p. 126). The second attempt is obviously too heavy-handed. With dialogue, the power is in the words spoken and not in any qualification of how they were spoken.

What about plot creation? A story with a good plot is roughly analogous to a complicated meal prepared by a good chef. Lots of important things happen that contribute to its flavor and quality in a sequence that has the best final effect, and it all comes done at the same time. In *The Art of Fiction: Notes on Craft for Young Writers,* Gardner (1983) suggests that there are three basic ways to do this from which every plot developer chooses. The writer either "borrows from traditional story . . . works backward from the climax . . . or works forward from an initial situation" (p. 165). By traditional story, we take Gardner to mean one such as Pygmalion, which yielded the play My Fair Lady, or the Arthurian legend, from which is derived just about any story in which the main character develops a utopian society only to be betrayed by a spouse, a friend, and an evil sorceress (truly magical or not). Mythology and classical literature provide plenty of models.

Gardner's other two options each present advantages and disadvantages of their own. If the writer starts with a really exciting climax and works backward, there will be no danger of a disappointing or anticlimactic ending. Tony Hillerman, whose murder mysteries take place on the Hopi and Navajo reservations of northern Arizona and New Mexico prefers this method. By the same token, the writer may have a hard time coming up with an intriguing opening that doesn't give away the ending. Keeping the ending from being predictable may be hard, but at least all of the clues will lead fairly to the ending.

The other option of creating an exciting, intriguing opening first and then moving toward a climax makes it easier to grab the readers' attention. The problem may lie in getting painted into a corner from which the author can't write her or his way out. The protagonist may have wandered so far down an exciting, interesting path that the writer can't think of a good resolution. The term *deus ex machina,* Latin for "*God from a machine,*" is often used to describe, as *Merriam-Webster* (2003) puts it, "a person or thing (as in fiction or drama) that appears or is introduced suddenly and unexpectedly and provides a contrived solution to an apparently insoluble difficulty." This term came from Greek playwrights who wrote their protagonists into impossible situations and then lowered an actor who portrayed a god arriving just in time to save the protagonist.

The modern-day equivalent of *deus ex machina* would be the writer who puts the protagonist in an impossible situation but then solves it by having the whole problem sequence turn out to be just a dream. Again, this sounds like bad television.

Whichever plot-building technique students want to use, it will have its own problems and advantages. Students may enjoy experimenting with all three or doing a little combining, such as borrowing a traditional story and working backward from the climax. The story of Icarus and Daedalus, for example, might be the plot skeleton for a story about two snowboarders who discovered professional competition as the way to escape the perceived prison of life in a small mountain town and tried to perform acrobatics that were so dangerous as to prove disastrous. The climax, an actual disaster, could be the starting point at which the writer begins creating the plot (backward, obviously), and all the events that lead up to it could be created working backward to the main characters' discovery of snowboarding.

Regardless of which plot creation model a writer uses, good plot builds tension, but not too much. In fact, a master plotter knows when to release a little tension so that readers don't get so saturated that the climax finds them numb. The reader will not know whether the writer started with the climax decided upon or created an opening attention grabber and spun the tail hoping to think of a strong ending on the way toward it; instead, the reader will read the narrative in the order it is told.

Writers may be helped by knowing about the elements of plot, elements currently covered in most eighth- or ninth-grade English classes, such as the following:

- An *initiating incident,* the event that introduces the conflict.
- *Rising action,* a series of minor confrontations between the two sides of the conflict, building in suspense and intensity as the plot moves forward.
- An *actual climax,* the high point in the story's action, in which the conflict is resolved.
- The *denouement,* the final conclusion after the climax in which the consequences are explained and loose ends are tied up.

Knowing the elements of plot does not automatically translate to being able to employ them in the writing of a well-written narrative, but it will provide a vocabulary for feedback and discussion.

EXPOSITION

Exposition could also be called informative writing. In this case, the writer is passing on information to the reader. Expository writing products include brochures, lab reports, research papers, multiple forms of journalism (straight news articles, feature news items, press releases, community reports—to name a few), consumer reports, genealogical work, some forms of book and movie reviews, and more.

A journalist might call this the five W's and an H (*who* did *what, when* he did it, *where* he did it, *why* he did it, and *how* he did it). The writer is not a passive instrument of conduction, however, because good expository writing requires that the writer analyze the information and decide what is important to pass on, what further questions to ask, what needs development, what questions the reader may have, how to answer those questions, and how best to organize the written delivery of this information for the desired effect on the reader.

Details, Details, Details!

In exposition, as in most writing, the strength is in the details, and good details are specific. The writer must look closely to *write small,* meaning the writer needs to focus *in* with a magnifying glass rather than *out* with a telescope.

Exposition is not low-level cognitive work by any means. The writer must consider at all times both the subject matter and the audience. What information is worth passing on to this particular group? Knowing what information to include means, conversely, knowing what information to leave out, and that requires evaluation. The good expository writer is not satisfied with summarizing common knowledge about a topic but rather will search out new (or previously unknown) and interesting details.

Finding new information means knowing where to look, so good exposition goes hand in hand with superior research skills. Writers must be able to place the findings of their research in some form of hierarchy, consciously or unconsciously, so they can decide what to omit, what to keep, and how much attention and development to give each piece of information.

Format Is Crucial

The organization of the expository piece is important in order to have the desired effect on the target audience. The writer can choose from a number of forms that have been proven over time. If the paper is to inform about how something is done, such as a paper on refinishing furniture, it should be organized according to *process.* If the paper is intended to tell the audience what result a topic may produce, such as in an article about aerobic exercise, *cause and effect* may be the best organizing principle. If the writer is simply trying to explain the characteristics of something with which the reader is unfamiliar, such as a travel article about a vacation destination, *description* may be the organizing schema. If the writer is trying to explain what qualifications the topic must have to fit within a category that is new or unfamiliar to the reader, such as a new arena of expertise brought on by computer technology (Web designer, for example), *definition* may be best. An *analysis* format would describe and assess characteristics, such as in a consumer report. A *classification* format might be used to distinguish among individuals in a large group, such as in an exposition about popular music, as might a *compare and contrast* form of organization.

These formats for expository organization based on rhetorical forms are not the only possibilities, nor do we mean to imply that an exposition needs to fall into one and only one of them. The writer of exposition may create any hybrid that best imparts the information.

Expository writing is the mode of the investigative journalist, so students might benefit from thinking of themselves in that way. What's the real story here? We have all read feature news stories that left us thinking we knew nothing new after the reading than before, but we've also all read feature stories that left us thinking we were given a look at a side of the topic we had never seen before, an important side, finally revealed to the outside world.

Does expository writing ever include narrative or persuasive segments? Absolutely. The writer is not a potted plant sitting next to the story. Rather, the expository writer makes decisions about how best to convey information, and often this means using an illustrative anecdote or making a brief attempt to persuade the reader of the significance, value, or importance of something before moving on in the written piece. Expository writers must remember that the reader comes to this piece with hopes of getting the inside story from someone in the know, someone who can tell stories about the topic and place value on or characterize aspects of it that only an insider could do. Otherwise, the piece is of no value to the reader.

Expository writing is the mode of writing students will use most often in their other subjects, including social studies and science. Lab reports, for example, should follow some basic principles common to expository writing. In her article on the concept-based lab report, Lummis (2001), a high school chemistry teacher from Sewell, New Jersey, lists some characteristics of the well-written lab report, characteristics common to all good exposition. Lummis says students need to "write as clearly and concisely as possible. Any technical jargon should be defined if necessary and avoided when possible. . . . Clarity is the key" (p. 31). In addition, Lummis instructs the writer to reach out to the reader and "anticipate and answer every question readers might have" (p. 31).

PERSUASION

The basic purpose of the persuasive paper is to convince a reader that the writer's opinion about a topic is correct or is at least a valid one among many. Persuasion requires that the writer understand the construction of arguments to support an opinion. Historically, some composition courses were once called "rhetoric and logic," and this applies well to persuasive writing: The writer attempts to show the reader a logical path of thought that leads to the same conclusion that the writer has arrived at and is espousing.

A persuasive writer should first assess the information about the chosen topic. Does the writer really know enough about it to generate a valid opinion? Some research is required to make certain that the writer starts down the path with an opinion that won't fall apart under scrutiny once the facts are discovered. In part, this requires the writer to distinguish fact from opinion and opinion from argument.

Defining the Elements of Persuasion

A *fact* is a point of information that cannot be disputed, a point that can be proven to be true. It is a fact that the capital of Texas is Austin. An *opinion*, on the other hand, is a value judgment about something. It is a matter of opinion whether or not Austin is the best location for the capital of Texas.

An *argument* is an arrangement of facts supporting a structure of logic intended to convince a reader of the correctness of an opinion. An argument for the opinion that Austin is the best location for the capital of Texas would be that it has a geographically advantageous position due to the fact that it is nearly equal in distance from the state's northern and southern borders and is culturally similar to both southeastern and western Texas communities.

The *format*, the organization or order, of a persuasive paper must take whatever form the writer can most effectively use to convince the reader of the validity of the writer's opinion; effective sequencing should be valued over a set format. Writers must focus on the feedback readers give them about the effectiveness of their organization or order and not on whether or not the paper follows a mandated outline form. If writers need an initial model schema for putting the persuasive paper together, however, they might try what Payne (1965) has referred to for some years as "the psychology of argument" (p. 40).

Payne's hierarchy suggests that the writer order the parts of the persuasive paper in a way most likely to achieve the desired effect given the nature of human psychology. She uses the example of a teenager trying to persuade his father to lend him the family car for an evening, and she compounds the difficulty by adding the qualification that the last time the car went out with the young driver, it came back with a dented fender (Payne, 1965, pp. 40–41).

Psychology of argument order outlines a procedure for walking the young driver's father through a series of steps least likely to provoke a negative response and most likely to elicit the desired response and includes the following parts in the following order. First, introduce the audience (the paper's reader, or in Payne's illustration, the father) to the topic in general, without stating an opinion or request. Next, give some background as to how the situation reached the point at which it now stands. In Payne's example, this means reviewing past events with the car, including the moratorium on teenage use of it.

The next step in the best use of psychology is to state the writer's opinion. In our illustration, the son makes the request for borrowing the car and indicates that there are reasons that are about to be discussed. The first reasons that the persuader discusses, however, are reasons that contradict his or her opinion. In the case of borrowing the car, the young driver admits that he made a mistake and that his father was absolutely right in rescinding his driving privileges (Payne, 1965, pp. 41–42).

Although this may seem counterproductive, it is actually a way of manipulating the reader's thinking. Rather than pretending that con arguments don't exist, the writer minimizes them by admitting early on that they do exist but then moving on to the pro arguments. As Payne (1965) points out, the reader will not be convinced of the reasonableness of the writer's opinion if obviously valid con arguments are merely discounted. By dealing with those first, the writer is encouraging the reader to check them off on a mental list and move on to what the writer really wants the reader to buy into, and that would be the pro arguments (p. 41).

Again, following a strategic plan that considers the psychology of the reader, if the writer has arguments to counter the con arguments, he or she pairs them up, each con with its corresponding pro. In Payne's illustration, for example, the young man admits that he dented the fender, but he promises to pay for fixing it.

At this point, the reader is most prime for the writer to move on to the *pro arguments*, the structures of logic that support the writer's opinion. Finally, Payne (1965) recommends continuing the strategy of manipulating the reader's thinking about the topic by ordering what the reader sees from what the writer least wants to focus on to what the writer most wants to focus on. This means placing the pro arguments in ascending order, saving the best one for last. The last thing the reader will consider then is the best reason for agreeing with the writer's opinion (p. 42).

POETRY

Although English teachers often feel inadequate to teach their students how to write poetry, they really don't need to feel that way. Students love poetry. As small children, they were delighted by the rhythm and rhyme in nursery rhymes and picture books and loved rhyming authors from Mem Fox to Dr. Seuss. As they grew older, their love of meter and rhyme continued with the works of Shel Silverstein and others, but they also developed an affinity for free verse, such as that written by Sonya Sones or Sara Holbrook specifically for young people. By the time they reached middle and high school, their taste for poetry may have transferred to song, which is simply poetry set to music. No matter what their taste in music, they still enjoy words in verse, their sounds, and their meanings.

Not all teachers feel well-equipped with methods for facilitating students in the writing of poetry; however, a sentiment we have identified with in the past is that:

> Even though most of us would love to see our students write poetry, we often avoid it more than any other form of writing. Why is that? Perhaps we think of it as something magical, something so artistic or ephemeral that it just can't be taught. We feel awkward, clumsy or simply inept at helping students write poetry, and so we touch upon it briefly and quickly move on to other things. (Blasingame, 2002, p. 109)

Methods for helping students write their own poetry do exist, however. Some are methods to "demystify the magic," as Winter (1994), a high school English teacher at Olathe North High School, in Olathe, Kansas, has entitled her book. She helps students to see that writing, in various modes, is not a matter of magic but of strategies and methods that produce magical results.

Cowboy poet Paul Zarzyski remembers the day in high school when he discovered that all poetry was not written far away and long ago about things he knew nothing about. In fact, he learned, poetry could be about his very own life and penned by his very own hand:

> Poetry, like a friendly ghost, like lightning you could hug without harm, had struck close to home, and I instantly loved the notion that my tiny life might be worthy of such power and song and sentiment. Poetry, all of a sudden, made sense and mattered. (2000, p. 240)

Zarzyski has written volumes of poetry since those high school days and won multiple awards, including the Cowboy Hall of Fame's Western Heritage Wrangler Award.

Most teachers who have seen their way clear to provide time and technique for students to compose verse have seen similarly positive consequences: "Any teacher who has tried a coffeehouse style reading of students' poetry knows that little inspires the level of students' sincere engagement in literature as much as writing and reading their own poetry" (Blasingame, 2002, p. 109).

Poetry is art, and art takes time, so patience is required. We recommend devoting a respectable amount of writing workshop time to the writing of poetry, and we also recommend not expecting it to be produced in huge quantities. Poetry is to prose what espresso is to coffee: a highly charged concentrate. Poetry distills the writer's ideas into a powerful substance and, consequently, has great power to express the writer's thoughts and feelings. A poet takes life experiences that might fill a story or book and concentrates them in a form that may take up no more space than a single page.

Helping Beginning Poets

If students are new to writing poetry, teachers might want to use a progression of activities, each more complex than the previous one, to help them ease into the process. We have had success taking students through the following sequence of activities, beginning with an activity called "found poetry." Found poems come from selecting key words and phrases from a story or novel and arranging them into a form that has the look and feel of poetry and also conveys the essence of a character or event in that selection of literature. The order and placement of words on the page can be done in any fashion that the students desire. To create the final product, students can add words of their own choosing as needed. Following is an example of a found poem we composed about the character Johnny from S. E. Hinton's book *The Outsiders* (1967):

Johnny
Scared of his own shadow
Sixteen
Had it awful rough at home, awful rough.
" . . . killed a kid . . . How'd you like to live with that?"
Never noticed colors and clouds and stuff until you.
Never thought of himself but saved the children in the church from death.
Dying
Sixteen years isn't enough
But then:
"I don't mind dying now.
It's worth it. It's worth saving those kids.
Their lives are worth more than mine."
Nature's first green is gold,
The hardest hue to hold.
Stay that way.

In creating a found poem such as the preceding one, a student practices choosing a relatively small number of words, then combining and arranging them for poetic effect. It does not require that students create the words, but it gives them a feel for composing.

The next step in the progression that we recommend is a step in which the students do provide the words and phrases, do provide the content, by mining their own life experience, but in this step a form of some kind is provided. We suggest that students be given a wide variety of possible formats to use rather than be forced into one. Eventually, when they compose poems completely from scratch, they will create or choose a form that fits the content rather than start with a form in mind.

For their own poetry, many poetry teachers (and many poets) have borrowed or mimicked a form used in a well-known poem. A wonderful source for this is Creech's (2001) young adult novel, *Love That Dog,* which centers on a young man's experience in English class writing poems that mimic the work of famous poets. Creech's book places the original poems in an appendix and the mimicked poems throughout the book.

In particular, we have had success imitating a couple of William Carlos Williams poems that are often studied in U.S. literature classes. Students read Williams's "This

Is Just to Say" and "The Red Wheelbarrow" and then try to imitate their simple but artful forms. Following are two samples:

This Is Just to Say

I have not forgotten
The barbs
That you tossed my way
At the party

And which
You probably
thought
I would forget.

I have not;
They were unforgivable,
So cruel
And so cold.

So Much Depends

So much depends
Upon

A blue
Pickup truck

Turning down the
Street

And returning to a lonely white
Dog.

Formula poems are another strategy for helping students begin to believe they can write poetry. We have had success with one particular formula that works especially well in getting students to move away from the literal language of prose and into the figurative language of poetry. We borrow this formula from Hise (1995), and his book *Patterns: The How to Write a Poem Program,* a collection of suggested poem formulas for young poets. The formula we like best is C + C + WD + E = P, which means *c*omparison plus *c*omparison plus *w*ild *d*ream plus *e*motion equals a *p*oem. We ask students to choose a topic, maybe a person, and then to do some brainstorming about the topic in which they let their minds run free and loose and a little crazy. Following is an example of a C + C + WD + E poem about a grandfather.

Grandpa Harry

Grandpa Harry is like a bottle of Alka Seltzer for an upset stomach.
He is like the answer page in the back of my algebra book.
He dreams of a garden two miles long with tomatoes like bowling balls and peppers like footballs.
He dances with delight at his granddaughter's wedding.

Students find that using the patterns can elicit words and phrases that appear to have deep meaning. We suggest that two things are happening. One is that the students' natural sense of metaphor and simile and their natural ear for sentence fluency are freed up by the formula, which does not require them to come up with a narrative to fit a form. The second may be a subliminal or subconscious selection of images that the poet associates with the subject.

Getting More Advanced

Ultimately, students will want to create their own poetry from scratch. They will want to step outside the bounds of assigned forms, topics, or tasks—and when they do: fantastic! At this point the classroom climate, the community of writers, and the trusting and safe environment the writing teacher has created, will pay off tremendously, especially in the area of sharing and responding.

To give classroom teachers some help on how best to facilitate students in the writing of poetry, we once asked seven accomplished poets some practical questions about how they write. The questions were about finding a topic, finding the words, rising above literal language, choosing a form, using devices of poetry, and revising (Blasingame, 2002, pp. 109–113). Some of their thoughts and ideas follow.

Students' first concerns as they enter the writing workshop to write poetry may be *what to write about* and *how to get started*. Our recommendation for topic selection is that students pull topics right out of their personal experience (no Grecian urns, please). As Arizona poet Alberto Rios, Western Literature Association's 2002 Poet of the Year, advises, the best place to look for subject matter is in your own memories: "When you speak from memory, the heart forgets what doesn't matter and reduces life to its essence" (Blasingame, 2002, p. 110). In Chapter 3, we have suggested a means for students to accumulate topics or writing territories where they can mine the wealth of their life experiences. Perusing that list of topics close to their hearts, student writers will find a more than sufficient number of potential topics.

Getting started can be a real stumbling block. Students may be under the impression that a poem should jump out of their minds fully formed, and that's just not true. A couple of words with an appealing sound may be enough.

Paul Zarzyski usually begins by writing down just a few words that have an interesting sound:

> When I am occasionally given a gift from the Cowpoke Cosmos, I'm not trying real hard to say something smart; I'm not trying real hard to put together words that will dazzle the reader's eye. I'm just trying to put a few notes together, a few chords that I haven't heard before that are interesting to my ear. (Blasingame, 2002, p. 110)

Students can benefit from this successful poet's technique of starting with just a few words that sound appealing or unusual together and building the poem from there. A few sessions of free writing will often yield just such a kernel or combinations of words, providing a starting place for the student poet. By reading their work aloud and listening to peers read their work aloud, student writers may catch potential poem starters that reading silently did not bring to the surface. Sound is important, as is meaning, and since sound can often underscore meaning, poets must read and reread out loud and often as they work.

When we refer to a combination of a few words as a poem starter, we do not mean that those words are the first line of the poem, but rather they are the starting point around which the poet builds the rest of the poem. Those words could occur at any point in the poem.

As students start writing down words, it is important to forge forward without self-doubt. The poet must get words on paper. Words will inspire more words. As Sara Holbrook explains, "Art is an intertwining of inspiration and doing. Feeding the muse is a journey to that magic, scary and emotional place that not only sparks ideas, but also creates in you the almost obsessive desire to *do*" (Blasingame, 2002, p. 111).

Students are often too preoccupied with choosing words to fit a form. Professional poets find that it can be counterproductive if they start with a predetermined form in mind for their poems. Forcing ideas and words to fit into a physical space of set length or required rhyme scheme can easily diminish the quality of work. If rhyme or meter arise as the poet works, so be it, but if not, the poet should arrange the words as he or she sees fit. Arizona poet Jeanine Savard explains why her work often takes the form of free verse: "I surrender myself completely to what form the poem wants to take. . . . You can insist on a sonnet form [for example], but I don't . . . . I am not interested in that challenge; there are enough challenges in free verse for me" (Blasingame, 2002, p. 111). Too often, students have become frustrated or compromised the quality of their verse as they manipulate the syllables and sounds to arrive at the right number of feet or rhyme. We see no benefit in this.

One of the most surprising discoveries for us was that poetry is as much perspiration as inspiration: Hard work pays off. As Zarzyski said about the importance of hard work:

> I know that if I work hard and long enough this is not a long shot. It's not like winning the lottery. I know that if I am putting in the time, putting in the work like a baseball player putting in the practice time in the batting cage, I'm going to be rewarded. (Blasingame, 2002, p. 113)

In summary, we reiterate our recommendation for generous time in the writing workshop for poetry writing, utilizing a progression of steps for the beginning poet, and patience for poets and teachers.

RESEARCH

The traditional research paper has often been called the "library research paper," and for good reason: It was basically a report with the information gathered from reference works, books, and periodicals of various kinds, whatever the budget of the library would allow. Students might find more and better resources in a larger library, such as can be found in a large university or large metropolitan area, but the process and product were basically the same: looking up a topic, recording the information found, and summarizing it in some form for the final work. It was simply the high school version of that elementary school report we mentioned in the multi-genre chapter, but instead of copying out of encyclopedias, students were using a greater variety of sources and, we hope, following appropriate citation and quotation practices so as not to commit plagiarism. Some teachers may have successfully raised the level of performance for their students by requiring that the paper not simply report on a topic but actually take a stance of some kind and defend it. However, even at that, the stances were not generally unlike positions already taken by writers who produced the materials that students researched.

We suggest a different approach: the I-Search paper as espoused by Macrorie (1984) in his work by that name.

I-Search

The I-Search paper is different from the traditional research paper in a number of ways, ways which better prepare students for the real world by providing lifetime skills, even academic research skills. Beginning with the very name, the paper is not just a rehashing of what has already been said on a topic, not just a report or summary of information, but rather a search in first person done by the writer, the very *I* in I-Search. Choice of topic is also different since the students are not restricted to a pre-established list (How many teachers accumulated "good topics" over the years based on what was in the books and magazines in the school library (if they weren't stolen)? In the I-Search paper the student picks the topic based not on what is in the library and available to be checked out but rather on the basis of what he or she is passionate about investigating. The source of these topics becomes the students' lives, their interests, their worlds, or the worlds they want to create or visit. Within the investigation of the major topic may be minor topics that provide pieces of the puzzle, too. For example, if a student wanted to do an I-Search paper about her grandfather, and she discovered that he stormed the beach at Normandy, she might want to do a little side investigation into the Allied Forces invasion at Normandy during World War II. A student who wanted to do a paper on scuba diving might want to do a side investigation on the nature and cost of scuba vacation packages.

A good starting point for the I-Search paper writer, after brainstorming potential topics, is to choose the one that seems most appealing and try it out in a short piece of writing about why that topic is attractive. This could take the form of a (1) What I Know Now and (2) What I Want to Find Out paper (Macrorie, 1984, p. 100). The audience will be both the student's peers and the teacher. The voice, the excitement, the sincerity of the paper will need to be such that the reader is convinced that the writer really does have a heartfelt need to investigate this topic and how he or she will benefit, materially or spiritually from the information gathered, the conclusions drawn, or even the process itself.

The students will read their beginning papers—sometimes called "topic papers"—to the class or to the members of their writing groups, who will provide feedback. Their peers can easily judge how sincere the writer is or what level of interest appears to drive this investigation and so give a prediction of the success or failure of the project.

In addition, peers may have suggestions for sources to investigate of which the writer was unaware. For example, perhaps it is not widely known, but a teacher was once a rodeo rider and could be interviewed by a student who is interested in bull riding. Perhaps a student interested in touring Canada by motorcycle could visit a motorcycle mechanic about the mechanical concerns involved. Upon hearing what the other class members are doing, peers are likely to come up with all kinds of resources about which the lonely writer would be unaware. This first topic investigation might best be considered tentative, however, until the I-Search paper writer has moved deeply enough into the investigation to determine whether or not adequate information is available.

Examples of the I-Search paper will help students to see what it is and understand how it is constructed. Examples can come from past students whose work is exemplary, for example, and if a teacher is just beginning this approach, excellent examples are available in Macrorie's (1984) book.

Once the students have tentative topics, they need to make a list of potential sources for seeking out information. Although the library is still a viable source for investigation, it is not the only source, not necessarily the best source, and also not necessarily the best place to start. The best place to start might be the Internet, just to get ideas, but at some point early in the process the writer needs to turn to interviewing to find out what the experts know about the topic and what resources they believe are the best on the topic. Following are some hypothetical examples:

> "If you want to know about the career of an astronomer," a local university professor might say during an interview, "you need to go to the observatory on Mount Starchart and talk to Dr. Orbit, the man who discovered the existence of Planet X–575."
>
> "If you are interested in African elephants," the veterinarian at the city zoo might say, "you really should read Dr. Pachyderm's book, *My Trunk, Myself.*"
>
> "If you want to know the most challenging slopes in the world, the local ski school instructor might say, "you should check out **www.blackdiamondsand brokenlegs.com** (not a real Website) because it reports on the daily conditions at the hardest hills worldwide and changes its ratings accordingly."

Interviewing skills are included in many states as part of the state standards for language arts. The I-Search paper provides a means for teaching these skills. Perhaps the most crucial interviewing survival skills that students can learn is to come prepared and to use an effective means for catching and storing the interview dialogue. By coming prepared, we mean that the interviewer must come with prepared questions, good questions that have been designed to elicit information in several dimensions.

Some questions should be created that will result in concrete, specific information that the investigator can employ in answering the "what I want to know" question. Some questions should be open-ended enough that the interviewee can take them in whatever direction he or she wants. Interviewers should consider the level of ignorance that brought them into researching this topic and realize that they may not know enough initially to ask all the good questions that someone already knowledgeable in this area would. For this reason, a fruitful question might be along the lines of "If you were me, what question would you ask, and/or what question would you like to be asked?" In addition, a question in the affective domain—such as "How do you feel when you hang glide at 5,000 feet elevation?"—will help elicit emotional responses from the interviewee that may provide valuable information, the kind of information a book could not accurately provide.

Student interviewers must find some means for recording and transcribing their interviews. Practice or simulated interviews in class can be effective for underscoring the difficulties inherent in accurately recording an event. The uninitiated interviewer may find that a plan to write down everything the interviewee says is unrealistic, and the interviewer planning to rely solely on the tape recorder may find that one technological misstep could mean a valuable interview is completely lost from record. A little practice with a set of questions, a notepad, and a tape recorder may prove to be the ounce of prevention needed to ensure success. Students also need some guidance in transcribing interview tapes. Also useful might be some modeling of appropriate editing to leave out the vocalized pauses and help with irrelevant grammar and usage errors but attempts for the most part to stay true to the words of the interviewee.

Appropriate Use of the Internet

Students are probably more adept than most of their teachers at using the Internet for accessing information. They know from experience which search engines (such as Metacrawler and Google) actually tie several search engines together at once and yield the greatest number of matches or "hits."

What students may not know is that all information on the Internet is not of equal credibility. The Internet might be called one of the last truly unregulated wildernesses, one in which no gatekeepers make sure that information vendors are policed. In fact, faulty information, even intentionally false information, is perfectly legal on the Internet. For that reason, students would be well-served by a little guidance—perhaps through a demonstration with an LCD projector and a live Internet feed—about what sites are likely to be reputable and which are not, which quotations need to be looked up in hard copy or on more legitimate sources before quoting them, and which sites might be best to ignore. Certainly a class period or part of one could be used for this.

Using References

The writer's need to document the sources of information is in no way diminished by the I-Search paper format. In fact, the documentation page for this style of research paper will look more like an actual research study, the kind published in research journals, since this paper includes some primary sources. Students may follow a school district or school English department style guide for documenting sources, or they may use the *Chicago Manual of Style,* the *Publication Manual of the American Psychological Association,* or the Modern Language Association (MLA) format, or any other format that a teacher requires.

Regardless of which format is followed, students' I-Search paper final drafts will need a "works cited" or similar page in which all sources are documented. Students should have guidance and practice in class on the proper methods, not only for the physical form of the citation and the quotation or paraphrasing that the citation accompanies but also on the actual legal need for citing the source of information. Make certain that students know that information—paraphrased or taken word for word (and both are equally the intellectual property of the source from which they were obtained)—must be credited to the person and document from which it came. If the writer did not personally experience the information, the source has to be credited, unless the information is common knowledge.

The practices that encouraged students to copy reports out of the encyclopedia when they were children are not acceptable at this point, and information, text, pictures, and anything else taken from the Internet are just as much governed by these rules as is any book or magazine.

Plagiarism and incorrect documentation of sources may or may not be two different things, but regardless, the issue can turn from one of academic procedure to one of ethics very quickly. For this reason, teachers and schools must have policies in place about plagiarism, as well as a written plan for enforcing and making public notification of them. Consider the controversy in which a Piper, Kansas, teacher found herself when she discovered that a large number of her students' research papers had been taken verbatim from Internet Web sites with no indication that they were not the students' ideas and words and were without documentation or credit given to the true source.

When the teacher, high school, and school district administrators and school board members failed to agree on how this should be handled, the teacher resigned, only to find herself the object of a media feeding frenzy. According to the Kansas City Star, after her resignation, the teacher "told her story Thursday to CNN's worldwide audience. [and] On Friday, CBS and The New York Times called. Next week, NBC plans to visit" (Carroll, 2002, B2).

Surely this kind of controversy is in no one's best interest, and we contend that the best way to prevent it is to teach appropriate documentation of sources, including the ethical ramifications, and to enlist the help and support of the school administration in creating school policy that has been approved at the district level.

If the I-Search paper topic is something that the researcher can experience firsthand and write about, it is an excellent investigative and journalistic approach. For example, a paper on hunting elk might include the writer's own experience on a guided hunt—not a bad idea, especially considering the possibilities for narrating the story and interviewing the people involved, such as the guide, the other hunters, and a game warden. A paper on sky diving might set the whole experience up with interviews and empirical data from print media, but ultimately a primary source such as a narrative of an actual parachute jump—especially if moments of it can be tied back to data discovered in the research— will communicate information to the reader that an objective source, one removed one or two steps from the actual event, cannot. Of course, these are just examples and not recommended topics.

The Write-Up

The actual write-up of the I-Search paper has a less formal tone and a much more personal voice than the traditional research paper. It can be narrated in first person as the researcher tells the story of what happened to him or her from the first urges to learn something about this topic, through the plan for investigation, through the actual research and reporting on what information the search yielded. Macrorie (1988) states this as "What I Knew," "Why I'm Writing This Paper," "The Search," and "What I Learned," the last of which, he points out, also includes what I "didn't learn" (p. 64).

We would add that, as in a good story, some sort of denouement is needed, not just the ending but the significance of it. By this we mean that the I-Search paper conclusion should discuss how the results of this investigation will or will not affect the writer. As Macrorie (1988) puts it in his conclusion to "Why I'm Writing This Paper," "The writer demonstrates that the search may make a difference in his life" (p. 64).

BIBLIOGRAPHY

Atwell, N. (1998). *In the middle: New understandings about writing, reading, and learning,* 2nd ed. Portsmouth, NH: Boynton/Cook Heinemann.

Blasingame, J. (2000). Conversations: Sharon draper. *The Writer's Slate, 15.2,* 1–6.

Blasingame, J. (2002). Seven poets answer seven questions for the classroom teacher. *English Journal, 91.3,* 109–113.

Carroll, D. (2002, February 9). Former teacher at Piper deluged with calls. *The Kansas City Star,* B2.

Creech, S. (2001). *Love that dog.* New York: HarperCollins.

Danziger, P. (1986). *This place has no atmosphere.* New York: Delacorte.

Fletcher, R. (1993). *What a writer needs.* Portsmouth, NH: Heinemann.

Gantos, J. (1995). *Heads or tails: Stories from the sixth grade.* New York: Farrar, Straus and Giroux.

Gantos, J. (1999a). *Jack on the tracks: Four seasons of fifth grade.* New York: Farrar, Straus and Giroux.

Gantos, J. (1999b). *Jack's black book.* New York: Farrar, Straus and Giroux.

Gardner, J. (1983). *The art of fiction: Notes on craft for young writers.* New York: Random House.

Hillocks, G., Jr. (1995). *Teaching writing as reflective practice.* New York: Teacher's College Press.

Hinton, S. E. (1967). *The outsiders.* New York: Bantam, Doubleday, Dell.

Hise, J. (1995). *Patterns: The how to write a poem program.* Carlsbad, CA: Interaction Publishers, Inc.

King, S. (2000). *On writing.* New York: Simon and Schuster.

Kinneavy, J. L. (1971). *A theory of discourse.* New York: W. W. Norton and Company.

Lamott, A. (1994). *Bird by bird.* New York: Anchor Books.

Lummis, J. (2001). Teaching technical writing: switching to concept-based lab reports. *The Science Teacher, 68*(7) 28–31.

Macrorie, K. (1988). The *I-Search paper.* Portsmouth, NH: Boynton/Cook.

Merriam-Webster. (2003). *Merrium-Webster collegiate dictionary,* 11th edition. Springfield, MA: Merriam-Webster, Inc.

Nelson, L. (1994). *Writing and being.* Philadelphia: Innisfree Press.

Payne, L. (1965). *The lively art of writing.* New York: Mentor.

Tapahonso, L. (1998). *Sáanii dahataall: The women are singing.* Tucson: University of Arizona Press.

Willis, M. S. (1984). *Personal fiction writing.* New York: Teachers and Writers Collaborative.

Winter, Teena. (1994). *Demystifying the magic: Strategies for teaching the writing of the narrative, the essay, and the poem.* Ottawa, KS: The Writing Conference, Inc.

Zarzyski, Paul. (2000). The lariati versus/verses the literati: Loping toward Dana Gioia's dream come real. *Cowboy Poetry Matters.* Ashland, OR: Story Line in Paul Zarzyski Press, (pp. 239–252).

PART II

Assessment

CHAPTER 6

Assessment

Assessment of students' achievement is fundamental to
all school reform efforts because effective instruction
relies upon assessment and because the merits of any
reform are usually judged by relative gains in
assessment data.

Scott G. Paris

THE NATURE AND IMPORTANCE OF ASSESSMENT

A variety of substantive concepts affects and informs all disciplines in schooling. One
such concept is assessment of student work. Assessment is an integral and ongoing
process in the daily lives of all in education including, but not limited to, students, parents, teachers, and administrators. It is apparent that although there is agreement on
the general importance of assessment, the practices that are found in the schools are
as varied as the students we teach.

"Assessment is one of the most important and pressing issues facing the literacy
community. At every turn, we are hearing and telling others that we must reform assessment if we are going to help students become thoughtful, critical, responsible, and effective readers and writers" (Valencia, Hiebert, and Afflerbach, 1994, p. 1). We all know
that assessment is not new in curriculum in general and in language arts in particular.
However, assessment has taken on an increasingly high profile due to the public and
political demand for the elusive measure of accountability in our public schools.

Informal assessment has been taking place in almost every classroom every day.

Teachers have always viewed their ongoing interactions with children as occasions for
assessing students' learning processes, abilities, and accomplishments. Sometimes
these occasions are documented in written notes—about students' participation in a

writing conference, their interactions during literature circle discussions, or their scores on a comprehension quiz. At other times teachers' notes are mental—they observe responses of particular students and file this information away in memory. (Valencia, Hiebert, and Afflerbach, 1994, p. 6)

Many have argued that these processes are not enough. Many call for high-stakes testing as a means of demanding accountability.

The Advent of High-Stakes Testing

The emphasis put on high-stakes testing was born out of a variety of historical and sociological elements taking place soon after the conclusion of World War II. It continued as the United States became involved in the arms race with the Soviet Union. During this time, anxiety was understandably high, and when the Soviet Union launched Sputnik in 1957, many critics of the U.S. public school system wondered about the strength of the public schools. The anxiety continued with the publication of *A Nation at Risk* (Gardner, 1983). The effort was on, and has continued to the present day, to move from the "subjective," often formative assessment, and toward "objective/high stakes," often summative assessment.

To understand the implications of the high-stakes test one must first examine the rationale for assessment as a whole. Assessment in its most elementary form is designed as a tool with two distinct functions: (1) improving learning and teaching and (2) providing a measure of performance for accountability, whether formative or summative (Paris, 1998, p. 201). Formative assessments provide diagnostic information about the products and processes of students' learning so educators can adjust curriculum and instruction to better foster learning. These ongoing assessments take many forms, such as teachers' observations, conferences, and performance feedback intended to motivate students to improve their own learning (p. 189) In contrast, summative assessments are usually externally imposed, often carry high-stakes, and may not be directly related to classroom curriculum content or instructional methods; summative assessments are usually reported as test scores that compare students, classrooms, teachers, and schools (p. 189).

"Whereas tests were once used largely as monitoring devices, they now have enormous consequences for many people, hence the catch-phrase 'high-stakes testing'" (Bracey, 2000, p. 5). High-stakes testing merely means that the consequences for good (high) or poor (low) performance on a test are substantial; important decisions such as promotion/retention, teacher salaries/bonuses, school district autonomy, and funding all can hinge on a single test score (Irvin, 1995, p. 101).

Problems Inherent in High-Stakes Testing

Many involved in the world of education are expressing strong concerns about the true value of high-stakes testing (Paris, 1998; Bracey, 2000; and Valencia et al., 1994). The International Reading Association (IRA) contends the following:

The important thing about a test is its validity when used for a specific purpose. Thus, tests that are valid for influencing classroom practice, "leading" the curriculum, or holding schools accountable are not appropriate for making high stakes decisions about individual student mastery unless the curriculum, the teaching, and the tests are aligned; all too often, they are not. (*High-Stakes,* 1999, p. 2)

The IRA is not alone in its contention that high-stakes tests are being misused and abused. They are joined by other notable professional organizations such as the American Psychological Association (APA), the National Council of Teachers of English (NCTE), the American Educational Research Association (AERA), and the Alliance for Childhood. "The use of standardized tests as the sole measure of learning is condemned as insupportable by every professional testing organization; yet such tests are required by nearly every state in the union" (Pick, 2000, p. 3). Bracey points out that the standards for test use supported jointly by the American Psychological Association, the American Educational Research Association, and the National Council on Measurement in Education clearly state that one single test score should determine no decisions about human beings (2000, p. 3). This is supported by the findings of a committee of the national Academy of Sciences that concluded in its 1999 study of the appropriate and inappropriate uses of tests, titled High-Stakes, "Tests are not perfect. No single test score can be considered a definitive measure of a student's knowledge" (Pick, 2000, p. 4).

Serious misgivings about these tests range from their validity to their sociocultural implications. The Alliance for Childhood reports "This massive experiment, intended to raise educational achievement, is based on misconceptions about the nature and value of testing and about how children develop a true love of learning" (*American Educational Research Association Alliance,* 2001). This concern is echoed by the IRA, which reports that the primary concern of its members is that the testing has become a means of controlling instruction as opposed to a way of gathering information to help students become better readers (*High-Stakes,* 1999, p. 4). It urges teachers, administrators, and policy makers to ask themselves a simple question: "Is the primary goal of the assessment to collect data that will be used to make better decisions that impact the individual students taking the test? If the answer is 'no,' the high stakes tests are inappropriate" (*High-Stakes,* 1999, p. 2).

Yet another set of unintended consequences can be categorized as arguments against high-stakes testing based on the holistic approach to the learner. Although standardized tests can be useful as one measure of a student's knowledge, it is imperative that they be viewed in the context of the whole child. This is achieved by combining standardized test data with other forms of assessment as well as input from a teacher who intimately knows the student's strengths and weaknesses (*American Educational Research Association Alliance,* 2001, p. 5). This is especially important in the cases of the student who "freezes" on tests, the student who reads adequately but too slowly to finish the test, the student who understands concepts but has difficulty retrieving details, the student with learning disabilities, and the English language learners or limited English proficiency students (LEP) (*American Educational Research Association Alliance,* 2001 p. 5).

Growing evidence indicates that the pressure and anxiety associated with high-stakes testing are highly unhealthy for children and may undermine the development of positive social relationships and attitudes toward school and learning. This idea is addressed by the NCTE resolution that "High-stakes testing often harms students' daily experience of learning, displaces more thoughtful and creative curriculum, diminishes the emotional well-being of educators and children, and unfairly damages the life-chances of members of vulnerable groups" (National Council of Teachers of English, 2000, p. 1)

While defenders of standardized testing often acknowledge the shortcomings of high-stakes testing, they argue that it is the best present measure we have. In light of the magnitude of its negative track record, the idea that there isn't anything better seems ludicrous. The National PTA's position statement on testing offers an alternative: "Children deserve to be judged as whole human beings, embodying the full range of human intelligences and abilities. Such assessments should be performance based, reflecting the different kinds of knowledge and skills that a student is expected to acquire" (*American Educational Research Association Alliance*, 2001, p. 8). This holistic approach, characterized as performance-based assessment, is a subset category under the broad heading of "authentic assessment." Such assessments are the most compelling alternatives to high-stakes and standardized testing. It is important to note that "Authenticity in assessment resides not in its response format, but in its content, the underlying constructs it taps, and the correspondence among the assessment, the instruction from which it samples, and the purpose for which the assessment will be used" (Valencia, et al., 1994, p. 6).

AUTHENTIC ASSESSMENT

Traditional assessment relies most heavily on indirect or "proxy items" that are intended to successfully simulate a student's performance on valued challenges. Authentic assessment demands that students must be effective performers by using acquired knowledge, whereas traditional tests demand only that students recall what was learned and plug it in out of context. Authentic tasks mirror the real world as opposed to the "drills" of rote memory that traditional tests stress. The pitfalls of traditional testing lie in the inference that one has mastered the performance of a particular skill merely because one can describe the steps of said skill.

> *Assessment is authentic when we directly examine student performance on worthy intellectual tasks.*
>
> Grant Wiggins

> Authentic assessments present the student with the full array of tasks that mirror the priorities and challenges found in the best instructional activities: conducting research; writing, revising, and discussing papers; providing an engaging oral analysis of a recent political event; collaborating with others on a debate, etc. Conventional tests are usually limited to paper and pencil, one-answer questions. (Wiggins, 1989, p. 704)

Selecting the correct response from a list of options does not truly assess in any significant way the measure of one's performance or product of learning. Authentic assessment achieves validity and reliability by stressing and standardizing the appropriate criteria for scoring such a myriad of products. Traditional testing standardizes objective "items" and, hence, the one right answer for each.

Too often, multiple-choice tests mislead both students and teachers about the types of work to be mastered. Right answers become more valuable than the cognitive process.

"Norms are not standards; items are not real problems; right answers are not rationales" (Wiggins, 1989, p. 704). Authentic assessment leads to clarity on the part of the students as to what their obligations are, while teachers are empowered to believe that assessment results are both meaningful and useful for improving instruction.

The real issue with authentic assessment is whether or not the student can demonstrate a good grasp of the material being studied by providing some kind of performance or portfolio at the end of a unit, which requires personal translation of key ideas (McKenzie, 1994, p. 1). According to Bloom's taxonomy, this skill would be that of "synthesis," the ability to invent a new version of something through the application of learned material with prior learning. This type of assessment is designed to draw the student's learning into the open so the teacher can accurately evaluate what is going on within the student's mind. It will supply the teacher with useful data on an ongoing, daily basis, and this information will suggest modifications in instructional strategy for each individual student ("What Is," 1997, p. 1).

Much has been written in general terms about authentic assessment as it relates to an alternative to high-stakes testing. The following addresses the issue as it relates to the English classroom and, in particular, the writing curriculum.

Authentic assessment refers to tasks that resemble reading and writing in the real world and in school. Its aim is to assess many kinds of literacy abilities in contexts that closely resemble actual situations in which those abilities are used. For example, authentic assessments ask students to read real texts, to write for authentic purposes about meaningful topics, and to participate in such literacy tasks as discussing books, keeping journals, writing letters, and revising a piece of writing until it works for the reader. Both the material and the assessment tasks look as natural as possible. Furthermore, authentic assessment values the thinking behind the work—the process—as much as the finished product ("What Is," 1997, pp. 2–3)

English teachers have been using authentic assessment tools for many years. Most would agree the following assessment strategies fall under the heading of "authentic." These include, but certainly are not limited to, demonstrating literacy abilities by conducting research and writing a report, developing a character analysis, debating a character's motives, creating a mobile of important information, dramatizing a favorite story, drawing and writing about a story, or reading aloud a personally meaningful section of a story. These formats for performance assessments range from relatively short answers to long-term projects that require students to present or demonstrate their work. These performances often require students to engage in higher-order thinking and to show what they know and what they are able to do.

Thus, the casual observer visiting schools today may very well find desks in groups rather than in rows, the teacher moving about the room working with individual students or individual small groups, and students making noise—not chaotic noise but learning noise. The observer sees students engaged in a discussion of the Holocaust, or working on a cooperative project about the U.S. Civil War, or doing experiments with chemicals in a science class. What the observer may definitely see are students engaged with the content and with each other, and through this engagement, students may be showing their understanding through experiments, cooperative projects, and portfolios. These authentic assessments allow teachers to set up tasks that are meaningful and provide a connection between school and the real world (Lund, 1997, p. 25).

Students show what they know through various activities, instead of plowing through a test in which all answers may be forgotten within 10 minutes of finishing the test. Authentic assessment allows students to show their thinking processes and problem solving skills, as well as what they can do. This form of assessment also provides more accountability on the student's part. The student becomes responsible for his or her thinking.

Sometimes referred to as "authentic assessment," performance assessment is a type of student evaluation that attempts to make the testing process more realistic and more meaningful. Specifically, it aims to assess student performance in situations that closely match real world challenges and standards (Schurr, 1998, p. 22).

PORTFOLIO ASSESSMENT

As has been noted, portfolios are one type of authentic assessment. They are not new. Artists have used portfolios for some time. They are relatively new, however, in education. Many different forms exist, but the basic idea remains constant: The portfolio is a place to display one's work, to show off ability, and to record growth. While individual classrooms use portfolios, the educational establishment at the state level has not followed. Some states are leading the way. Vermont, Kentucky, New Mexico, Michigan, and Massachusetts are becoming more innovative and bold in their assessment techniques. All are moving toward portfolios for assessment (Viadero, 1999).

The case for using portfolios remains strong. Students must show how and what they are thinking, what they can do, and how well they can do it. It is important for students to take responsibility for their own learning. Students in our classrooms create and perform awesome feats every day, and they should have a place to display their efforts. Portfolios are authentic in that they show students' abilities, strengths, and weaknesses. They show thought processes and reasoning. They give a glimmer of talent and a glimmer of hope that students can actually achieve. Mondock (1997) discusses the processes before the finished project. She states, "It is the process behind the final product that shows the evidence of student growth" (p. 59).

Portfolios serve multiple purposes: They show a process as well as a product, they create a collection of work, they are useful to review instruction, and—maybe most important—they show a student's growth over time. Portfolios aid classroom teachers by allowing them to see strengths and weaknesses of students. Portfolios can provide a teacher with information about a child's progress. Teachers can begin to tailor classroom teaching to students and their learning styles and can see where strengths and weaknesses lie. A developmental portfolio documents improvements in any subject over the course of a school year. Showing a student's growth not only benefits the students but also aids the teacher when it comes to evaluation or parent conferences. In essence, the use of portfolios allows for stronger student–teacher communication and provides strong evidence of student accomplishments.

In addition to self-evaluation, the use of portfolios for assessment places more accountability on the student. Students become more responsible for their learning, whereas with standardized testing, teachers carry the majority of that burden (Bushweller, 1997). In portfolio assessment, students reflect on their work; they share what they have done, how they have done it, to what extent they believe they did a good job. By reflecting on the work, students assume more responsibility for the assessment. They work with the teacher in their assessment. For this process to work well, students should self-reflect on the work they choose to place in their writing portfolios. "Studies have shown, for example, that students become enthusiastic about learning when they feel the subject is relevant to their lives, when they can do real and challenging work, when they have control over what they do, when they feel connected to their schools, and when they do not feel compelled to compete against classmates for A's and high scores" (Viadero, 1999).

Portfolios strengthen the relationship between teaching and learning, but they also strengthen the relationship between school and life. Portfolios foster responsibility, self-evaluation, and accountability within students—characteristics we all need and use on a daily basis in the "real world." Portfolios are aligned with school curriculum but also with real life skills. By focusing on the metacognitive skills necessary for portfolio construction, students build skills like "awareness for the audience and the context for a portfolio, awareness of personal learning needs, development of skills necessary to complete a task, and an understanding of the conditions for success that enhance personal reflection within a portfolio evaluation" (Duffy, Jones, and Thomas, 1999, p. 35). Through the use of scoring guides or rubrics, students are able to self-assess. "Rubrics help students to focus on key elements and then emphasize them as they work toward mastery" (Lund, 1997, p. 26). In the world of work, people are constantly called upon to assess themselves. The rubrics clearly delineate what the expectations are for the portfolio, as well as for the teacher—skills that transfer to the world outside the classroom. In an online article entitled "Putting Portfolios to the Test," Graves (1999) refers to a study that compared skills of 100 graduating seniors to skills required for jobs. Almost half of the seniors studied could only fill in blanks and answer questions after reading a couple of paragraphs. These are the types of tasks that standardized tests ask students to do. "The new jobs are in problem solving and problem finding, but we're still turning out kids who are trained to answer questions."

Performance assessment is the most significant development in evaluation since the invention of the short-answer test during World War I. During that era, public schools began to follow the military's example and adopted standardized tests as the primary tool for assessing student performance (Sax, 1997, p. 5). For most of the 1900s, educational assessment focused on multiple-choice, standardized tests that divided knowledge and skills into discrete parts. Grady (1992) suggests that the U.S. dependence on standardized testing "may reflect our strong faith in science; we equate objective data with truth" (p. 9). When education consisted mainly of helping students memorize facts and information, and when drill-and-practice was the foremost teaching method, standardized testing served education's purposes well (Eisner, 1999, p. 658).

However, the shortcomings of standardized testing have become increasingly clear in recent years. Such tests rarely succeed in measuring students' thinking skills or their ability to synthesize content or solve problems. Standardized tests reduce content to fragmented "factoids" (O'Neil, 1992, p. 15). Yet to prepare to meet the challenges of the modern world, students now are encouraged to engage in tasks that require much more than basic recall of facts. To succeed today, students must know how to "frame problems for themselves, how to formulate plans to address them, how to consider relationships, how to deal with ambiguity, and how to shift purposes in light of new information" (Eisner, 1999, p. 658).

Teachers grow dissatisfied and frustrated because they recognize the necessity for young people to engage in activities that promote higher levels of thinking. Yet the district or the state often judges those students according to standardized tests that match neither curriculum guides nor classroom content (Herbert, 1992, p. 59). Wiggins, director of research for Consultants on Learning, Assessment, and School Structure (CLASS), points out that as stakes "get higher and higher for school reform, restructuring, and teacher accountability, the reliance on measure that teachers neither value nor have had a hand in designing becomes more and more unacceptable" (Vavrus, 1990, p. 51).

Better assessment can be the catalyst for more appropriate instruction, and better assessment can legitimize the practice of "teaching to the test." For example, California used a multiple-choice test to assess writing until 1987. Then the state switched to a performance assessment in which students produced a piece of writing in response to a prompt. A subsequent study revealed that more than 90 percent of English teachers in California changed their instruction by assigning writing more frequently and by requiring students to tackle different kinds of writing tasks (O'Neil, 1992, p. 16). Thus, California teachers encountered a test more worth "teaching to," resulting in a stronger alignment between instruction and assessment.

A very similar situation occurred in Kansas. The State Board of Education decided to move toward performance assessment in writing, reading, social studies, and science. The writing assessment included a writing sample that was assessed by teachers at the local level as well as at the state level. The assessment tool was the Six-Trait Analytic Model (see Chapter 7 for complete description). Prior to this performance assessment, writing teaching and writing assessment were grammar based. Most every school district in the state emphasized the teaching of grammar in isolation as the sole means of teaching writing. School districts used a variety of standardized tests (multiple choice) to show what students could do or not do when it came to writing. Of course, the test had no validity, for it did not ask students to write. After the shift in assessment emphasis from the state, school districts overwhelmingly shifted to a writing-based curriculum and the Six-Trait Analytic Model became the accepted tool not only for assessment but also for instruction. Teachers were using the model to assess students' writing and then using it to teach writing. Other states are now following this model. School districts in Iowa, Arizona, Utah, Illinois, Montana, Washington, and Oregon, to name only a few, have shifted the emphasis to teaching and using an analytic model for assessment and instruction.

The portfolio is one type of performance assessment that has gained favor among teachers, especially teachers of English and language arts. A writing portfolio in an English class serves a function similar to the artist portfolio mentioned previously. Students maintain a collection of their work, providing tangible and longitudinal evidence of their accomplishments.

Experts agree on four salient features that must be present for portfolios to serve as effective tools for instruction and assessment. First, portfolios are cumulative, students collect materials over an extended period of time (Stecher and Herman, 1997, p. 493). Unlike tests, which provide only a glimpse of a student's work at a particular time, portfolios "allow for a view of a student's work across time" (DeFina, 1992, p. 15). Second, portfolios are "embedded." They are part of regular instructional events, not unusual "on-demand" tasks (Stecher and Herman, 1997, p. 493). Third, students are responsible for selecting at least some of the entries. Finally, portfolios require reflection. Students comment on each selection, its quality, and its production (Tierney, Carter, and Desai, 1991, p. 41).

Writing portfolios include a number of features that are much more compatible with today's language arts classroom than standardized tests. In *Language, Literacy, and the Child*, Galda, Cullinan, and Strickland (1997) list the following as ways in which portfolios outshine traditional tests:

> Portfolios link assessment to teaching and learning.
> Portfolios show effort through many drafts.
> Portfolios allow for differences among students.
> Portfolios represent a range of learning activities. (p. 258)

In *Using Writing Portfolios to Enhance Instruction and Assessment*, Frank (1994) adds these benefits to the list:

> Students feel more free to take risks and try new approaches.
> Students assist in setting goals for improving their own work.
> Students think of themselves as writers. (p. 16)

Finally, in an article in *Schools in the Middle*, Schurr (1998) cites the following advantages of portfolios:

> Portfolios cater to alternative learning styles and multiple intelligences.
> Portfolios serve as discussion-starters.
> Portfolios highlight more complete tasks, not tiny bits of information.
> Portfolios encourage students to display what they do know and what they can do. (p. 24)

These succinct statements capture some of the benefits of portfolio use, according to respected educators. Yet what does the research say? How are portfolios being used, and are those applications successful? To what extent do portfolios encourage students to assume greater responsibility for their own learning? Recent research tells different stories about the effectiveness of portfolios, depending upon whether portfolios are used for large-scale assessment purposes or for instruction and assessment within a single class.

The use of portfolios for large-scale assessment has been rather limited, so research into this use of portfolios is not extensive. Furthermore, what research has been done in this area has produced inconsistent findings. The states of Vermont and Kentucky have implemented portfolio assessment, and some data are available from those programs.

During the 1990–1991 school year, the Vermont Portfolio Project was piloted with fourth- and eighth-graders in 137 schools (Abruscato, 1993, p. 475). After the year-long pilot test, portfolios in writing and mathematics became the cornerstone of the state's assessment system during the 1991–1992 school year. The new assessment program was designed to serve two purposes: First, to provide information about fourth- and eighth-graders' achievements and, second, to promote reform in curriculum (Stecher and Herman, 1997, p. 496).

Writing portfolios for grades 4 and 8 became part of Kentucky's statewide assessment (KIRIS, the Kentucky Instructional Results Information System) during the 1991–1992 school year. Math portfolios were added the following year. The assessment program is just one component of the Kentucky Education Reform Act (KERA), a sweeping state educational reform that was enacted in 1990 (Jones and Whitford, 1997, p. 276).

In *Handbook of Classroom Assessment*, Stecher and Herman (1997) analyze the reliability and validity of large-scale portfolio assessment in Vermont and Kentucky. In Vermont, inter-rater reliability was "disheartening." Writing portfolios contained six to eight pieces, and mathematics portfolios contained five to seven pieces. Raters used a four-point scale to analyze portfolios on different dimensions. By the second year of the assessment, inter-rater reliabilities for writing portfolios were. 56 for grade 4 and .63 for grade 8 (Stecher and Herman, 1997, p. 498). Ideally, reliability should be +1.00 (Sax, 1997, p. 293). Thus, Vermont could not use the data to report the proportion of students who had achieved each point on the scoring dimension, nor could it provide data on the comparative performance of districts (Stecher and Herman, 1997, p. 498).

In Kentucky, teachers used a holistic scoring guide to score portfolios locally. The raters at the district and state levels re-scored sample portfolios. As in Vermont, reliability proved to be a problem. Teachers in students' home schools rated students consistently higher than the state scorers rated them. For example, in grade 8, home teachers rated only 28 percent of the students as "novice" (the lowest rating on the rubric), whereas state scorers rated 51 percent of students as "novice" (Stecher and Herman, 1997, p. 498). As in Vermont, lack of inter-rater reliability meant that educators could not use the data to make any definitive reports to the public or to draw conclusions about the effectiveness of their own teaching.

Test "validity" refers to the extent to which measurements are useful in making decisions and providing explanations for various trends (Sax, 1997, p. 304). In other words, does the test result have the meaning it is intended to have? Does the test measure what it purports to measure? One kind of validity is "content validity," which refers to the extent to which an assessment represents the domain under scrutiny (Sax, 1997, p. 306). The procedure for establishing content validity usually involves garnering the opinions of experts regarding how well the assessment represents the domain. Since educators have played a pivotal role in the development of portfolios, everyone has simply assumed that portfolios contain content validity. However, there has been no deliberate attempt to document such validity.

Another kind of validity, "concurrent validity," is estimated by correlations with currently obtainable criteria. In other words, there is a correlation between test results and other valued indices of performance (Sax, 1997, p. 307). Limited study of concurrent validity of portfolio assessments has been done, but the evidence that does exist is not promising. Analyses of Kentucky's writing portfolios revealed that scores on portfolios were "related highly to both multiple-choice and open-ended tests of reading" and were "weakly correlated with scores from the on-demand writing assessment" (Stecher and Herman, 1997, p. 501).

Another aspect of validity is "comparability," in which the results of an assessment have the same meaning for different students. If two students achieve identical scores, we want to be able to say that those two students are equally capable. With portfolios, however, test takers make choices about which items to include. In essence, their tests are different, and this kind of variability creates doubt about the comparability of scores from different classes, schools, and districts (Stecher and Herman, 1997, p. 502).

Portfolio assessment in Kentucky entails an additional twist. To compel teachers to improve their instructional skills, KERA couples a high-stakes accountability system with the assessment program. If scores surpass the state's expectations, teachers and administrators can receive substantial bonuses; if scores do not meet expectations, or if scores do not show continuous improvement, teachers and administrators can be placed on probation (Jones and Whitford, 1997, p. 276).

KERA has had some positive effects. For instance, under the leadership of principal Jacqueline Austin, John F. Kennedy Elementary School in Louisville made great strides in writing. Writing had been one area where Kennedy students earned poor scores: 81 percent of fourth-graders ranked at the "novice" level, the lowest rating on the scale. Kennedy teachers chose strategies to address these problems, beefing up writing instruction at all grade levels and requiring writing across the curriculum. Between 1992 and 1994, writing scores quadrupled (Rothman, 1997, p. 275). The Kennedy Elementary School story is one of success, but the tide was turning across the state of Kentucky.

The original assessment program included the following: portfolios in writing and mathematics; open-response questions demanding short, timed, written responses; and performance assessments, such as group problem-solving activities. Considering the accountability involved, reliability of scores became a focus of concern.

"Portfolios have yet to achieve a level of reliability deemed acceptable for a high-stakes system" (Jones and Whitford, 1997, p. 277). The open-response items yielded the most reliable scores and, therefore, carried more weight in an "accountability index" that the state calculated to judge schools. It is no surprise, then, that the open-response questions gained a prominent position in the curriculum, with staff development activities and classroom activities striving to enhance students' abilities to handle these questions. Test preparation, not necessarily an increase in students' knowledge or abilities, created artificial increases in test scores. "Such corruption means that scores no longer generalize to the larger domain" (Stecher and Herman, 1997, p. 501).

Additionally, many performance assessments were discontinued, and multiple-choice items were reintroduced in state testing. Thus, linking KIRIS (Kentucky's statewide assessment program) with school accountability distorted the original goals of KERA (the Kentucky Education Reform Act), for educators lost sight of the instructional benefits of student performance assessment. Once again, at the classroom level, the curriculum has been narrowed, decontextualized bits of information have been overemphasized, and an inordinate amount of time has been devoted to test preparation (Stecher and Herman, 1997, p. 500)

Today, portfolio assessment in Kentucky still exists, but it receives less emphasis as teachers focus on "whatever is thought to raise test scores rather than on instruction aimed at addressing individual student needs" (Jones and Whitford, 1997, p. 277).

It is worth noting that the Vermont portfolio project differed from Kentucky's in that Vermont teachers played a significant role in designing the program. Furthermore, the Vermont portfolio project was not tied to a high-stakes accountability system (Wolcott and Legg, 1998, p. 49).

Most formal research about the large-scale use of portfolios for assessment yields findings that are inconclusive and/or discouraging. For example, few researchers have investigated reliability and validity, and those who have collected this kind of data report unattractive results. However (and this is a big however), practicing teachers' action research reports many positive findings about using portfolios for instruction and assessment within a single English classroom.

Teachers enthusiastically discuss the extent to which portfolios encourage students to take greater responsibility for and greater pride in their own writing. Two practicing teachers, Cooper and Brown, state in their *English Journal* article, "Our research has shown us that . . . the very act of compiling a portfolio can be a powerful process for many reasons, not the least of which is that it helps students see themselves as writers, particularly when it involves many opportunities for self-evaluation" (1992, p. 40). As students evaluate their own work, they internalize the standards. When they look over a body of their own work, judging it against a set of criteria they have internalized, they engage in the kind of thinking characteristic of professional writers.

Robert Tierney sees it this way: "Students are learning how to think for themselves and how to educate themselves over the course of their lives. When given ownership over the direction of their learning, they will work to their greatest capacity and in a creative fashion" (Tierney, Carter, and Desai, 1991, p. vii). Another teacher reports that portfolios provide the impetus for students to take more responsibility for their learning. "For instance, they evaluate their own work, deciding which pieces of writing deserve to be called 'the best.' In doing so, they come to value their own judgment and build self-confidence" (Five, 1993, p. 48). Teachers' experiences demonstrate that portfolios provide the avenue through which students not only finesse their writing skills but also cultivate the habits of lifelong learning.

In an article in *Educational Leadership*, Frazier and Paulson (1992) report similar observations. "Portfolio assessment offers students a way to take charge of their learning; it also encourages ownership, pride, and high self-esteem" (p. 64). Students gain confidence in their ability to comment upon their own writing, and they became more articulate in discussing their own writing. At the beginning of the year (October), one fourth-grader's self-evaluation read, "I think my ideas weren't too good." At the end of the year, that same student analyzed his writing more specificially:

> In the beginning of the year, I got 3.8 in my scores. Now I usually get a score of 3.5. My punctuation has improved. At the beginning of this year, I did not put periods at the end of sentences in my rough drafts. Now my rough drafts have the periods and capital letters where they should be. Spelling is still very hard for me, but I think I am slowly getting better at it. (Frazier and Paulson, 1992, p. 64)

This sounds like a student who has a vested interest in his writing, certainly more ownership than he would have in a file of test scores in the school's main office.

When Leslie Ballard needed to administer a final exam in her high school advanced composition class, she decided to use portfolios as an experiment. The portfolio was a success, as students spoke with "authority" about themselves as writers. She reports, "The first thing that struck me was their insight into their own strengths and weaknesses and their willingness to be honest about their efforts" (1992, p. 47). According to Ballard, when they looked over a semester's worth of work, many students realized the value of, for example, revision. "They saw the quality of papers that had not been revised at least once was not what they had come to demand of themselves by the end of the semester" (p. 47). To what extent do portfolios encourage students to assume more responsibility for their own writing? Clearly, portfolios contribute to students' development of self-discipline, self-direction, and self-evaluation.

Portfolios place just as much importance on process as on product. DeFina, in his book *Portfolio Assessment: Getting Started*, states that the process approach to writing has gained tremendous favor throughout the nation as "an excellent way to generate meaningful and grammatically correct written text" (1992, p. 49). Prewriting, drafting, conferencing, revising, and preparing a final copy are typical steps in writing, and the portfolio is the perfect vehicle for providing examples of students' work at the various stages of the writing process. In her book, *Using Writing Portfolios to Enhance Instruction and Assessment*, Frank (1994) goes so far as to say, "Writing portfolios only work where students are using the writing process" (p. 28). In an article in the *English Journal*, Raines (1996) concurs: "Portfolios are so aligned with the processes we now know how to facilitate effective student writing—time on task, active collaboration, authentic contextualized instruction, focusing on process as well as product. . . . " She also notes that students spend a significant amount of time on the prewriting, revising, and editing tasks necessary to produce effective work (p. 41). In *An Overview of Writing Assessment: Theory, Research, and Practice*, Walcott and Legg (1998) point out that portfolios record revision, for they contain "stacks of rough drafts that convey the process the student underwent" (p. 41). Thus, portfolios provide a much more complete picture of a student than a timed-writing assessment or a standardized test. Clearly, teachers value writing portfolios as a tool for documenting and validating the process approach to writing.

Within a classroom, portfolios inform teaching. Drawing on students' portfolio collections, teachers can "devise many alternate ways to assess mastery by identifying skills expected for the grade level and choosing ways for students to demonstrate mastery within a meaningful context" (Galda, et al., 1997, p. 259). For example, a teacher who is concerned about writers' use of commas could peruse students' portfolios to see if they are, in fact, using commas correctly. Thus, the teacher can check students' application of a skill in context, in a situation more natural than asking students to perform on a test about commas. A seamless integration of instruction and assessment is at work here.

The experience of teachers in one Vermont school provides another example of how portfolios inform teaching. When these teachers assessed portfolios, they noticed a significant absence of poetry. The explanation? Most teachers covered poetry as a last-minute unit at the end of the school year. Thus, the portfolios enabled the teachers to identify a gap in students' learning and to alter plans so they could eliminate that gap (Houston, 1992, p. 29).

As teachers become more focused on an individual student's growth, instruction becomes more student-centered. One teacher states, "you know, I'm constantly going back to those portfolios. I use them as a basis for writing lesson plans, setting goals for individuals and for small groups. So I'm constantly going back and in that way—that to me is the best use of the portfolio" (Roe and Vukelich, 1997, p. 24).

Writing portfolios also enable educators to provide parents and guardians with specific information about students' writing skills. Parents and guardians can see the difference between work done at the beginning of an academic term and the end (Galda et al., p. 260). Some teachers arrange meetings at which students present their portfolios to parents and guardians; this enables students to articulate their processes, growth, goals, and so forth (Herbert, 1992, p. 61). A visible collection provides parents and guardians with detailed information, as opposed to a letter in a grade book (a letter grade determined by assignments that students have long since tossed in the trash, thereby destroying a valuable snapshot).

Herbert wrote about her students' success in portfolio assessment the last eight years at Crow Island School. She states, "A fundamental notion I have come to recognize is that for an observer to understand the significance of a portfolio, it's necessary for its maker to explain it" (1996, p. 70). For students to understand the portfolio, the student must present it. The students invite their parents and guardians into their school for a "Portfolio Evening," sometimes called a "Portfolio Party." Herbert defines "Portfolio Evenings" as "nights when children review their portfolio with parents" (p. 70). During these evenings, students answer a series of questions that they prepare for in advance. Examples of these questions include the following:

1. How has your writing changed since last year?
2. What do you know about your writing now that you didn't know in September?
3. Let's compare a page from a book you were reading last year to one you are reading now.
4. What is unique about your portfolio?
5. What would you like Mom and Dad to understand about your portfolio? (p. 70)

When portfolios are part of the ongoing classroom activities, instruction and assessment mirror the pattern that learning and working follow in the "real world." In the workplace, an assessment follows the production of some item. The creator then revises the product on the basis of this assessment, and the creator then seeks further feedback. Again, the creator makes modifications and produces a final version. This process, with its recognition that few items are simultaneously created and perfected, stands in contrast to the lesson-test model of standardized testing (Grady, 1992, p. 13).

Current learning theory supports portfolio-based instruction and assessment. Humans do not acquire knowledge and skills in a tidy, orderly manner. Children's development differs in pace and style, and portfolios establish a structure for more individualized learning (Grady, 1992, p. 13). The collaborative and flexible nature of portfolios means that more students are given an opportunity to demonstrate what they do know and what they can do (Tierney et al., 1991, p. 105).

Before teachers implement portfolios in the classroom, they must do some soul searching about their own roles. One teacher explains that her role used to be one of a critical editor, and a student's role was one of producer. "The students spent varying (often minimal) amounts of time and effort on writing papers, and I spent an inordinate and unreasonable number of hours examining, editing, and commenting on every student error in their final products" (Raines, 1996, p. 41). Such a routine places little or no emphasis on writing as a process, little or no emphasis on student choice, and little or emphasis on student self-evaluation.

Teachers must rethink their relationships with students and begin to see themselves as coaches (Vavrus, 1990, p. 51). They have to relinquish some control over details, such as decisions about writing topics. After all, if one of the main objectives of writing portfolios is to enhance student autonomy, those efforts will be stymied if teachers allow students to be dependent on them for topics, direction, standards, and evaluation.

U.S. education in the 1900s—its goals, methods, and tests—was predicated on uniformity, conformity, and standardization; however, U.S. society in the twenty-first century demands a different set of skills and qualities: flexibility, problem solving, creativity, self-motivation, and lifelong learning, to name a few. Teachers' experiences show that portfolios are a viable and valuable tool for instruction and assessment in the English classroom. In addition to emphasizing writing as a process, portfolios encourage students to take greater responsibility for their own progress and encourage students to celebrate their individuality.

Portfolios will not produce tidy scores that are conducive to the kind of quick comparisons that the public likes to make. True curriculum reform and the development of students' higher-level thinking skills will require the public to stop worshipping standardized test scores. Eisner (1999) calls for a shift from "a conception of schooling as a kind of horse race or a kind of educational Olympics to a conception of schools as places that foster students' distinctive talents" (p. 660). In fact, good schools will not diminish students' individual difference. Rather, good schools might increase differences, capitalizing upon students' unique strengths. Portfolios make it possible to instruct, value, and assess individuals in just this fashion.

ASSESSING STUDENT PORTFOLIOS

Classroom teachers have often found it difficult to assess just what their students have learned. While every effort is often used to do this assessment, many times teachers are incapable of understanding whether standards are being met. Much emphasis has been placed on teachers to provide the most meaningful learning experiences possible, but little time, effort, or resources are given to helping those teachers assess the outcomes of those efforts.

It is important for teachers and students to grasp the impact on education that has taken place. The challenge, then, is to create an instrument to evaluate student learning that has taken place over time. Gilbert (1993) in her book *Portfolio Resource Guide: Creating and Using Portfolios in the Classroom,* offers the following questions when thinking of assessment:

Does the assessment appropriately reflect clearly defined achievement goals or outcomes?

Do the evaluation criteria for each piece and the portfolios as a whole represent the most relevant or useful dimensions of student work?

What kind of feedback will be helpful to the owner of the portfolio?

What level of knowledge and skills am I expecting from students?

What opportunities/options do students have to demonstrate their knowledge and skills?

How does assessment with portfolios fit in with other formal and informal assessments?

If portfolios will be used to evaluate programs or to formally document student learning, how can the progress shown in the portfolios be combined to show general group status and progress? (p. 19)

Gilbert also offers criteria that teachers should use when rating portfolios. They should:

provide an accurate measure of student achievement.

strengthen instruction by defining for students what is important.

provide specific information on what you will consider acceptable work.

reflect a value system that is consistent with desired objectives.

promote students' confidence in their ability to provide evidence of learning. (p. 19)

Teachers are developing rubrics as scoring guides to use in the assessment of individual pieces of writing and to use with the assessment of the portfolio as a whole. These rubrics can be developed, in a variety of ways. In whatever way rubrics are developed, specificity and clarity are the keys to success. Some create rubrics with the words "many," "some," and "few" to differentiate the scoring levels. For example, in a rubric on a piece of creative writing, one teacher used the following as one part of the rubric:

_____ Evidence of the writing process.

_____ Clear indication of improvement in word choice, description, organization, usage, and mechanics from first draft to final product.

_____ Some indication of improvement in word choice, description, organization, usage, and mechanics from first draft to final product.

_____ Little indication of improvement in word choice, description, organization, usage, and mechanics from first draft to final product.

This formula for the rubric was followed for each of the categories: Effective Description, Effective Figurative Language Devices, Effective Organization, Effective Title, Assigned Length, Mechanics, Usage, and Manuscript Form. This rubric form works fairly well, but it doesn't give as much specificity and clarity in each of the categories as needed to be an effective rubric. In addition, it may not provide students the necessary feedback that will help them in revision or that will help them understand specifically the learning that did or did not take place.

The following example is illustrated here and more fully developed and explained in the portfolio designs that follow. This teacher uses the Six-Trait Analytic Model for her rubric. Here she uses the six traits as her categories and then has a rating from 5 to 1 with descriptions for each rating score. The "voice" category is illustrated in Figure 6–1. For a complete look at this rubric, see Appendix B, Figure B–4.

Most who have had success with writing rubrics indicate that success occurs most readily when students are involved with their creation. Their language and their

Figure 6–1 The voice category

5 4	3 2	1
The writer's tone is lively, engaging, and appropriate for the topic. Hear me roar! I love this topic!	You hear a little of me in this topic. The writer's voice seems sincere. Moments of spontaneity enliven this piece.	The writer seems indifferent to either the topic or the audience. Exciting moments are absent.

thoughts about how they would like to be assessed must be considered. Of course, one result is that if students are involved in the creation of the rubrics, they cannot claim that they didn't know what was expected of them.

CLASSROOM PORTFOLIOS

Two portfolio designs are illustrated in the following pages: one for middle school, created by Jill Adams, Ph.D. candidate at the University of Kansas, and former 7th grade English teacher at Southwest Junior High School in Lawrence, Kansas; and one for high school, created by Michael Trendel, Wellsville High School, Wellsville, Kansas. Readers will note that the portfolio designs include the processes by which the portfolios will be created, the forms that will be used by students, the rubrics for the contents that will be assessed, and the choices that the students may make.

Team Writing Portfolio

Level: Seventh grade
Purpose: To promote students' understanding of themselves as writers and learners and to show growth over the year in improvement in writing across core classes (English, transition math, life science, and geography).
Contents:
    Portfolio table of contents
    Portrait of myself as a writer
    Writer's reflections
    Goal setting/evaluation sheets for each quarter
    Six-Trait track record reflection
    Two most satisfying pieces (assessed) from English
    Unsatisfying piece (assessed) from English
    Free pick writing piece (assessed) from any core class
    Three picks from any core class writing activities
       (may or may not be assessed)

Most satisfying science writing piece (assessed)
Most satisfying geography writing piece (assessed)
Most satisfying math writing piece (assessed)
   (The six previous pieces would be assessed in their respective classes.)
The best of the Six Traits
How I Have Changed as a Writer: A Final Reflection

Process: All year, students write pieces in all of the core team classes. In English class, they go through the entire writing process, and must show the process before the piece is handed in. When students hand in a piece for published copy, they first assess it using the six traits. I then do the same. The next step is to conference about the piece and the difference between the two scorings.

Students will also set/evaluate two writing goals each quarter and will conduct peer interviews and student/parental responses each semester. The students select the majority of items in the portfolio. Each writing piece they select must be dated and have either an introduction or reflection attached to it. The student and teacher will assess the portfolio at the end of the year and have a conference to discuss it. In addition, after the assessment a portfolio party will occur to showcase the portfolios.

Forms: (see complete forms in Appendix B)

Portfolio cover assignment/rubric
Six-Trait track record
Six-Trait essay rubric
Goal setting/evaluation
   sheets (each quarter)
Checklist for organization
Peer portfolio evaluation
Parent-to-student
   portfolio response
Team writing portfolio

Writer's reflections
General Six-Trait rubric
Six-Trait research rubric
Best of Six-Traits sheet

Items to use Free Bees
Student/parent portfolio
Eighth-grade writing goals

ASSESSMENT RUBRIC

Reflection is a major part of this portfolio; therefore, Adams creates some material for her students so that they have some success in creating their reflections on what they have done.

ENGLISH 7: WRITER'S REFLECTIONS

Directions: Please answer the following questions on a separate sheet of loose-leaf paper. Answer the questions as thoroughly as possible and write in complete sentences. When possible, refer to specific pieces of writing you have done or specific books you have read as you answer the questions.

1. What does someone have to do in order to be a good writer?
2. What are the different kinds of writing you do—for yourself or for others?
3. What is the easiest part of the writing process for you (prewrite, rough draft, peer edit, self-revise and edit, publication)? Explain.
4. What is the hardest part of the writing process for you? Explain.
5. Where and how do you get ideas for writing?
6. Do you ever draw or doodle as part of the writing process?
7. Have teachers, their writing assignments, and their comments helped or hurt you in learning how to write? In what specific ways?
8. What helps you the most to make your writing better?
9. Under what conditions do you write best (quiet, radio on, with others, by yourself, etc.)
10. What do you like about writing?
11. What happens to your finished pieces of writing?
12. Do you ever reflect or assess a piece of writing after you have a presentation copy?
13. How do you recognize a piece of effective writing?
14. How important is writing in your life?
15. Why is it important for you to be able to write well?
16. What simile best describes your view of the writing process?
17. What metaphor best describes your style of writing?

An important part of any portfolio program is the goal setting that students do. Over the course of the portfolio year, students assess themselves periodically and then set goals for the next period. In this case, students complete Goal Setting Sheets for each of the four quarters of the school year (see Appendix B, Figure B–2). All figures for the portfolio discussed here appear in Appendix B for your convenience.

To track the progress of students' writing, students and teachers use the Six-Trait Track Record (see Appendix B, Figure B–3). With this form, students and teachers can see at a glance how writers are improving over time with each piece of writing. This track record allows for eight pieces of writing to be shown. Students and teachers are able to track at a glance a student writer's accomplishments in each trait over the eight papers.

Students and teachers use the rubric in Figure B–4 to assess general writing assignments, the essay, and the research writing. It is important to note that both students and teachers use these rubrics. Students make self-assessments prior to the teacher using the same rubric to make the final assessment. Conferences are held to review the rubric.

As students begin building their portfolios, they rely on the reflection process (see Appendix B, Figures B–5 and B–6): They begin to think about what they have learned when working with the various pieces of writing. During this process, they ask themselves why they chose the pieces that they did, what it is about the pieces that makes them particularly significant. At this time, students also reflect on other significant issues:

Which piece did you select?
Why do you characterize this piece as satisfying? Give specific reasons.
What did you learn about yourself as a writer from your work and reflection on
    this piece?
Why do you characterize this piece as unsatisfying?
Why would you like to have this piece in your portfolio?
What are the piece's strengths and weaknesses?

We hope you find the forms in Appendix B (B–7 through B–14) helpful in creating your own classroom writing portfolios.

At the end of the process, teachers ask students to look through their writing folders and their portfolios. Teachers offer the following questions to guide students as they write a reflective essay describing how their portfolio pieces show the ways they have grown and changed as writers. When they finish this essay, students are ready to write their goals for the eighth grade.

What do you notice when you look at your earlier work?
How do you think your writing has changed?
At what points did you discover something new about writing?
What do you think your greatest strengths are in writing?
How do the changes you see in your writing affect the way you see yourself
    as a writer?
What do you still need to work on in your writing?

A somewhat similar portfolio design is offered by Michael Trendel, who teaches at Wellsville High School in Wellsville, Kansas. The following is his portfolio design, including the portfolio expectations (the forms that he uses are given in Appendix B). The design is presented here as he created it and presented it to his students.

Writing Workshop Portfolio

Level: The portfolio may be used with middle school through high school grades; however, some adaptations may have to be made according to grade level.

Purpose: The portfolio will demonstrate your growth as a writer and learner. The portfolio will document your personal approaches to the writing process, contain your own reflections regarding your development, and showcase your best work.

Process: The writing portfolio will be turned in quarterly in a three-ring binder, and you will turn in works that meet the criteria for the required portions each nine weeks. The first and third quarter portfolios will be graded on completeness and quality of work in the portfolio. However, the semester portfolio and final portfolio will be graded not only on completeness and quality of work, but progress you have made as a writer. At the beginning of each grading period, you will receive a table of contents for your upcoming portfolio, and you will be given grading rubrics. It is your responsibility to read the rubrics and to make sure you understand the criteria.

Contents: As previously stated, I will give you a list of the contents your portfolio will contain each quarter. The portfolio will function as a Working Portfolio, where all writing and work are organized. However, during the final quarter, you will work on creating a Showcase Portfolio, one that will give an accurate picture of your development. Most of your portfolios will contain the following:

Table of Contents: You will provide a table of contents to help in organizing the portfolio.

Writing Survey: Before we begin writing in the class, you will complete a brief survey regarding your writing experiences and attitudes.

Reading Survey: This is similar to the writing survey, only you will share your reading experiences and attitudes.

Autobiography: You will include a short piece of writing that gives some background information about yourself.

Introduction and Reflection of Each Piece: For each piece of writing contained in your portfolio you will include an introduction of that piece and a reflection of that piece.

Polished Writing Pieces: Each quarter you will complete three polished pieces of your choice.

Best Short Piece: Each quarter you will write several short pieces of writing on topics that I assign. At the end of the quarter, you will be asked to include your best piece.

Best Time Writing: Each quarter we will write several in-class timed pieces. You will be asked to turn in your best timed writing at the end of the quarter.

Free Pick: You may pick any piece you choose.

Best Piece from Another Class: At the end of the year, you will include your favorite writing piece from another class.

Reading Projects: During each quarter, you will read three books and complete a reading project for each book. The projects will be included in your portfolio.

Writing Assessments: At the end of each quarter, you will read through and assess your portfolio. You will record your assessment on the Writing Assessment rubric. In addition, you will create new goals and a plan for achieving those goals for the next semester.

Reading Assessment: At the end of each quarter, you will list the books that you have read, and you will assess your reading choices.

Parent Assessment: At the end of the first semester and the second semester, you will have your parents read your portfolio. They will answer questions and sign the form, so it can be included as part of your portfolio.

Evidence of Goal Achievement Form: At the end of each semester, you will fill out this form using your writing goals from the previous quarter. You will list the goals and cite evidence that you have achieved these goals.

Growth Chart: At the end of the year, you will create a graphic organizer that shows your growth as a writer.

Final Writing, Reading, and Learning Assessment: To complete your portfolio, you will write a three-page reflection that explains your growth as a writer, reader, and learner.

Miscellaneous: This section will contain your rough drafts, revisions, peer evaluations, teacher conference forms, past polished pieces, past reading projects, shorter writing pieces, and any handouts that have been given. While this portion will not be specifically assessed, it is part of your portfolio, and its contents might offer evidence of growth and development.

Forms: Writing Survey (illustrated in Figure 6–2 and with complete portfolio in Appendix B, Figure B–15), Reading Survey (illustrated in Figure 6–3 and with complete portfolio in Appendix B, Figure B–16), Writing Self-Assessment (Figure B–17), Peer-Evaluation Form (Figure B–18), Six-Trait Rubric (Figure B–19), Writing Goals Worksheet (Figure B–20), Writing the Final Reflection and Self-Assessment: Questions to Ponder (Figure B–21), Growth Graph for First semester (Figure B–22), Portfolio Requirements: First Quarter (Figure B–23), Portfolio Rubric: First Quarter Completeness of Portfolio (Figure B–24), Portfolio Requirements: Final Showcase Portfolio (Figure B–25), and Portfolio Rubric: First Semester Progress (Figure B–26).

Assessment: Once again, the portfolio will be graded quarterly using rubrics that will be given to you at the beginning of each quarter. The first and third quarter portfolios will be assessed on quality and completeness of work. The semester and year-end portfolios will be graded on quality, completeness, and progress.

In this writing portfolio, Mr. Trendel shares with his students a variety of expectations for writing, including the following:

- Find topics and purposes for your writing that matter to you, to your life, to who you are and who you want to become.
- Try new topics, purposes, audiences, genres, forms, and techniques.
- Make your decisions about what is working and what needs more work in pieces of your writing. Be the first responder to your writing. Learn to work from multiple drafts.
- Listen to, ask questions about, and comment on others' writing in ways that help them move the writing forward.
- Produce at least three to five handwritten pages of rough draft each week and bring at least three pieces of writing to completion every nine weeks.

Trendel also has a few tips for his writing workshop, which is a part of the writing portfolio:

- Save everything. It's all a part of the history of the piece of writing, and you never know when or where you might want to use it.
- Date and label everything you write to help you keep track of what you've done.
- When a piece of writing is finished, clip everything together, including the drafts, notes, lists, editing check sheet, and peer conference form, and file it in your working portfolio.

Figure 6–2 Writing survey

WRITING SURVEY

NAME _____ **DATE** _____

1. Are you a writer? _____
   (If your answer is YES, answer question 2a. If your answer is NO, answer 2b.)

2a. How did you learn to write?

2b. How do people learn to write?

3. Why do people write? List as many reasons as you can think of.

4. What does someone have to do or know in order to write well?

5. What kinds of writing do you like to write?

6. How do you decide what you'll write about? Where do your ideas come from?

7. What kinds of response helps you most as a writer?

8. How often do you write at home?

9. In general, how do you feel about what you write?

Figure 6–3 Reading survey

READING SURVEY

NAME _____ **DATE** _____

1. If you had to guess . . .
   How many books would you say you owned? _____
   How many books would you say there are in your house? _____
   How many books would you say you've read in the past year? _____

2. How did you learn to read?

3. Why do people read? List as many reasons as you can think of.

4. What does someone have to do or know in order to be a good reader?

5. What kinds of books do you like to read?

6. How do you decide which books you'll read?

7. Who are your favorite authors? (List as many as you'd like.)

8. Have you ever reread a book? _____ If so, can you name it/them here?

- Record every piece of writing you finish on the form in your permanent writing folder.
- Collect data about yourself as a writer, look for patterns, and take satisfaction in your accomplishments over time.
- Get into the habit of beginning each workshop by reading what you've already written.
- Establish where you are in the piece and pick up the momentum.
- Understand that writing is thinking. Do nothing to distract other writers. Don't put your words into our brains as we're struggling to find our own.
- When you need to confer with peers, use a conference area and record responses on a peer-conference form so the writer has a reminder of what happened.

Trendel also suggests possible types of writing from which students may choose:

Personal narrative	News story
Fictional narrative	Editorial
Short story	Children's book
Parody	Monologue
Tall tale	Interviews
Fable	Autobiography
Fairy tale	Biography
Romance	Research report
Historical fiction	Script
Science fiction	News story
Western	Diary entry
Review	Letters
Movie	Letter to a friend
CD	Business letter
TV show	Letter of request
Performance	Letter of complaint

Trendel suggests that students find topics and purposes for their writing that matter to them, to their lives, to who they are and who they want to become.

Again we hope you find the forms included in Appendix B helpful in creating your own classroom writing portfolio.

Since students working with this portfolio will complete reflections on pieces of writing that they finish, Trendel makes important suggestions for students to follow as they create their reflections. He states, "With each piece of writing, you will write a self-reflection." This is an opportunity for you to evaluate your piece and share your personal insight into the writing. The following are questions that you might want to explore in your reflection:

- How did you get the idea for this piece? What was your purpose for writing this piece? What goals did you hope to achieve? Did you achieve those goals?
- Describe the process of writing this piece from beginning to end. Where did you add items? Where did you cut?
- What problems did you struggle with as you wrote this piece? Did anything frustrate you as wrote?

- How did your peer evaluator and others help you with this writing?
- Tell the parts that you like the best and why.
- How is this piece the same or different from the work you have done in the past?
- Was this piece risky for you? Describe any other stories or pieces that might grow out of this piece. What goals do you have for your next piece?
- Was your personal writing process the same for this piece as it has been for others or was it different? Describe.
- What do you hope to achieve with your next piece? What new territory do you hope to explore?

BIBLIOGRAPHY

Abruscato, J. (1993). Early results and tentative implications from the Vermont portfolio project. *Phi Delta Kappan, 74,* 474–477.

American Educational Research Association: Position statement concerning high-stakes testing in preK–12 education. (2000). Washington, DC: Alliance for Childhood.

American Educational Research Association Alliance for Childhood: High-stakes testing position statement. (2001). College Park, MD: Alliance for Childhood.

Ballard, L. (1992). Portfolios and self-assessment. *English Journal, 81.2,* 46–48.

Bracey, G. (2000). *Short guide to standardized testing: Fastback 459.* Bloomington, IN: Phi Delta Kappa.

Bushweller, K. (1997). Teaching to the test. *American School Board Journal.* Retrieved July 3, 2002, from **www.asbj.com.**

Cooper, W., and Brown, B. J. (1992). Using portfolios to empower student writers. *English Journal 81.2,* 40–45.

DeFina, A. A. (1992). *Portfolio assessment: Getting started.* New York: Scholastic.

Duffy, M. L., Jones, J., and Thomas, S. W. (1999). Using portfolios to foster independent thinking. *Intervention in School & Clinic, 35,* 34–39.

Eisner, E. (1999). The uses and limits of performance assessment. *Phi Delta Kappan, 80,* 658–660.

Five, C. (1993). Tracking writing and reading progress. *Learning, 21.6,* 48–51.

Frank, M. (1994). *Using writing portfolios to enhance instruction and assessment.* Nashville, TN: Incentive Publications.

Frazier, D. M., and Paulson, F. L. (1992). How portfolios motivate reluctant writers. *Educational Leadership, 49. 8,* 62–65.

Galda, L., Cullinan, B. E., and Strickland, D. (1997). *Language, literacy, and the child.* Orlando, FL: Harcourt Brace.

Gardner, D. (1983). *A nation at risk: The imperative for educational reform. An open letter to the American people. A report to the nation and the secretary of education.* Washington, DC: National Commission on Excellence in Education.

Gilbert, J. (1993). *Portfolio resource guide. Creating and using portfolios in the classroom.* Ottawa, KS: The Writing Conference, Inc.

Grady, E. (1992). *Fastback 341: The portfolios approach to assessment.* Bloomington, IN: Phi Delta Kappa.

Graves, D. (1999). Putting portfolios to the test. *Teacher Magazine.* Retrieved April 17, 2002, from **www.edweek.org.**

Herbert, E. (1992). Portfolios invite reflection from students and staff. *Educational Leadership, 49.8,* 58–61.

Herbert, E. (1996). The power of portfolios. *Educational Leadership, 53.4,* 69–74.

High-stakes assessments in reading: A position statement by the International Reading Association.

(1999). Newark, NJ: International Reading Association.

Houston, N. (1992). Evaluation: Picture of a portfolio. *Instructor, 101.7,* 23–29.

Irvin, Judith L. (1995). *Reading and the middle school student: Strategies to enhance literacy.* Boston: Allyn & Bacon.

Jones, K., and Whitford B. L. (1997). Kentucky's conflicting reform principles: High-stakes school accountability and student performance assessment. *Phi Delta Kappan, 79,* 276–281.

Lund, J. (1997). Authentic assessment: Its development and applications. *The Journal of Physical Education, Recreation & Dance, 68,* 25–30.

McKenzie, J. (1994). *Site-based decision-making: Authentic assessment and formative program evaluation.* New York: Correct Change Press.

Mondock, S. (1997). Portfolios—The story behind the story. *English Journal, 86,* 59–64.

National Council of Teachers of English, *Position statement concerning the use of high-stakes testing.* (2000). Urbana: National Council of Teachers of English.

O'Neil, J. (1992). Putting performance assessment to the test. *Educational Leadership, 49.8,* 14–19.

Paris, S. G. (1998). *How students learn: Reforming schools through learner-centered education.* Washington, DC: American Psychological Association.

Pick, G. (2000). Taking the road less traveled: Authentic assessment in other locales. *Catalyst: Voices of Chicago School Reform, September, 9,* 1–5.

Raines, P. A. (1996). Writing portfolios: Turning a house into a home. *English Journal, 85.1,* 41–45

Roe, M., and Vukelich, C. (1997). That was then and this is now: A longitudinal study of teachers' portfolio practices. *Journal of Research in Children's Education* 12, 16–26.

Rothman, R. (1997). KERA: A tale of one school. *Phi Delta Kappan, 79,* 272–275.

Sax, G. (1997). *Principles of educational and psychological measurement and evaluation.* Belmont, CA: Wadsworth.

Schurr, S. L. (1998). Teaching, enlightening: A guide to student assessment. *Schools in the Middle, 6.5,* 22–31.

Stecher, B. M., and Herman, J. L. (1997). Using portfolios for large-scale assessment in Gary D. Phye, ed. (pp. 491-516). *Handbook of Classroom Assessment: Learning, Adjustment, and Achievement.* Gary D. Phye, ed. San Diego, CA: Academic Press: 491–516.

Tierney, R. J., Carter, M. A., and Desai, L. E. (1991). *Portfolio assessment in the reading–writing classroom.* Norwood, NJ: Christopher–Gordon.

Valencia, S. W; Hiebert, E.; Afflerbach, (Eds.). (1994). *Authentic Reading Assessment: Practices and Possibilities.* Newark: NJ International Reading Association.

Vavrus, L. (1990). Put portfolios to the test. *Instructor, 100.1,* 48–53.

Viadero, D. (1999). Lighting the flame. *Teacher Magazine.* Retrieved April 17, 2002, from **www.edweek.org.**

What is authentic assessment? (1997). Houghton Mifflin Reading/Language Arts. Retrieved June 2, 2001, from **www.eduplace.com/rdg/res/litass/ auth.html.**

Wiggins, G. (1989). A true test: Toward more authentic and equitable assessment. *Phi Delta Kappan, 70,* 703–713.

Wolcott, W., and Legg, S. M. (1998*). An overview of writing assessment: Theory, research, and practice.* Urbana, IL: National Council of Teachers of English.

CHAPTER 7

The Six-Trait Model

"I'm so *happy* you're teaching *quality* this quarter.
Hardly anybody *is* these days."
What the hell was she talking about? *Quality?*

Robert Pirsig

THE SIX-TRAIT MODEL FOR WRITING INSTRUCTION AND ASSESSMENT

The Six-Trait Model provides a means for teachers to help students achieve quality writing and a model for both teachers and students to assess their writing and the writing of others.

QUALITY WRITING

In his 1974 work *Zen and the Art of Motorcycle Maintenance,* Robert Pirsig recalls his struggle to define quality writing and help his students at Montana State University attain it. After a fellow professor exhorts him to "teach quality," he and his students discover that they actually know good writing when they read it and can agree on which pieces are good and which are not. Pirsig identifies good writing as having "aspects of Quality such as unity, vividness, authority, economy, sensitivity, clarity, emphasis, flow, suspense, brilliance, precision, proportion, depth and so on" (p. 186).

The qualities of good writing are no mystery; as early as 1961, research had established what they are and how readers prioritize them. In order "to find out what qualities in student writing intelligent, educated people notice and emphasize when they are free to grade as they like" (Diederich, 1974, p. 5). Paul Diederich, John French, and Sydell Carlton asked 60 professionals, including 30 college professors, 10 writers and editors, 10 lawyers, and 10 business executives to read 300 papers from college freshmen at three universities (Diederich, 1974, p. 5). The readers were to rate the papers between 1 and 9 and write comments about what they liked or disliked in each paper. A factor analysis of the readers' ratings and comments yielded five distinguishable clusters or groupings of qualities or traits the raters used to evaluate the papers. The largest group of raters most emphasized the quality of ideas, the next largest emphasized mechanics, the third largest emphasized organization, and the last two clusters, which were of equal size, emphasized wording/phrasing and flavor. Within the five categories were such sub-points as "richness, soundness, clarity, development and relevance to the writer's topic" within the category or trait of ideas (Diederich et al., 1974, p. 6).

THE SIX-TRAIT MODEL AND QUALITY WRITING

Diederich's research validated a set of traits for defining quality writing, and by the mid-1980s the need for a means to teach and assess these traits seemed to reach critical mass. Teachers in a variety of locations including (but not limited to) Montana, Florida, and Oregon were arriving at rubrics, often remarkably similar, for analyzing students' writing based on a set of traits and descriptors for quality writing. As Ruth Culham, unit manager in the Assessment Program at the Northwest Regional Educational Laboratory (NWREL) in Portland, Oregon, explains about this moment in the history of writing instruction:

> During the mid-1980's something comparable to spontaneous combustion occurred in multiple sites across the nation as educators experimented with analytic assessment. Everyone seemed to be asking the same questions and coming up with the same answers. Now that we have a writing process in place, how on earth do we assess it? All that we had access to was a collection of standardized, norm-referenced tests. Those didn't seem to measure anything beyond students' mastery of conventions. Holistic assessment was gaining popularity, but it was only when the writing process took firm hold that people recognized the need for an analytic system, one that would be more descriptive of student performance. (Culham, 2003, p. x)

One of the most widely used and easily accessed versions of the Six-Trait rubric is NWREL's copyrighted Six-Trait Rubric (Figure 7–1), which can also be downloaded from **www.nwrel.org/assessment**. Much of the early work for the NWREL rubric must be credited to the 1983–1984 Analytical Assessment Committee, a group of 17 teachers from the Beaverton, Oregon, schools who were charged with creating a rubric that could be used at all levels to give writing evaluation consistency across the district. In collaboration with Vicki Spandel (2001), a research associate at the Northwest Regional Educational Laboratory, they created a flexible, basic rubric (p. 41). Spandel continues her work in traits-based writing instruction and assessment through Great Source Education Group, a Houghton Mifflin company.

Individual teachers, English departments, individual schools, entire school districts, and state education departments nationwide have adopted various forms of a traits-based writing rubric as they work to improve writing instruction. These rubrics assign numbered ratings to levels of proficiency in each trait according to descriptors similar to Diederich's sub-points. The NWREL rubric uses a rating scale of one through five points, but a six-point rubric has also become popular with state departments of education and testing companies more recently, as have various other scales of more or fewer rating levels. Proponents of five- and six-point rubrics alike make a good case for their own versions, but regardless of the numbers in the rating scale, the qualities of good writing are comparable across rubrics.

The Discrete Traits

Diederich's research isolated discrete traits of writing only for the purpose of identifying what readers value in writing. Teachers are more likely to find the traits are in many ways interrelated or mutually influential. Rather than tell students that the boundaries between traits are rigid, teachers may want to compare them to colors on an artist's palette that are sometimes blended together. For example, purposeful word choice, sentence fluency, and ideas combine to create strong voice in the way that red, blue, and white combine to create lavender.

The Six-Trait Model in the Classroom

We cannot overemphasize the common misapplication that teachers, school districts, and state departments of education make if they regard this model primarily as a means of testing. Educators who use the rubric to arrive at scores, and especially those who apply statistical tests to compare scores among student populations but fail to make the model an integral part of their writing instruction, are essentially testing without teaching. Considering all the research done to discover what readers in the real world value, all the analyses to sift out the variety of major and minor characteristics of quality writing, and the years of effort to arrange

> *It is interesting and illuminating that we found five and only five distinct schools of thought among these fifty-three distinguished readers, emphasizing ideas, mechanics, organization, wording and flavor respectively. There is some room for argument as to the interpretation of these five factors, but there is no reasonable doubt that our study revealed just five different bases for the judgment of our sample of 300 papers, or that the distinctive emphases of these five ways of looking at student writing could be described fairly accurately by the labels we chose.*
>
> *Paul Diederich*

them into an easily understandable, student-and-teacher-friendly hierarchy, it is illogical to reduce the model to a set of numbers only. Of what value are the assessment numbers reflecting students' writing performance without a means for improving their performance?

From a curriculum planning perspective, the model is a gold mine for providing or enhancing every aspect of the writing program. It gives teachers not only a consistent

Figure 7–1 Six-trait rubric

Ideas and Content
(Development)

5 *This paper is clear and focused. It holds the reader's attention. Relevant anecdotes and details enrich the central theme.*
  - **A.** The topic is **narrow** and **manageable.**
  - **B.** **Relevant, telling, quality details** give the reader important information that goes **beyond the obvious** or predictable.
  - **C.** Reasonably **accurate details** are present to support the main ideas.
  - **D.** The writer seems to be writing from **knowledge** or **experience;** the ideas are **fresh** and **original.**
  - **E.** The reader's questions are **anticipated and answered.**
  - **F.** **Insight**—an understanding of life and a knack for picking out what is significant—is an indicator of high level performance, though not required.

3 *The writer is beginning to define the topic, even though development is still basic or general.*
  - **A.** The **topic is fairly broad;** however, you can see where the writer is headed.
  - **B.** **Support is attempted,** but doesn't go far enough yet in fleshing out the key issues or story line.
  - **C.** **Ideas are reasonably clear,** though they may not be detailed, personalized, accurate, or expanded enough to show in-depth understanding or a strong sense of purpose.
  - **D.** The writer seems to be drawing on knowledge or experience, but **has difficulty going from general observations to specifics.**
  - **E.** The reader is **left with questions.** More information is needed to "fill in the blanks."
  - **F.** The **writer generally stays on the topic** but does not develop a clear theme. The writer has not yet focused the topic past the obvious.

1 *As yet, the paper has no clear sense of purpose or central theme. To extract meaning from the text, the reader must make inferences based on sketchy or missing details. The writing reflects more than one of these problems:*
  - **A.** The writer is **still in search of a topic,** brainstorming, or has not yet decided what the main idea of the piece will be.
  - **B.** Information is **limited** or **unclear** or the **length is not adequate** for development.
  - **C.** The idea is a **simple restatement** of the topic or an **answer** to the question with little or no attention to detail.
  - **D.** The writer has **not begun to define the topic** in a meaningful, personal way.
  - **E.** **Everything seems as important as everything else;** the reader has a hard time sifting out what is important.
  - **F.** The text may be **repetitious,** or may read like a collection of **disconnected, random thoughts** with no discernable point.

Organization

5 *The organization enhances and showcases the central idea or theme. The order, structure, or presentation of information is compelling and moves the reader through the text.*

  A. An **inviting introduction** draws the reader in; a **satisfying conclusion** leaves the reader with a sense of closure and resolution.

  B. **Thoughtful transitions** clearly show how ideas connect.

  C. Details seem to fit where they're placed; **sequencing is logical** and **effective.**

  D. **Pacing is well controlled;** the writer knows when to slow down and elaborate, and when to pick up the pace and move on.

  E. The **title,** if desired, is **original** and captures the central theme of the piece.

  F. Organization **flows so smoothly** the reader hardly thinks about it; the choice of structure matches the **purpose** and **audience.**

3 *The organizational structure is strong enough to move the reader through the text without too much confusion.*

  A. The paper has a **recognizable introduction and conclusion.** The introduction may not create a strong sense of anticipation; the conclusion may not tie-up all loose ends.

  B. **Transitions often work well;** at other times, connections between ideas are fuzzy.

  C. **Sequencing** shows **some logic,** but not under control enough that it consistently supports the ideas. In fact, sometimes it is so predictable and rehearsed that the **structure takes attention away from the content.**

  D. **Pacing is fairly well controlled,** though the writer sometimes lunges ahead too quickly or spends too much time on details that do not matter.

  E. A **title (if desired) is present,** although it may be uninspired or an obvious restatement of the prompt or topic.

  F. The **organization sometimes supports the main point or storyline;** at other times, the reader feels an urge to slip in a transition or move things around.

1 *The writing lacks a clear sense of direction. Ideas, details, or events seem strung together in a loose or random fashion; there is no identifiable internal structure. The writing reflects more than one of these problems:*

  A. There is **no real lead** to set-up what follows, **no real conclusion** to wrap things up.

  B. Connections between ideas are **confusing** or not even present.

  C. **Sequencing needs** lots and lots of **work.**

  D. **Pacing feels awkward;** the writer slows to a crawl when the reader wants to get on with it, and vice versa.

  E. No **title is present** (if requested) or, if present, **does not match** well with the content.

  F. Problems with organization make it **hard for the reader to get a grip** on the main point or storyline.

© Northwest Regional Educational Laboratory

Continued

Figure 7–1 *(Continued)*

Voice

5 *The writer speaks directly to the reader in a way that is individual, compelling, and engaging. The writer crafts the writing with an awareness and respect for the audience and the purpose for writing.*

A. The tone of the writing **adds interest** to the message and is **appropriate for the purpose and audience.**

B. The reader feels a **strong interaction** with the writer, sensing the **person behind the words.**

C. The writer **takes a risk** by revealing who he or she is consistently throughout the piece.

D. **Expository or persuasive** writing reflects a **strong commitment** to the topic by showing **why** the **reader needs to know this** and why he or she should care.

E. **Narrative** writing is **honest, personal, and engaging** and makes you **think about, and react to,** the author's ideas and point of view.

3 *The writer seems sincere but not fully engaged or involved. The result is pleasant or even personable, but not compelling.*

A. The writer seems aware of an audience but discards personal insights in favor of **obvious generalities.**

B. The writing communicates in an **earnest, pleasing, yet safe** manner.

C. Only **one or two moments here or there** intrigue, delight, or move the reader. These places may **emerge strongly for a line or two, but quickly fade away.**

D. **Expository or persuasive** writing **lacks consistent engagement** with the topic to build credibility.

E. **Narrative** writing is **reasonably sincere,** but doesn't reflect unique or individual perspective on the topic.

1 *The writer seems indifferent, uninvolved, or distanced from the topic and/or the audience. As a result, the paper reflects more than one of the following problems:*

A. The writer is **not concerned with the audience.** The writer's style is a **complete mismatch** for the intended reader or the writing is **so short** that little is accomplished beyond introducing the topic.

B. The writer speaks in a kind of **monotone** that flattens all potential highs or lows of the message.

C. The writing is **humdrum and "risk-free."**

D. The writing is **lifeless or mechanical;** depending on the topic, it may be overly technical or jargonistic.

E. The development of the topic is **so limited** that **no point of view is present**—zip, zero, zilch, nada.

© Northwest Regional Educational Laboratory

Word Choice

5 *Words convey the intended message in a precise, interesting, and natural way. The words are powerful and engaging.*

A. Words are **specific** and **accurate.** It is easy to understand just what the writer means.

B. **Striking words and phrases** often catch the reader's eye and linger in the reader's mind.

C. Language and phrasing is **natural, effective,** and **appropriate** for the audience.

D. **Lively verbs** add energy while **specific nouns** and **modifiers** add depth.

E. Choices in language **enhance** the **meaning** and **clarify** understanding.

F. **Precision** is obvious. The writer has taken care to put just the right word or phrase in just the right spot.

3 *The language is functional, even if it lacks much energy. It is easy to figure out the writer's meaning on a general level.*

A. Words are **adequate and correct in a general sense,** and they support the meaning by not getting in the way.

B. Familiar **words and phrases communicate,** but rarely capture, the reader's imagination.

C. **Attempts at colorful language** show a willingness to stretch and grow but sometimes reach beyond the audience (thesaurus overload!).

D. Despite a **few successes**, the writing is marked by **passive verbs, everyday nouns,** and **mundane modifiers.**

E. The words and phrases are **functional** with only **one or two fine moments.**

F. The words may be **refined in a couple of places,** but the language looks more like **the first thing that popped into the writer's mind.**

1 *The writer demonstrates a limited vocabulary or has not searched for words to convey specific meaning.*

A. Words are so **nonspecific and distracting** that only a **very limited meaning** comes through.

B. Problems with language **leave** the **reader wondering.** Many of the **words** just **don't work** in this piece.

C. Audience has not been considered. **Language is used incorrectly,** making the message secondary to the misfires with the words.

D. **Limited vocabulary** and/or **misused parts of speech** seriously impair understanding.

E. Words and phrases are so **unimaginative** and **lifeless** that they detract from the meaning.

F. **Jargon or clichés** distract or mislead. **Redundancy** may distract the reader.

© Northwest Regional Educational Laboratory

Continued

Figure 7–1 *(Continued)*

Sentence Fluency

5 *The writing has an easy flow, rhythm, and cadence. Sentences are well built, with strong and varied structure that invites expressive oral reading.*

A. Sentences are constructed in a way that underscores and enhances the **meaning.**

B. Sentences **vary in length as well as structure.** Fragments, if used, add style. Dialogue, if present, sounds natural.

C. **Purposeful** and **varied sentence beginnings** add variety and energy.

D. The use of **creative and appropriate connectives** between sentences and thoughts shows how each relates to, and builds upon, the one before it.

E. The writing has **cadence;** the writer has thought about the sound of the words as well as the meaning. The first time you read it aloud is a breeze.

3 *The text hums along with a steady beat, but tends to be more pleasant or businesslike than musical, more mechanical than fluid.*

A. Although sentences may not seem artfully crafted or musical, **they get the job done in a routine fashion.**

B. Sentences are **usually constructed correctly;** they **hang together;** they are **sound.**

C. **Sentence beginnings** are not ALL alike; **some variety is attempted.**

D. The reader sometimes has to **hunt for clues** (e.g., connecting words and phrases like *however, therefore, naturally, after a while, on the other hand, to be specific, for example, next, first of all, later, but as it turned out, although,* etc.) that show how sentences interrelate.

E. **Parts** of the text **invite expressive oral reading;** others may be stiff, awkward, choppy, or gangly.

1 *The reader has to practice quite a bit in order to give this paper a fair interpretive reading. The writing reflects more than one of the following problems:*

A. Sentences are **choppy, incomplete, rambling, or awkward;** they need work. **Phrasing does not sound natural.** The patterns may create a sing-song rhythm, or a chop-chop cadence that lulls the reader to sleep.

B. There is little to **no "sentence sense"** present. Even if this piece was flawlessly edited, the sentences would not hang together.

C. Many **sentences begin the same way**—and may follow the same patterns (e.g., *subject-verb-object*) in a monotonous pattern.

D. **Endless connectives** (*and, and so, but then, because, and then,* etc.) or a **complete lack of connectives** create a massive jumble of language.

E. The text **does not invite expressive oral reading.**

Conventions

5 *The writer demonstrates a good grasp of standard writing conventions (e.g., spelling, punctuation, capitalization, grammar, usage, paragraphing) and uses conventions effectively to enhance readability. Errors tend to be so few that just minor touch-ups would get this piece ready to publish.*

A. **Spelling is generally correct,** even on more difficult words.

B. The **punctuation is accurate,** even creative, and guides the reader through the text.

C. A thorough understanding and consistent application of **capitalization** skills are present.

D. **Grammar and usage are correct** and contribute to clarity and style.

E. **Paragraphing tends to be sound** and reinforces the organizational structure.

F. The writer **may manipulate conventions** for stylistic effect—and it works! The piece is very close to being **ready to publish.**

> *GRADES 7 AND UP ONLY: The writing is sufficiently complex to allow the writer to show skill in using a wide range of conventions. For writers at younger ages, the writing shows control over those conventions that are grade/age-appropriate.*

3 *The writer shows reasonable control over a limited range of standard writing conventions. Conventions are sometimes handled well and enhance readability; at other times, errors are distracting and impair readability.*

A. **Spelling** is usually **correct or reasonably phonetic on common words,** but more difficult words are problematic.

B. **End punctuation is usually correct;** internal punctuation *(commas, apostrophes, semicolons, dashes, colons, parentheses)* is sometimes missing/wrong.

C. **Most words are capitalized correctly;** control over more sophisticated capitalization skills may be spotty.

D. **Problems with grammar or usage are not serious** enough to distort meaning but may not be correct or accurately applied all of the time.

E. **Paragraphing is attempted** but may run together or begin in the wrong places.

F. **Moderate editing** (a little of this, a little of that) would be required to polish the text for publication.

1 *Errors in spelling, punctuation, capitalization, usage, and grammar and/or paragraphing repeatedly distract the reader and make the text difficult to read. The writing reflects more than one of these problems:*

A. **Spelling errors are frequent,** even on common words.

B. **Punctuation** (including terminal punctuation) is often **missing or incorrect.**

C. **Capitalization** is **random** and only the easiest rules are correctly used.

D. **Errors in grammar or usage are very noticeable,** frequent, and affect meaning.

E. **Paragraphing is missing, irregular, or so frequent** (every sentence) that it has no relationship to the organizational structure of the text.

F. The reader must **read once to decode,** then again for meaning. **Extensive editing** (virtually every line) would be required to polish the text for publication.

© Northwest Regional Educational Laboratory

Continued

Figure 7–1 *(Continued)*

Presentation

(optional)

5 *The form and presentation of the text enhances the ability for the reader to understand and connect with the message. It is pleasing to the eye.*

A. If handwritten (either cursive or printed), the **slant is consistent,** letters are clearly formed, **spacing is uniform** between words, and the text is easy to read.

B. If word-processed, there is **appropriate use of fonts and font sizes** which invites the reader into the text.

C. The use of **white space** on the page (spacing, margins, etc.) allows the intended audience to easily focus on the text and message without distractions. There is just the right amount of balance of white space and text on the page. The formatting suits the purpose for writing.

D. The use of a **title, side heads, page numbering, bullets,** and evidence of correct use of a style sheet (when appropriate) makes it easy for the reader to access the desired information and text. These markers allow the hierarchy of information to be clear to the reader.

E. When appropriate to the purpose and audience, there is **effective integration of text and illustrations, charts, graphs, maps, tables, etc.** There is clear alignment between the text and visuals. The visuals support and clarify important information or key points made in the text.

3 *The writer's message is understandable in this format.*

A. **Handwriting is readable,** although there may be **discrepancies in letter shape and form, slant, and spacing** that may make some words or passages easier to read than others.

B. **Experimentation with fonts and font sizes** is successful in some places, but begins to get fussy and cluttered in others. The **effect is not consistent** throughout the text.

C. While margins may be present, **some text may crowd the edges.** Consistent spacing is applied, although a different choice may make text more accessible (e.g., single, double, or triple spacing).

D. Although some markers are present (titles, numbering, bullets, side heads, etc.), they are not used to their fullest potential as a guide for the reader to access the greatest meaning from the text.

E. An **attempt is made to integrate visuals** and the text although the connections may be limited.

1 *The reader receives a garbled message due to problems relating to the presentation of the text.*

A. Because the letters are irregularly slanted, formed inconsistently, or incorrectly, and the spacing is unbalanced or not even present, it is **very difficult to read and understand the text.**

B. The writer has gone **wild with multiple fonts and font sizes.** It is a major distraction to the reader.

C. The **spacing is random and confusing** to the reader. There may be little or no white space on the page.

D. **Lack of markers** (title, page numbering, bullets, side heads, etc.) leave the reader wondering how one section connects to another and why the text is organized in this manner on the page.

E. The visuals do not support or further illustrate key ideas presented in the text. They may be **misleading, indecipherable, or too complex** to be understood.

yet flexible means of assessing student writing but also an effective platform for instruction. One of the quintessential works in curriculum development, Tyler's *Basic Principles of Curriculum and Instruction* (1949), suggests that educators can most effectively develop plans for instruction by answering four questions, summarized as follows:

1. What are the desired learning outcomes, meaning what do we want students to know and be able to do?
2. What learning activities will accomplish those outcomes?
3. What is an effective way to arrange those learning activities?
4. How can we assess the degree to which students have gained the targeted skills or knowledge? (p. 1)

The Six-Trait Model easily provides the means for answering those questions as we plan writing instruction in the following ways:

1. The scoring rubric rating descriptors provide a listing and concrete descriptions of what it is that we want students to know or be able to do as writers.
2. The traits and their rating descriptors also provide a target at which teachers can aim their instruction when choosing or designing learning activities.
3. Teachers can arrange and employ the Six-Trait techniques to whatever degree and in any combination they feel best enhances or supplements the curriculum already in place.
4. The scoring rubric provides a means for measuring the degree to which students and teachers have succeeded in reaching these outcomes.

THE SIX-TRAIT MODEL: A ONE-YEAR STUDY

Teachers participating in a 1-year study (Blasingame, 2000) to examine the effects of implementing the Six-Trait Model eventually came to a consensus that it was not in conflict with anything they were already teaching. Instead, they found it to be a means to enhance and more effectively organize their instruction. During the study they identified a number of successful instructional strategies. It's important to note that these strategies seem to closely reflect the levels of Bloom's Taxonomy of Cognitive Development—that is, knowledge, comprehension, application, analysis, synthesis and evaluation, arranged in a logical progression to move students to the highest level. We share those strategies here in six steps. These steps can be used in their entirety and in order when introducing traits to students for the first time, but they don't have to be. Teachers can mix and match them, adapt or modify them, and assimilate them into current curriculum and instruction according to how the teacher judges they will best serve the students' needs.

Following are the steps as observed, discussed, and explained by the researchers and participants in the 1999–2000 study of the Williams Bay School District in Williams Bay, Wisconsin (Blasingame, 2000).

QUICK TIPS

**LITERATURE TO ILLUSTRATE EACH TRAIT:
SOME CROSS-CURRICULAR IDEAS**

Ideas

English—Christopher Paul Curtis, *Bud, Not Buddy;* **Biology**—Stephen Pinker, *How the Mind Works;* **Social Studies**—Stephen Ambrose, *A Band of Brothers;* **Math**—David Blatner, *The Joy of Pi;* **Phys Ed**—A feature article from *Sports Illustrated;* **Auto Mechanics**—*Car Talk,* syndicated newspaper column.

Organization
English or Business—A business letter; **Auto mechanics**—*Chilton's Manual.*

Voice

English—Luci Tapahonso, *Saanii Dahataal: The Women Are Singing—Poems and Stories;* **Social Studies**—Hunter S. Thompson, *Fear and Loathing on the Campaign Trail.*

Word Choice

English—N. Scott Momaday, *House Made of Dawn;* **Social Studies**—election year editorials.

Sentence Fluency

English—James Hurst, "The Scarlet Ibis."

Science—Carl Sagan, *Cosmos.*

Conventions

English—Daniel Keyes, *Flowers for Algernon.*

1. Introduce Each Trait by Reading and Discussing Age-Appropriate Literature (Make the Reading/Writing Connection)

This can happen in a number of ways—probably the more often and more diverse, the better. Teachers sometimes used only a passage from literature for a quick introduction to a trait and sometimes used the traits as one means of discussing the literature that was already in their curriculum. High school teachers in the study were observed using canonical works including Ernest Hemingway's *The Old Man and the Sea* and F. Scott Fitzgerald's *The Great Gatsby* to analyze and discuss the traits of voice and sentence fluency. Middle school teachers were observed using children's picture books such as Jon Scieczka's *The Stinky Cheese Man* to introduce the concept of voice at the setup for a major writing assignment, moving on to more difficult literature. Another middle school teacher used a short story with a teenage protagonist from *Read* magazine to introduce the trait of word choice. In that word choice lesson, the teacher use reading and writing activities to teach the students how an author uses powerful word choice to accomplish characterization and how they, the students, could use it to write character sketches. We observed a middle school teacher use a collection of riddles, announcements, definitions, and famous quotations as part of a lesson on the trait of organization.

In addition to literary works already in the curriculum, a collection of written works of all kinds for introductory or trait-targeting lessons is a valuable tool. One middle school teacher in the study successfully requested the district for a paid summer curriculum project to create a collection of written pieces "that illustrate individual traits dramatically and in an entertaining fashion" (Blasingame, p. 176).

The possibilities for choosing literature to illustrate a targeted trait are limited only by the teacher's resourcefulness and creativity; for example, we have seen menus used to introduce the trait of word choice and birthday cards used to introduce the trait of voice. Look for works that will not only illustrate the targeted trait but will also grab the students' interest. Pieces that read aloud well work especially well. A few genres to consider for all age groups include the following:

1. Picture books
2. Young adult literature
3. Song lyrics
4. Poems
5. Newspapers
6. Magazine articles
7. Advertising of all kinds
8. Greeting cards
9. Nonfiction works

Each of the teachers in the study was careful to introduce and discuss illustrating literature using terminology from the Six-Trait rubric, thereby providing students with a language for talking about writing, a language they may not have possessed previously. Teachers are well advised not only to couch the discussion in Six-Trait language but also to facilitate students in their use of it by putting the descriptors in places in the classroom where students can easily find them as needed. Every student needs to have his or her own Six-Trait rubric.

We highly recommend the "Student Friendly" and/or "One-Pager" versions created by and available from NWREL (NWREL, 2001), but similar materials are available from many vendors and in recent years have begun to appear in students' desk reference books and literature anthologies. Ambitious teachers may choose to create their own materials for students and modify them to suit their own needs. One teacher we observed hung large posters (2 feet by 3 feet) of each trait and its descriptors from the ceiling near the front of the room. As students discussed literature and as they participated in writing workshop discussions, they only had to look at the posters in front of them for reminders as needed. By our observations, after a full school year the students appeared to no longer need the posters and discussed both their reading and their writing adeptly in the language of the traits.

Making the Reading/Writing Connection

One high school teacher in the study reported a new reading–writing connection as a result of her use of literature as a Six-Trait teaching strategy:

> Deborah saw an interesting connection between reading and writing unfolding. She believed that her students were developing the ability to read literature differently than they had in the past. She described this as "seeing a piece of literature through a writer's eyes and not just a reader's eyes." What she meant by this was that as they read, they now had the tools for analysis in the Six-Trait model. . . . they could turn that analytic stance on the literature that they were reading. Deborah believed this was enabling them to understand what the writer of a story or novel did rather than just understand the plot line. They rose to a higher level. The effect was cumulative; the more they read, the more they learned about writing, and the more they wrote, the greater became their understanding of literature. (Blasingame, 2000, p. 144)

2. Use Hands-On Activities with the Traits to Help Students Understand What They Are and How to Improve Them in Their Own Writing

In the second step, students engage in activities designed to address one aspect of writing, an aspect connected to one or more traits. These are not exercises or drills but enjoyable writing or reading activities. Teachers might refer to these as target lessons, mini-lessons or, as NWREL does, focus lessons. Typically, these lessons will target specific descriptors from the Six-Trait rubric and will give students tools for recognizing them and skills-building activities for developing them. These are not major writing assignments but brief activities that help to break down learning into manageable chunks. They are easily blended with other language arts lessons.

The difference between a hands-on activity and a major writing assignment is the narrow focus of the hands-on activity. By separating out individual writing skills and practicing on those alone, these activities enable all writers, but especially beginning writers, to concentrate on one task rather than an entire writing project, a prospect that beginning writers often find overwhelming.

Good focus activities do the following:

1. Help students understand the descriptors of a given trait.
2. Illustrate those descriptors in some sort of model.
3. Give students specific, concrete strategies for improving those qualities in their own writing.
4. Provide a narrowly focused writing task that will give them a means to try out their new skills.

A focus lesson on word choice, for example, might look like this:

Come to Beautiful Downtown Music City for the Rhyme of Your Life

(Using Good Word Choice to Create a Travel Brochure for Your Hometown)

You and the other members of your group will be learning about the trait of word choice as you create a brochure advertising your neighborhood or hometown.

1. Look at your copy of the Six-Trait rubric for word choice and consider the descriptors for good word choice as you review and discuss the travel brochures from Hawaii, Alaska, and Disneyland with which you have been provided.

In particular, find seven examples in each brochure of the descriptor: "Words are specific and accurate."

Here are two helpful strategies: (a) Are there words that appeal to the senses of sight, smell, taste, hearing and touch? (b) Are there descriptions that use specific, concrete adjectives and precise nouns?

For example, do we read about what a warm Hawaiian breeze feels like on the skin or what a slice of roast pork roasted in fresh pineapple tastes like at a luau? Exactly how tall is Mount McKinley? What are the names of the animals we might see in Denali National Park?

2. Using the paper and colored markers provided (composing these in a computer lab would be even better), create a tri-fold travel brochure about your hometown or neighborhood using the brochures you have just analyzed as models. For each of the six panels of your brochure, be ready to explain how you used good word choice by applying the strategies for "Words are accurate and specific."

Each group will share its brochure with the class, and then brochures will be displayed on our Six-Trait bulletin board.

One teacher in our study took advantage of her U.S. literature curriculum to create a focus lesson designed to help her students make the reading/writing connection. She designed a lesson for the combined traits of ideas and organization to help students understand how to write what the Six-Trait rubric describes as "an inviting opening" that "holds the reader's attention." She read aloud each of the openings from a number of stories in an anthology of American short stories. After reading the first two paragraphs, she would stop and ask her students if they would like to hear more. Using the descriptors from the Six-Trait rubric, the class analyzed each story's opening for elements of writing that were successfully or unsuccessfully accomplished (Blasingame, 2000, p. 148).

Trait focus lessons are available from a number of sources. They can be found in abundance at the NWREL Web site (**www.nwrel.org/assessment**), where they are listed by grade level and trait. They also are available in *6+1 Traits of Writing* (Culham, 2002), in *Creating Writers* (Spandel, 2001), and in *Using the Six-Trait Analytic Scale* *for Instruction: Activities for the Classroom 6–12* (Bushman, Goodson, and Blasingame, 1999). Complete teaching kits are available from Write Source, a division of Houghton Mifflin, and a great variety of materials, including focus lessons, are available from the Carson Delarosa Company in Raleigh, North Carolina.

3. Give Students Practice in Analyzing Anonymous Sample Papers from Students of Their Own Age Groups

Teachers guide students through analysis of sample papers that do not belong to them or anyone they know. Teachers should use transparencies to facilitate pointing out specific words, phrases, clauses, or passages in the paper as they are discussed. These papers are completely anonymous and available from a number of sources. Suggested scorings usually accompany the papers. Although in the past teachers have been advised to use a pair of papers—one with a high rating and one with a low rating—to illustrate a given trait through contrast, we have found a much more fruitful practice is to use two versions of the same paper, one from before revision and another from after revision.

Comparing a first draft and a revised version of the same paper reinforces the concept of writing as a process and helps to teach revision. Students become accustomed to thinking that the first draft is only a step toward a much better piece later in the process. They feel less vulnerable and defensive about early drafts as they come to see that first draft as anything but sacred and definitely inferior to what they can produce after feedback from readers and the opportunity to revise. Students come to think of papers as existing on a continuum of process, a process through which the writer moves the paper until he or she is satisfied and ready to publish.

In addition, using a first draft and revision set of papers enhances students' ability to see improvement in the analyzed trait. If "wildlife" is identified as a weak word choice in the first draft, for example, then "grizzly bears, elk, mountain lions, and bighorn sheep" are easily recognized in the revised version as improved word choice. If sentence fluency is weak in the first draft, then students can easily see where clauses and phrases were joined with effective transitions or separated with punctuation in the revised version. The second paper shows the improvement that might only be told about if there were no second paper for students to see, and showing is always better than telling.

Once students learn the vocabulary and the technique on risk-free practice papers, they can apply their new skills to their own papers and those of their classmates. Having come to view the process of analyzing a first draft for a given trait and applying strategies for improving it as completely normal, students are less likely to balk at analyzing their peers' papers or to refuse to consider suggestions for improving their own written work.

Suggested Practice for Using Anonymous Sample Papers

1. Model First

A. Show students a transparency of a first draft and identify for them some of the paper's characteristics as you would analyze them using the rubric for a given trait. Refer to specific descriptors rather than using a rating number.

B. Show students a revised version and point out the specific revisions of words, phrases, or passages you flagged in the analyzing the first draft.

C. *(Crucial step)* Identify the strategy the writer used to make the improvement. For example, analyzing for the trait of ideas in the first draft, the teacher noted the lack of "interesting details" (direct quotation from the rubric) in one paragraph's discussion of a topic. Checking the revised version, the teacher points out three specific and interesting details that the writer added.

2. Guide Next

A. Let the students work in groups to go through the same steps you just used: Analyze the first draft for a given trait using the rubric descriptors, compare it to the revised version and identify changes, and identify the strategy the writer used to make changes.

B. Discuss the two papers now as a whole class by letting the groups take turns sharing their findings one at a time.

3. Move Up Bloom's Taxonomy

A. Show the class a transparency of another rough draft and again analyze it for a given trait.

B. Identify and list the descriptors from the rubric that fit the paper and the specific word, phrase, or passage to which they apply.

C. For each descriptor on the list, discuss a strategy for revision.

D. Discuss application of those strategies to the sample paper.

Obviously, this work with anonymous sample papers will be most fruitful if it centers on a trait with which the students have had some work in class. If the students have had a focus lesson and discussed illustrating literature, they have past knowledge and experience to draw on and make connections. The teacher will also have specifics from past learning to refer to, such as what a teacher might say while helping students analyze sample papers for sentence fluency:

> "Does everyone remember how Luci Tapahonso's piece, 'Hill's Brothers,' sounded out loud?"
> (Response from students)
> "Does this piece we're reading today sound as good?"
> (Response from students)
> "Thinking back to the focus lesson activity we did for sentence fluency, the Super Sentences activity, what are some strategies we could use to improve sentence fluency?"
> (Response from students)

This use of sample papers is an important key for unlocking students' potential to improve their writing skills. Teachers in our 1-year study at Williams Bay agreed that students would be slow to improve without practicing meaningful revision as part of the writing process, but revision in most teachers' past practice meant a step in which students would rewrite their papers according to the correction marks teachers made on them before passing them back days or weeks later. If students would ever improve their skills, they would need the ability to evaluate writing themselves and a repertoire of skills for improving a word, a phrase, a clause, a passage, or a whole piece. This requires practice with papers and terminology for giving meaningful feedback.

As the study began, teachers acknowledged that before adopting the Six-Trait Model and using anonymous sample papers to practice scoring, their past experiences with peer assessment had been unsuccessful for three reasons:

1. Students seemed unable to identify specific examples of strengths or weaknesses in their own paper or papers of their peers.
2. Students had little vocabulary to express their analysis.
3. Students seemed reluctant to make any critical comments beyond minor proofreading concerns, such as spelling or punctuation.

Since peer and self-assessment provided no meaningful, useful feedback, teachers had abandoned those practices.

Since adopting the step of teaching analysis of each trait by guiding students through analysis of anonymous sample papers, teachers at Williams Bay believed that revision was greatly improved. The success of this instructional strategy seemed to have three facets:

1. Students could practice making critical analysis of peer-age writing without any social risk since the papers did not belong to their classmates.
2. The Six-Trait rubric gave them a set of terms to apply without having to invent a language for expressing their analysis.
3. Students were reinforcing their understanding of the qualities of good writing and the Six-Trait Model every time they analyzed another paper without having to go through the lengthy writing process as a group.

4. Use a Major Writing Assignment to Focus on One or Two Traits at a Time

Considering Bloom's Taxonomy, this step is logical in the progression from *knowledge* to *comprehension* to *application* to *analysis* and now to *synthesis*. At this point, students have read and discussed the interesting, age-appropriate literature to show them what a given trait looks like at its best (knowledge and comprehension). They have done short, engaging exercises to break down the trait into its component skills and develop them individually (application), and they have analyzed and discussed anonymous sample papers using the rubric and its descriptors (analysis). Now they are ready to create their own written products from scratch, focusing on performance in the target trait or traits (synthesis).

If the teacher is trying to lead the student writers through an effective learning progression, the major writing assignment should be aligned with the trait lessons that preceded it. In other words, if the class worked on word choice recently, a paper that uses a lot of description would be fertile ground for extending that learning.

Teachers need not disassemble the curriculum they have been using and rearrange the order in which they have previously assigned papers. Instead, they can simply choose which traits they want to teach with which writing assignments (writing assignments that are already in the curriculum) and place the trait lessons where they will be the most helpful. Even in a class that does not focus on writing, we have seen an

American literature teacher choose to teach voice in tandem with Ernest Hemingway and sentence fluency in tandem with F. Scott Fitzgerald.

5. Use the Six-Trait Rubric to Provide Feedback to the Writer Through Peer, Self, and Teacher Assessment and/or Conferencing

The key here is to make this step as similar as possible to the first half of step 3. Students are still analyzing a paper based on their knowledge of a given trait and identifying words, phrases, and passages that fit the descriptors for that trait. Some of these descriptors will indicate strength and some weakness, and those indicating weakness will locate the need for revision in a given part of the paper. The only difference between step 3 and step 5 is that the papers are no longer anonymous but rather are the papers of their peers and the students themselves.

An excellent peer conferencing form designed to use the Six-Trait Model can be found in Chapter 3. We recommend that students work in groups of three to five and center their discussion of each member's work on the peer conferencing form or some similar form that the students have learned to work with and that will prevent their feedback from being unfocused. Other members of the group should have a copy of the student's paper and listen as the writer reads it out loud, sometimes twice, before the group members respond first to the paper's message and then to its form. Remember to use the praise, question, polish (PQP) technique here so that the student writer hears what is done well in the paper and how it affected the readers first. Suggestions for revision come in the polish portion of the peer conference. At the end of the conference, the student writer will receive the conferencing sheets from the other group members for further consideration and for future reference during the revision process. We recommend modeling this conferencing format for the students before they begin with each other.

One impulse students may have that teachers should warn them against is the urge to go beyond saying where a paper needs improvement and what kind of improvement by actually suggesting the text of a rewritten word or passage. This violates the writer's ownership of the paper since those words are not his or hers but were actually written by someone else. Peers may tell the writer, for example, that a passage about a car accident would benefit from better word choice through more accurate and specific descriptions. They should not suggest, however, actual wording such as "a 2002 Cadillac Escalade broadsided our tiny Ford Focus at 45 miles an hour."

Accomplishing step 3 successfully is crucial to the successful transfer to step 5, but unless the proper classroom climate has been established, as we describe in Chapter 1, such that students have developed a trust and rapport with one another and the teacher, they will not be able to make the transfer from working with anonymous papers to working with each other's papers. Cooperative learning theorists use the term "positive interdependence" to describe this "situation in which students (a) see that their work benefits groupmates and their groupmates' work benefits them and (b) work together in small groups to maximize the learning of all members" (Johnson, Johnson, and Holubec, 1988, p. 1:17) (Refer to Chapter 1 for suggestions on how to establish such a classroom culture.)

Although student writers will grow to understand the nature of the traits through seeing them in literature, doing focus lessons, and analyzing anonymous sample papers from peer-age writers, the model's greatest potential for improving students' writing skills resides in steps 5 and 6 because this is where they will actually employ this knowledge in the act of writing. Unfortunately, teachers and students often miss out on the full benefit of using the Six-Trait Model by failing to invest the time and effort needed for effective revision.

Don't Mistake Editing for Revision

Rather than using steps 5 and 6 in the writing process, the focus of writing classes at this point in a writing project historically has been for students to get their drafts back with a grade, some comments, and a red tattooing of marked mistakes in the use of conventions. Little or no meaningful feedback was given other than the editing of surface errors.

Rather than apply a set of criteria for quality about which students had been educated, in the past teachers often evaluated papers by applying whatever criteria occurred to them at the time according to how the paper affected them. Students and teachers were unlikely to have a detailed understanding of what a well-written paper should look like, let alone a shared vocabulary with terms that everyone had practiced identifying and re-creating, as writing classes would have accomplished by using steps 1, 2, and 3 to learn about the traits. Typically, students would either accept the grade they were given or make editing corrections according to the teacher's marks. Editing should be distinguished from revising and might better be referred to as proofreading. Revising is not proofreading for errors; rather, it is evaluating and changing deeper aspects of the paper, such as whole ideas and general organization, along with other aspects of wordsmithing, such as choice of words, phrasing, and transitions.

6. Provide Students Time, Resources, and Credit for Revision

Just as step 5 should resemble the first half of step 3, step 6 should resemble the second half, again with the major difference that students are not considering how to apply revision strategies to an anonymous paper but rather how to apply them to their own writing. The student writer has received verbal feedback accompanied by peer conferencing sheets from the members of his or her writing group, and if there has been adequate practice in applying revision strategies from the anonymous sample paper work, the writer can go to work making changes. He or she can refer to the focus lesson material or reference works provided in the classroom or can ask for help from the teacher on improving specific aspects of the paper.

The writer of the paper still owns the written piece, however, and must decide which revision suggestions to accept and which to reject. We want to emphasize that although we encourage the writer to be open to the responses of his or her peers, and we encourage the teacher to create a climate where trust facilitates the giving and taking of constructive criticism, ultimately the paper belongs to its author. If the writer makes changes that he or she does not agree with or does not believe improve the paper, not only is ownership diminished but so is improvement in writing skills because the writer is blindly following someone else's ideas rather than his or her own. This practice would be no better than what has gone on in many writing classrooms for years in which the student writes the paper, the teacher marks it according to how she or he would have written the paper, and the student obediently makes changes he or she doesn't believe in or even understand in some cases.

For this reason we recommend that, although students should get points or credit for the revising step in the process, the credit should not be based on whether or not the writer made all the changes the assessors suggested. This is not to say that in a final conference the teacher might not ask the student to explain why he or she chose not to make a given change.

7. Final Assessment

At the same time a paper is assigned, students should be informed of exactly how it will be graded. The grading system can be as complicated or as simple as the teacher wants to make it, although we recommend it be simple enough for students to easily understand and not so complicated as to be a mystery to them when they see the final grade on the paper. The more closely a student can connect the grade and its elements to the work they are doing, especially while they are doing it, the more the grade will benefit both the teacher and student.

Six-Trait writing authorities such as Vicki Spandel (2001), and Ruth Culham (2003) advise against translating Six-Trait rubric scores directly into grades. Instead, they recommend using the traits as part of the grade but giving additional credit for other aspects of a writing project, such as the quality of the students' steps taken in the writing process. The individual teacher needs to decide how much of the final grade should be based on the students' performance as assessed using the Six-Trait rubric and how much should come from other considerations. Since the Six-Trait rubric is meant to give no consideration to the student's personal effort, we recommend the teacher give it a weighting of no more than 50 percent of the paper's total grade.

We recommend some form of rubric that shows the specific qualities of the paper to be assessed, the steps in the process for which they will be given credit, and exactly what amount of the final grade will be associated with each. Again, this can be as simple or complicated as the teacher wants to make it. For example, the rubric might reflect a final grade that includes 50 percent (or 100 points out of the 200 point total) of the total given for steps in the writing process, including 5 percent (10 points out of a 200 point total) for the prewriting work attached to the project. The rubric might show that 35 percent of the grade will be based on the Six-Trait rubric (70 points out of a possible 200), and since the paper is a descriptive one, the trait of word choice will be more heavily weighted than the other traits and will count for 15 percent of the total grade (or 30 points). The remaining 15 percent (30 points out of 200) will be given for filling out the metacognitive/reflective forms that accompany this piece into the writing portfolio. Such a rubric is reflected in Figure 7–2.

At some point teachers must decide when, if ever, assessment of a paper really is final. Some teachers we know have a policy in which papers can be rewritten repeatedly for a better grade until the student decides to stop.

Figure 7–2 Assessment rubric

Steps in the Writing Process 100 pts. (50%)		
Prewriting 10 pts. (5%)	Pts.	%
Drafting 30 pts. (15%)	Pts.	%
Conferencing 20 pts. (10%)	Pts.	%
Revision 20 pts. (10%)	Pts.	%
Publishing 20 pts. (10%)	Pts.	%
Six-Trait Performance 70 pts. (35%)		
Ideas 5 pts. (2.5%)	Pts.	%
Organization 5 pts. (2.5%)	Pts.	%
Voice 5 pts. (2.5%)	Pts.	%
Word Choice 30 pts. (15%)	Pts.	%
Sentence Fluency 5 pts. (2.5%)	Pts.	%
Conventions 20 pts. (10%)	Pts.	%
Portfolio 30 pts. (15%)		
Written Reflection 15 pts. (7.5%)	Pts.	%
Metacognitive Question Sheet 15 pts. (7.5%)	Pts.	%
Total 200 pts. (100%)	Pts.	%

BIBLIOGRAPHY

Blasingame, J. (2000). Six case studies of first year implementation of the Six-Trait model for writing instruction and assessment. (Doctoral Dissertation, University of Kansas). *Dissertation Abstracts International, 61–12A*, 4705.

Bushman, J., Goodson, F. T., and Blasingame, J. (1999). *Using the Six-Trait analytic scale for instruction: Activities for the classroom—6–12, second edition.* Overland Park, KS: The Writing Conference, Inc.

Culham, R. (2003). *6+1 traits of writing.* New York: Scholastic.

Diederich, P. (1974). *Measuring growth in English.* Urbana, IL: National Council of Teachers of English.

Johnson, D. W., Johnson, R. T, and Holubec, E. J. (1988). *Advanced cooperative learning.* Edina MN: The Interactive Book Company.

Northwest Regional Educational Laboratory. (2001). *6+1 traits of an effective writer.* Portland, OR: NWREL.

Pirsig, R. (1974). *Zen and the art of motorcycle maintenance.* New York: Bantam Doubleday Dell.

Spandel, V. (2001). *Creating writers.* New York: Addison, Wesly, Longman.

Tyler, R. (1949). *Basic principles of curriculum and instruction.* Chicago: University of Chicago Press.

PART III

Planning for Instruction: A Compendium of Instructional Resources

> Thou hast most traitorously corrupted the youth of the realm in
> creating a grammar school. . . . It will be proved to thy face that thou
> hast men about thee that usually talk of a noun and a verb, and such
> abominable works as no Christian ear can endure to hear.
>
> *Shakespeare, Henry VI, Part II.*

INTRODUCTION

Part One of this book presents instructional techniques and strategies to help novice and experienced teachers enliven their classrooms with activities for teaching writing. It has been our intent to share tried and true activities based on research—current and past—on the writing environment, the process of writing, and the writing workshop and the multi-genre approach to writing. Part Two presents theory, research, and classroom models about the use of authentic assessment, specifically the use of portfolios and the Six-Trait Model for instruction and assessment.

Part Three of this text highlights some of the troublesome areas of teaching writing, including the following issues: teaching grammar and mechanics, when and how to facilitate spelling, service learning, the involvement of the community in a writing program, the importance of establishing communication with administrators and parents, and teaching writing to English as a Second Language (ESL) students.

GRAMMAR AND MECHANICS

The study of grammar and mechanics as they relate to oral and written composition has been a thorn in the side of English teachers for many, many years. The research has been very clear, the results from practice have been very clear, but to this day, teachers—especially in the upper elementary grades and middle schools—seem to think that a steady dose of grammatical drill is in the best interest of student writers. As recently as June 2002, a group of teachers was overheard bemoaning the "fact" that the students in their classes were just "terrible" with the use of conventions (yes, they were Six-Trait enthusiasts) and that they felt they should return to more serious drill and practice with grammar and mechanics.

Does the research on the teaching of grammar in isolation support this practice? We think not. As early as 1906, Hoyt made one of the first inquiries into what the knowledge of grammar provides students. He tested 200 ninth-graders in grammar, composition, and the ability to interpret a poem. Among his conclusions are the following: "(1) About the same relation exists between grammar and composition, and grammar and interpretation, as exists between any two totally different subjects, such as grammar and geography; (2) grammar is of little avail in strengthening one's power to use language" (as cited in Meckel, 1963, p. 975). In other words, Hoyt's study indicates that there is little relationship between knowing grammar terminology and the ability to write and interpret literature.

Boraas (1917), another early investigator, discovered even more surprising evidence. He "reported finding a lower correlation between knowledge of grammar and ability in composition than he found between knowledge of grammar and knowledge of history and arithmetic" (as cited in Meckel, 1963, p. 976). The research continues.

Hatfield's *Report of the Curriculum Commission* of the National Council of Teachers of English (1935) summarizes research studies published up to the time of his report. The content and method of instruction in grammar should be determined "by the purposes which grammar can serve. . . . Scientific investigations have failed to show the effectiveness of grammar in the elimination of usage errors. . . . There is no scientific evidence of the value of grammar, which warrants its appearance as a prominent or even distinct feature of the course of [language arts] study" (p. 228).

More than a decade later, Gordon (1947) expresses what has become traditionally accepted language arts pedagogy: "Grammar not merely has a use in the English classroom, but is indispensable. It is not, and never should be taught as an end in itself. Its value is that it provides part of the technique for good writing" (p. 27). We must add our enthusiastic interpretation to Gordon's point. It is not to be taught in isolation but always, as it is needed to help in the revision stage of the writing process. Many studies reported in *Encyclopedia of Educational Research* (1950), *Research in Written Composition* (Braddock, Loyd-Jones, and Schoer, 1963), and *Research on Written Composition: New Directions for Teaching* (Hillocks, 1986) all confirm that instruction in formal grammar has no effect on the quality of students' writing. A somewhat more recent study (Warner, 1993) reaffirms these general conclusions. In summary, grammar by itself does little or nothing to the quality of writing. We hasten to add that grammar, or at least portions of what we have come to call grammar, might be part of the mini-lessons that accompany the writing workshop. We can't be any more emphatic than this: If grammar is to be taught, writing must follow immediately. Students must make the error before the error can be corrected.

SPELLING

In much the same way that we incorporate the teaching of grammar and mechanics into our writing program, we incorporate the teaching of spelling. Spelling rules and conventions are usually taught systematically in the elementary grades, but at the middle and high school levels, the emphasis should shift from the *rule-based process* to the *use-based process*. We do know that teaching spelling in isolation is not successful. We have all been through the spelling list approach at one time or another: list on the board on Monday, pretest on Wednesday, and final spelling test on Friday. What usually takes place next is "forget the words on Saturday." The words are usually taken from a spelling book; they are in alphabetical order. An interesting problem usually arises: Students never get to words beginning with R or the remaining part of the alphabet because time in the school year runs out.

Difficult as this process of running out of time is, it is not the major concern. What we know about isolated grammar instruction is the same for spelling: Students do not keep the words in their short-term or long-term memories, primarily because they do not have any ownership of the words they are asked to spell. These words are seldom used in their reading, writing, or speaking due to the source of the words. They are taken from a spelling list not associated with the writing or reading they do. It is quite evident to us that students must know how to spell words that they use regularly.

We believe that students must be nudged a bit into incorporating new words into their writing and speaking vocabularies. They can do that in many ways. We mention a few here. Discussion of words that are new from literature helps to increase students' vocabularies. New words are added to vocabularies during active involvement in the study of literature, not by learning words on isolated lists. Secondly, when teachers and students use the Six-Trait Analytic Model, they are working toward increasing vocabularies when working with word choice, one of the traits.

QUICK TIPS

A SPELLING GUIDE

1. Say the word and distinguish each syllable as the word is spoken.
2. Visualize how the word appears with your eyes closed.
3. Look at the word again on paper to see if the visual impression was accurate.
4. Write the word on paper and check its spelling.
5. Repeat step 4 twice.
6. Write a short piece of discourse in which the word is used.

Quick Tips

Common Spelling Rules

Nouns ending in *y* preceded by a vowel add *s* when making the plural form. Those ending in *y* preceded by a consonant change the *y* to *i* and add *es*.

Words ending with a silent *e* drop the *e* before a suffix beginning with a vowel and retain it before a suffix beginning with a consonant.

Words of one syllable that end in a consonant preceded by a single vowel double the consonant before adding *ing* or *ed*. If the word has more than one syllable, the same process occurs if the accent is on the last syllable.

Place *i* before *e* when the sound is long *e*, except after *c*; after *c*, the spelling is *ei*.

It seems to us that spelling in the middle and upper grades should be primarily an individual matter. While the emphasis on rules and spelling lists may be effective and, therefore, worthwhile at the elementary level, the emphasis must change to an individual spelling program in the middle and high schools.

An Individual Spelling Program

To begin this spelling program, teachers should secure a list of spelling demons. Many lists are available: 25 most misspelled words, 100 spelling demons, and so on. Lists also exist for particular grade levels. We recommend that teachers use such a list as a basis for students' individual spelling lists. Students spell the words as they are dictated. Those words they misspell go on their individual lists. Students do not receive a grade on this first spelling activity; it is for diagnostic purposes only. Words that are misspelled from then on are placed on the students' individual lists. These words come from a variety of sources, such as revised writings, essay examinations, and daily written lessons. Students are responsible for correctly spelling those words that they are using. If words are misspelled, they add them to the list of words to be studied and eventually to be assessed.

Periodically throughout the semester, teachers test students on the words that appear on their individual spelling lists. This testing may occur weekly, every 2 weeks, or monthly. Teachers should devise a method for this testing that best suits their programs. We offer two possibilities: (1) Teachers place students in pairs and have each student test the other student on his or her words. The students may evaluate the spelling tests at that time, or they may be turned in for teacher evaluation. If this approach is used, teachers may need to move about the room during the testing to see that students are remaining on task and are following the appropriate procedure. (2) Teachers have students come individually to the teacher's desk for an evaluation session. This approach is workable if teachers periodically plan a lesson in which students can be working by themselves so that the teacher is free to test individual students. This may be a free reading time, journal-writing time, or general study time. If teachers are using the writer's workshop approach, they may find it workable to briefly interrupt students and have them come to their desks.

This second approach may demand more of a teacher's time but may be more beneficial due to the quality control it provides.

Whichever approach is considered, the following comments about the spelling program may be useful.

In the best interest of students, we urge that students be tested on only 10 words at a time. Some students will, of course, have many words on their lists, perhaps 30 or 40. However, other students may have only 5 words. It would be unacceptable to punish those students with just 5 words, so only 5 words would be on the list to be tested. The student who has 30 or 40 words should not be tested on all 40 at one time. Teachers should simply ask for 10 at a time. It may take three or four tests over time to reduce this list, but it will happen.

Students should be encouraged to keep their word lists where they will be safe and secure. The journal works well for this purpose. It is frequently kept in the classroom and, therefore, is readily accessible. If teachers are using the portfolio system and have hanging files or portfolio collection boxes, they might have students keep their spelling lists there. Teachers may find that they want to keep a master copy of individual spelling lists. One teacher who has used this approach for teaching spelling for some time has a small three-ringed binder in which she keeps the spelling list for each student in her classes. While she agrees that it takes more time to do this clerical recording, she believes it is the best procedure. As she assesses assignments from which misspelled words are taken, she adds these words to the appropriate lists in the binder. When the periodic tests are completed, she removes the appropriate words from the lists. This approach works particularly well for students who fail to keep an up-to-date list. These students are still held responsible for the words that they have failed to place on their lists. They might even have to check with the teacher's notebook.

Many teachers have taken our classes and have learned about this spelling program. Most are very eager to try it. What they report back to us is that it works. One important consideration is that students are held accountable for the words that they use and not words that come from a standard list. Students find the program beneficial as well. They find relevancy in the program since they are dealing with words that are in their vocabularies. What we are told is that the teachers find the lists get shorter and shorter. It is interesting that students are more concerned with spelling since they will, in all probability, meet the word again if they misspell it in their writing.

SERVICE LEARNING

As the name implies, service learning describes a project in which the participants, while actively engaged in learning and reflecting, provide a service that is needed in the community. As Brack and Hall (1997) explain, students have the opportunity and responsibility to "research real problems, struggle to find solutions, and to articulate the challenges they face and the solutions they find in the papers they write" (p. 144).

By the very nature of experiential learning, the depth of a service-learning experience has the potential to be far greater than a classroom experience alone. Students are likely to learn about themselves, their community, and the differences among their own lives and the lives of the people they serve. Service learning is ideal for teaching writing not only because much of a project's operation may require writing in various genres—from business letters to informational brochures—but also because much of the students' own processing of their learning, especially reflection, will also require writing. Since service-learning projects put students face to face with fellow human beings who can benefit from their help, the service-learning students often invest their own spirits in a project, thereby creating an intrinsic motivation to write well enough to accomplish important goals both for the project's success and for accurately expressing their thoughts and feelings about the whole experience.

The design for our own service-learning project (an after-school writing center for students at Fees Middle School in Tempe, Arizona, staffed by Arizona State University [ASU] students from our Methods of Teaching Writing class) was based on the model provided by the Service Learning Department at ASU. In our project, the ASU students were responsible for creating valuable yet enjoyable writing activities based on the state standards and the Six-Trait Model and implementing one new writing activity each week with a group of sixth-, seventh-, and eighth-graders. Writing activities included such things as researching on the Internet and creating a travel brochure, reading excerpts from the autobiographical works of young adult authors and writing similar personal narratives, and creating a variety of features and news items for the student newspaper. From these writing activities, the Fees Middle School students developed a portfolio of written work in various stages of completion, work that they used for class assignments, for submission to literary publications, for the school newspaper that the club initiated, or just for their own enjoyment. The ASU students took the middle school students through the writing process individually to help them develop their skills and some pride in their work and abilities. The ASU students gave every student personal attention at every session, usually at a ratio of one tutor for every two students.

The ASU participants were also required to write about their experiences on a daily and weekly basis, to participate in an asynchronous online discussion, and to jointly create an article to submit for publication.

Some important elements of this service-learning project plan include the following:

1. *A partnership* with a community organization or organizations to identify a need, create a plan, pool resources, and provide support.

2. *A detailed project plan* that includes a description of the need and the objectives that describe how the need will be served. The plan should also indicate who is responsible for each part of the plan, what the timeline is, and how the project's success will be measured.

3. *A detailed service-learning curriculum* to coexist with the project plan. Not only will the students be participating in the project by contributing their time and effort, but they also will be writing, and perhaps reading, about their experiences (rather than writing about someone else's experience as they might in a traditional composition class). The curriculum will outline in detail exactly what the students in the service-learning project will have to do in addition to their work on the project, including writing assignments such as research papers on the project's topic, personal narratives, opinion pieces, daily reflections, and any other written products the curriculum designer deems appropriate.

4. Providing *a training program for the participants* so that they know what to expect and how to respond in the project environment. This could include some simulations, but at the least should include directions for interaction with the community served and policies for behavior. A participants' handbook is helpful.

5. *Supervision,* including a set structure outlining the persons responsible for supervising the service-learning students and for what exactly they are accountable. Supervision includes the project's real-time operation, as well as the learning activities the students participate in outside of the project's operation time.

We have found that although student reflection is crucial to a service-learning program that emphasizes writing, the reflections need guidance. Students must be facilitated in their critical thinking skills and in the ways that they write about their thoughts. A simple log or journal in which they describe their day on the project and what they thought or felt is fine as a starting point and will probably provide better writing than a report on some topic a student cared nothing about, but deeper reflection and more sophisticated writing will come from more carefully designed reflective tasks. Facilitating metacognitive analyses of their experiences, for example, will push students to think about their own previous assumptions and how they see these changing as a result of their experiences.

We have been especially pleased with the online discussion of our service-learning participants in which they have a chance to respond to a provocative question and then respond to each other's postings. The end result of these discussions showed up in the final papers describing participants' perceptions of the effects the writing center service-learning project had on their formation as teachers.

An excellent resource for getting started with a service-learning program or sharing ideas with those who are refining theirs can be found at the National Service-Learning Clearing House online at **www.servicelearning.org.**

INVITING PARENT, COMMUNITY, AND ADMINISTRATOR PARTICIPATION

Criticism of parts or even the whole of this approach to teaching writing by those in the community, parents of students in the writing program, and administrators who have to respond to parents' concerns may occur. There are those who for whatever reasons simply cannot accept change and come hell or high water will not give up teaching the parts of speech in a writing program. Others, of course, may criticize out of ignorance; they do not know the research that supports the process approach to teaching writing. They are not familiar with the writer's workshop or the use of portfolios as useful methodologies.

It is important for teachers to take the initiative in telling colleagues, parents, and administrators about programs that work well and that are good for students. Teachers often have to defend what they are doing, and most of that defense occurs in the negative, complaining context. By the time this situation arises, the problem already exists, and teachers find it very difficult to discuss general philosophies, theories, and research findings when confronted with a person who is concerned with one very specific problem. For example, it would seem to be more difficult to defend

Quick Tips

RESOURCES

For colleagues and administrators:

- *Picture Books: An Annotated Bibliography for Teaching Writing* (5th ed.) (book)
- *Picture Books: An Annotated Bibliography for Teaching Writing* (5th ed.) (video)
- *Putting Portfolios to Work* (Video)

For parents and the community:

- *Dear Parent: A Handbook for Parents of Six-Trait Writing Students* (book)
- *Dear Parent: A Handbook for Parents of Six-Trait Writing Students* (video)

From Northwest Regional Educational Laboratory (**www.nwrel.org**).

the lack of teaching of the thesis statement to eighth-graders to the sophomore English teacher if a solid foundation about the sequence of writing and cognitive development had not been set forth first. To say simply "I don't want to teach it to my eighth-graders" probably will not convince this sophomore English teacher that you are not shirking your professional responsibility.

A better way, perhaps, is for teachers to go on the offensive—not *be* offensive, just take the initiative in sharing with other teachers, administrators, parents, and the community what students are doing in the classroom. Writing teachers should not wait until a problem surfaces before they communicate their writing program with all of its parts to those who need to know.

To Other Teachers and Administrators

It would seem important to us that teachers who are working with the writing programs suggested in this book share as much as possible with their colleagues and, of course, with their administrators. This sharing is not intended in any way to force other teachers to conform to these practices but to suggest that this methodology is working for the teacher and it may, in fact, work for the colleagues. Administrators must be aware of what is going on in the classroom so that they will be informed and able to answer questions raised by parents. It is also important for teachers to ensure administrators that, indeed, they are meeting the objectives/standards that have been agreed upon by the profession and the local school and district. These objectives can be shared with both groups in private conferences or in faculty meetings. In addition, teachers should consider sharing the materials and methods that they are using to achieve these objectives. Perhaps one of the most important ways to show that what you are doing is working is to share the product that has been achieved—that is, share the student writing with those who are interested. If colleagues are complaining that doing the writer's workshop won't work and students are not being taught the necessary skills for effective writing, the best way to combat that criticism is to show the writing that students are doing.

Perhaps as important as the student's work is the sharing of the research and theory that have been suggested and documented in this book to support the practice of teaching writing. The documentation would be of some help when talking to colleagues and administrators about the writing process. Writings from Donald Graves, Donald Murray, Janet Emig, Nancy Atwell, Vicki Spandel, Ruth Culham, Ralph Fletcher, Grant Wiggins, and Peter Elbow laid a solid foundation in the teaching of writing. In addition, when teachers read pertinent articles in the *English Journal, Voices from the Middle, The Middle School Journal, Educational Leadership*, and *Journal of Adolescent and Adult Literacy,* to mention a few sources, they should share their findings with their colleagues and administrators. A copy of a classroom activity described by another classroom teacher and published in a national journal may have tremendous influence.

It seems to us that it is also very productive to invite colleagues and administrators to visit your classroom to see firsthand what is taking place in the writing program. Casually walking by an open door to a room in which students are involved in a writer's workshop event may lead the observer to question what in the world is going on. Students are moving about, working in groups, working with partners, and some may be just sitting on the floor reading to themselves. Observers need to be in the classroom, observing what is happening. To make this observation most beneficial, it should take place over 2 or 3 days so that the observer can see the sequence as it develops.

Frequently, when "portfolio day" arrives, most classrooms are very busy. Students are in groups of three or four or they are with a partner trying to decide what writing is best to take from the "hanging files" or "working files" to place in their portfolios. This workday can be very busy, very noisy. Therefore, a close observation by personnel who are usually not connected with the process is important. Many teachers invite colleagues and administrators, as well as parents, to join in the process of portfolio selection.

To Parents

In previous years, parents did not contribute much to the educational process of their students. Many times it was difficult to get parents to participate at all. Today, a shift has taken place and parents, on the whole, have become much more involved in the life of the classroom. Some would argue that they have become too involved. Some teachers complain that if a group of parents, albeit a small group of parents, doesn't particularly like what is going on in the school, change occurs. Teachers have argued that administrators do not support them enough when it comes to parental involvement.

We argue, as we have noted earlier, that teachers must go on the offensive. As soon as possible, teachers should involve parents in what they are doing in the classroom. We note that many teachers with whom we are working believe that most parents want to participate and want to do what is in the best interest of their children. We also note that the informed parent is more likely to agree with what is being done than to disagree with the creative methods that teachers are using in the classroom.

QUICK TIPS

HOW TO INVOLVE PARENTS
- Share at back-to-school nights.
- Invite parents to work as aides in the classroom.
- Sponser an "English Fair."
- Have students write a newsletter.
- Include parents on assessments of portfolios.
- Have portfolio parties.
- Create a Web site.

It is imperative that teachers present as much detail as possible about the writing programs when they meet parents at after-school meetings or back-to-school nights. If teachers can provide examples of multi-genre papers, portfolios, or various kinds of writing from previous years' students, parents will see firsthand what can be accomplished with this new methodology. Parents must hear about what happens in groups when students present their drafts to each other for critiques. They need to hear the benefits of choice and ownership in the writing program.

Since writing is of utmost importance in the classroom, it seems appropriate that students use that medium to convey what is happening in the classroom. Newsletters home to parents can be used to highlight what activities students are participating in and the success that they are having. Brad Dunlap, teacher at Desert Arroyo Middle School, Cave Creek, Arizona, and his students create a newsletter periodically to share what writing products the students are working on. Not only does this help in the communication with the parents, but it also makes a very important statement to students that writing is important and that this writing can be used effectively to communicate important information to other people.

Letters home to parents can provide additional information about structure, content, and methodology about the writing class. Angie Flax, teacher at Ottawa High School, Ottawa, Kansas, creates a letter to parents to present at back-to-school night in which she presents the format for the forthcoming year. She also sends that letter home to parents who were not at the school event. Flax goes into great detail about how the portfolios are constructed, how pieces of writing are kept in the classroom and not sent home, how the pieces are selected, and how the portfolio will show growth of the student's writing ability over the course of the semester.

Perhaps one of the most gratifying events that could showcase student writing to parents is the English Fair. For years, science teachers have been involved with science fairs. In fact, some districts have districtwide science fairs. It would seem appropriate for the English department to create an English Fair. This approach could, in fact, showcase student writing, or it could be broader than that and include all academic programs, including social studies projects, math projects, and other content area creations. If this were done, writing teachers may want to encourage other content teachers to make writing a part of their projects so that, again, writing could be seen as important in a variety of ways.

To the Community

If teachers of writing can work with groups in the community, it fosters a great deal of credibility with students as they participate in the writing program. Whenever possible, teachers can make connections with the community and their students. Writing projects can be displayed around the community, often in financial institution foyers, U.S. post offices, libraries, malls, and community-based Web sites.

Professional writers often live within the community. Teachers can and should invite them to visit their classrooms to talk about how they write. It is often the case that these "hometown" authors will come in and talk without charge. Through the auspices of the local or state arts commission, author-in-residence programs draw frequently on local community authors. Most often, these visits come without costs to the local school. Of course, schools will bring in nationally known authors to visit in classes, but while we encourage schools to do this, we are not advocating that specific program here. Many local, talented writers reside in local communities and are most eager to participate in their community/school programs.

We have noted in previous chapters the importance of the I-Search paper as an important vehicle to make the research component of the writing program credible for young writers. The I-Search paper calls on young writers to investigate community resources as their sources of information for the topic they are investigating. For example, a student may have a pet dog that suffers from parvo, a viral infection. As part of the I-Search investigation about this disease, students may visit the local animal hospital and gather pertinent information from the local veterinarian. They may also visit with the local animal shelter to gather additional material. Community resources can be of great help when working with authentic searches.

We also suggest teachers secure sources in the community for which their students can write. Many times the Girls and Boys Clubs or the Kiwanis Club, for example, need brochures written. Writing classrooms can take on these projects, again making the statement that writing is something that is done outside the classroom as well as inside.

Many community agencies frequently have writing contests that students may enter. Often the VFW, Chamber of Commerce, and supporters of special events such as El Día de Los Libros y Los Niños (**http://www.nlci.org/activity/dlnintro.htm**) and Black History Month offer young people opportunities to enter their writing contests. Teachers should be on the lookout for such contests and support their students in that endeavor. Other writing contests offered by national organizations or by the local schools system should be a part of the writing program. In any event, winners of these writing contests should be supported. Teachers may announce winners through in-school means, as well as through the local media. Such announcements should celebrate the winners by sharing their names through the community media with community members.

THE ENGLISH AS A SECOND LANGUAGE (ESL) STUDENT

We believe that best practice in writing instruction for ESL students follows the same basic tenets as writing instruction for native English speakers with a few additions, a belief well grounded in ESL research. Scholars of second-language learners advise using

> *Our methods are, in turn, increasingly oriented toward cooperative, learner-centered teaching in which learner strategy training plays a significant role.*
>
> H. Douglas Brown,
> *San Francisco State University*
> From "TESOL at Twenty-Five:
> What Are the Issues?"

the process approach to teaching writing, much the same as we have detailed in Chapter 2. As we address later in this section, however, research shows that ESL students need more than just writing activities; language acquisition requires an environment rich in input (verbal information). ESL students need to do a lot of reading and listening to acquire new vocabulary and constructions if we want them to improve their writing skills. All students, ESL or otherwise, will learn faster, develop stronger skills, and retain them longer when the pedagogy is learner centered and students are intrinsically motivated, so new verbal information based on areas of interest to ESL students is again vital. As we have said in previous chapters, student choice leads to student ownership and ultimately to success. The writing teacher with ESL students, then, must create a classroom environment in which students are reading, listening and writing constantly; students should be writing in a variety of ways, and writing about things they care about and want to communicate to others.

ESL writing teachers need to be aware of their students' first language literacy. There is a high correlation between first language literacy and second language literacy (Hudelson, 1987). In other words, language learners' reading and writing proficiency in their first language has a high correlation with the speed in which they learn to read and write in their second language. ESL students who were not proficient writers in their first language may not progress nearly as quickly as those who were already competent in the written word in their first language.

Teaching and Learning the Rules of Written English

A teacher newly entrusted with ESL students might be tempted to cover the rules of grammar and usage before ever allowing students to write. Actually, quite the opposite is best. Students will learn more slowly, have more difficulty with application, and remember less if the focus is on rote memorization of grammar rules and imitation of formulaic writing patterns. Imagine trying to learn the rules of a complicated card game like bridge before actually playing it; the rules will make much more sense in the context of the game.

According to second-language-acquisition scholars, it is important for the writing teacher to understand that students will benefit far more from "comprehensible input"—messages that the language learner can understand—than from direct grammar instruction or focus on correctness (Krashen, 2003, pp. 4–5). Krashen says that it helps "if the messages are interesting" (2003, p. 4).

Since rules of a language are so numerous, and since linguists now believe that these rules are learned in an order dictated by developmental readiness, teaching grammar rules one at a time just isn't effective. "We all remember grammatically based classes. Students focus on one rule at a time, the idea being to 'master' one rule and then move on to the next. It simply doesn't work" (Krashen, 2003, p. 5). Why not? Back to our bridge analogy: How long would a bridge club last if players studied the rules for weeks before ever actually playing? Probably not very long because it would be so boring.

The problems with direct grammar instruction in any substantial amount and removed from language interaction, however, are much deeper than just boredom. For the language learner to grasp a new concept, he or she must encounter the concept in a meaningful context. Studies have shown that ESL students in classes where the curriculum is based primarily on reading, writing, and speaking about topics of interest demonstrate not only greater fluency but also proficiency in grammar and usage equal to or greater than their counterparts in classes emphasizing description and drill of grammar rules (Isik, 2000; Nikolov and Krashen, 1997).

In this same vein, we believe that initial concentration on correctness can actually be counterproductive with ESL students in the writing classroom, just as it has been proven to be with native speakers, in which case the individuals studied chose to abandon words and constructions that they had been penalized for using with incorrect punctuation (Hartwell, 1985, p. 121). Instead, students should be acknowledged for attempting complexity of constructions, accuracy of expression, and diversity of vocabulary beyond their past performances.

We do not at all propose abandoning the teaching of grammar with ESL students, but rather we propose doing so strategically within the writing process. This should be done in a number of ways simultaneously:

1. Students should be supplied with handbooks in which they can look up specific issues as questions arise during writing and conversation.
2. Mini-lessons in grammar and usage, as well as other conventions, should be taught in writing workshop and based on the problems that teachers see in students' writing.
3. The writing process should include an editing step in which the students' writing groups look for errors.
4. Read aloud to students and have them read, focusing on high-interest material written at a level just beyond the students' current proficiency, causing them to stretch to learn new and more advanced conventions of written expression.

Designing Writing Instruction for the ESL Student

Designing and implementing writing instruction for ESL students translates into some very specific practices as outlined by Brown (1993), including "teaching writing as a thinking process in which the learners develop their own ideas freely and openly" (p. 18). Brown goes on to recommend that students generate and work with their own topics and information, rather than "teacher assigned topics[s]" and that grammar be taught when students can see its value in making their communication more effective (p. 19).

Provide students with authentic writing tasks that involve interaction with peers and the outside world, such as writing letters (to the editor, to a company, to friends, to authors, to municipalities), creating a newspaper, publishing a literary magazine, writing a family history, and creating a guide to local history and culture. Other written products discussed in previous chapters can be especially effective, including short in-class pieces, such as the autobiopoem, and much longer projects, such as the I-Search or multi-genre papers.

Input Is Mandatory

Writing teachers with ESL students must understand another of Krashen's theories, "comprehensible output," which holds that output (i.e., speaking and writing) is not necessary for the acquisition of language (Krashen, 2003, p. 64), but "comprehensible input" (i.e., reading and listening) is a necessity. The significance of this for ESL is that writing class needs to be rich in input. Students must be reading and listening to language products in English to acquire the language in which they are learning to write. The curriculum must provide second language input, which might include literature, discussion, Internet research, interviewing, attending plays, poetry readings or other performances, and any other experiences in which the students can come in contact with the English language, especially in interesting contexts that will inspire them to stretch their understanding. ESL students will not improve their writing very quickly if there is no input from which to acquire new vocabulary, constructions, and other aspects of the English language.

Process Writing

The writing process, as we outline it in Chapter 2, is equally important for the ESL student and the first-language student. The benefits of breaking down the writing process for students have been acknowledged by ESL scholars as an example of the educational term "scaffolding:"

> One way to assist beginning and intermediate [ESL] writers is to provide them with temporary frameworks or supports that allow them to concentrate on one aspect of the writing process at a time. We refer to such temporary frameworks as literary scaffolds . . . the writing process itself is a powerful scaffold in that it breaks a complex process into smaller subprocesses, each of which is aimed at creating meaning. (Peregoy and Boyle, 1997, p. 202)

Writing process for ESL students involves the same steps as we have detailed in Chapter 2, but some become especially important in the scaffolding process, thus deserving of special attention, in particular, steps requiring teacher assistance or cooperative group work.

As we come to understand that comprehensible input is necessary for second-language acquisition, the idea of collaborative groups used during the writing process seems especially promising. "Cooperative groups not only promote better writing but also provide numerous opportunities for oral discussion within which a great deal of 'comprehensible input' is generated, promoting overall language development" (Peregoy and Boyle, 1997, p. 191). A classroom of students in single-file rows, all writing in silence, is not the goal; instead, we want students interacting with each other and with the teacher.

Writing teachers with ESL students also must be very careful about how they handle editing. As with first-language students, the step of editing needs to come at the end of the writing process when students have settled upon *what* they have to say and how to organize it and are preparing to publish the piece in some way, formally or informally. Time spent editing for spelling, punctuation, grammar, and usage (all the conventions) before this is analogous to sanding and varnishing boards before fashioning them into a beautiful grandfather clock: Why sand and varnish what may be thrown away by the time the product is finished? Since English language learners are already struggling with expressing themselves, we don't want to stifle their attempts by focusing on mistakes too soon in the process. "Finally, by setting the editing aside as a separate phase, process writing frees English learners to elaborate their ideas first and make corrections last. Yet through the editing process they grow in their awareness of English grammar, punctuation and spelling" (Peregoy and Boyle, 1997, p. 191).

Using the Six-Trait Model with ESL Students

Research strongly suggests that the Six-Trait Model for Writing Instruction and Assessment (see Chapter 7) is perfectly valid for ESL students; in fact in his 10-year, international study, involving 14 countries and a variety of languages, Purves arrived at very similar traits for rating papers across many languages and cultures (Purves, 1992). Purves chose to replicate the Diederich experiment of 1961, which arrived at the traits of ideas, mechanics, organization, wording and phrasing, and flavor, direct ancestors of the modern Six-Trait Model (Diederich, 1974; Purves, 1992). Purves used what he called an "international jury" to evaluate writing samples in various languages:

> The analysis of this jury's scores suggested to us five major factors involved in the rating of these compositions: content, organization, style and tone, surface features, and personal response of the reader. Of these, only the last differed from the findings of the Diederich study, and one could argue that his "originality" matched our personal response. (p. 116)

ESL scholars are already using similar systems for breaking down writing into its components. Consider the "writing traits matrix" Peregoy uses for assessing ESL writers in "Fluency," "Organization," "Grammar," "Vocabulary," "Genre," and "Sentence Variety" (Peregoy and Boyle, 1997, p. 200). Parts of it are almost identical to the Six-Trait Rubric used by writing teachers nationwide, such as Peregoy's descriptors for three levels of performance in Sentence Variety: "Beginning Level," "Uses one or two sentence patterns;" "Intermediate Level," "Uses several sentence patterns;" and "Advanced Level," "Uses a good variety of sentence patterns effectively" (Peregoy and Boyle, 1997, p. 200).

In other words, readers and writers, regardless of language, value the same things in a written piece. The beauty of the Six-Trait model is that it breaks down writing into identifiable, manageable, concrete specifics that students and teachers can examine and work with.

Resources to use with students, including rubrics and posters, are available in Spanish from the Northwest Regional Educational Laboratory, in Portland, Oregon (**www.nwrel.org**).

CONCLUSION

Best practice in writing instruction for ESL students does not differ radically from writing instruction for first-language students. In general, the teacher must take the students from where they are; provide them with a language-rich environment (comprehensible input); break down learning into manageable chunks (scaffolding); use appropriate strategies, such as cooperative groups, process writing, and the Six-Trait Model; and keep a learner-centered philosophy in mind.

BIBLIOGRAPHY

Boraas, J. (1917). *Formal English grammar and the practical mastery of English.* Unpublished doctoral dissertation, University of Minnesota.

Brack, G. W., and Hall, L. R. (1997). Combining the classroom and the community: Service-learning in composition at Arizona State University. *Writing the Community: Concepts and Models for Service-Learning in Composition.* Washington, D.C.: American Association of Higher Education, 143–152.

Braddock, R., Loyd-Jones, R., and Schoer, L. (1963). *Research in written composition.* Urbana, IL: National Council of Teachers of English.

Brown, H. D. (1993). TESOL at twenty-five: What are the issues? *State of the art TESOL essays: Celebrating 25 years of the discipline.* Bloomington, IL: TESOL, Inc., 16–31.

Diederich, P. (1974). *Measuring growth in English.* Urbana, IL: National Council of Teachers of English.

Encyclopedia of Educational Research (1950). New York: Macmillan.

Gordon, I.A. (1947). *The teaching of English.* Wellington: New Zealand Council for Educational Research.

Hartwell, P. (1985). Grammar, grammars, and the teaching of grammar. *College English, 47.2,* 105–27.

Hatfield, W. (1935). *An experience curriculum in English: A report of the curriculum commission.* New York: Appleton-Century.

Hillocks, G., Jr. (1986). *Research on written composition: New directions for teaching.* Urbana, IL: National Council of Teachers of English.

Hoyt, F.S. (1906). The place of grammar in the elementary curriculum. *Teachers College Record,* 7, 1–34.

Hudelson, S. (1987) The role of native literacy in the education of language minority children. *Language Arts, 64,* 827–841.

Isik, A. (2000). The role of input in second language acquisition: More comprehensible input supported by grammar instruction or more grammar instruction? *ITL: Review of applied linguistics,* volume 129–130, 225–74.

Krashen, S. D. (2003). *Exploration in language acquisition and use.* Portsmouth, NH: Heinemann.

Meckel, H. (1963). Research on teaching composition and literature. In N. L. Gage (ed.), *Handbook of Research on Teaching: A Project of the American Educational Research Association* (966–1,006). Chicago: Rand-McNally.

Nikolov, M., and Krashen, S. D. (1997). Need we sacrifice accuracy for fluency? *System, 25,* 197–201.

Peregoy, S. F., and Boyle, O. F. (1997). *Reading, writing and learning in ESL,* 2nd ed. New York: Longman.

Purves, A. C. (1992). Reflections on research and assessment in written composition. *Research in the teaching of English, 26:1,* 108–122.

Warner, A. (1993). If the shoe no longer fits, wear it anyway? *English Journal, 82, 5* (September), 76–80.

Appendix A

SAMPLE MULTI-GENRE PAPER AND RUBRIC

One 24-Hour Unit of Time During the Life Cycle
Process of an Adolescent Male Human
or
A Day in the Life of Chester Funderburk

Brian McGee
University of Kansas
T&L 718
Fall 2001

Something to consider:

The use of doublespeak can spread so that doublespeak becomes the language of public discourse, with speakers and listeners convinced that they really understand such language. After a while, we may really believe that politicians don't lie but only "misspeak," that illegal acts are merely "inappropriate actions." . . . If we really believe that such language communicates and promotes clear thought, then the world of *Nineteen Eighty-Four* with its control of reality through language is not far away" (42).

William Lutz
Rutgers University

November 19, 2001—An assignment in Chester Funderburk's Seventh Block English class, 1:36 P.M.

Understanding Doublespeak

"Doublespeak is language which pretends to communicate but really doesn't. It is language that makes the bad seem good, the negative appear positive, the unpleasant appear attractive, or at least tolerable. It is language that avoids or shifts responsibility, language that is at variance with its real or purported meaning. It is language that conceals or prevents thought. Doublespeak is language which does not extend thought but limits it" (Lutz, 40).

Euphemisms

In the course of time, some words acquire a connotation that many people find unpleasant. When this happens, people use a euphemistic term instead. (A euphemism is a better-sounding word or phrase used in place of one that seems too harsh or direct.) Thus "death" becomes "passing away" and a "janitor" becomes a "sanitation engineer."

Directions: Write euphemisms for the following words and phrases.

1.	spy	14.	slum
2.	insane asylum	15.	conceited
3.	old people	16.	crime
4.	garbage	17.	car mechanic
5.	weird	18.	rescue mission
6.	snobbish	19.	T-shirts
7.	touchy	20.	being broke
8.	undertaker	21.	drug addict
9.	crippled	22.	cutting trees
10.	false teeth	23.	pencil
11.	a lie	24.	dog catcher
12.	toilet	25.	prison
13.	fired		

Directions: Give new examples of euphemistic expressions not previously mentioned which would have the following purposes:

1. Gives a more prestigious title for a job or occupation.
2. Spares the feelings of another.
3. Attempts to cover up the truth.

Skipping ZZZZs for Stretch Pay

Chester's bedroom—November 20, 2001, 3:57 A.M.

I can't sleep. I guess that's pretty obvious, huh, since I bothered to put the time down in this journal entry. I think I'll start doing that from now on. Anyway, like I said, I can't sleep. My first instinct was to do something productive such as my algebra homework or read a book, but then my idealistic tendencies shrunk into tight, little granules of sand as they were overtaken by the colossal shadow which was (da, da, da) *<foreboding music sounds>* procrastination. C'mon, like I'm going to pass up some quality TV time for homework? Whatever.

But here's the weird thing: I can't stop thinking about the assignment I got in Mr. Koonce's class today. We talked about this idea called "doublespeak." Basically, it deals with manipulating language. I think back to how many times I was fooled as a kid with cereals, toys, and just information in general. It's pretty deep stuff.

The really strange thing is that a little while ago I flipped on the TV, hoping to catch a classic *Family Ties* episode or possibly a *Scooby Doo* cartoon, and what do I find but a dumb infomercial talking about abdominal muscles. The infomercial was apparently for something called the Ab-Deluxe. I have to admit I cracked up when I read the fine print at the bottom of the before/after photos: "A healthy diet is essential along with use of the Ab-Deluxe. Your results may vary." May vary? Hell, yes they will vary! I'm thinking that it should be illegal to advertise this way. But then I realized that this is what Mr. Koonce was telling us about. This is doublespeak. This is language manipulated for reason of personal gain. It is intentionally meant to fool us, the sheep consumers. Some fat dope is sitting in bed right now eating a Hostess Apple Fritter and thinking, "Gee, I need to buy one of those Ab thingys. I need to get in shape." You know he's not even bothering to read the fine print. He won't change his diet.

Oh get this. Now the handsome, athletic, ripped guy, who by the way is 100 percent opposite of what his clientele looks like, is speaking on behalf of the product and saying how 4 million people have already bought an Ab-Deluxe, how everyone is getting one, and how flexible the payment plan is. Okay, this is killer marketing here, man. You can buy this crap on multiple credit cards and stretch payments out to "three EASY payments of $19.95!" What a crock! If you stretch out payments on a credit card, then you'll be paying more than the cost of the Ab-Deluxe because of incredibly high interest rates on the credit cards. I tell ya, they sure stick it to ya. But ya know what? I take back what I said earlier; they should not make advertising this way illegal. I think, upon serious reflection, that if someone is dumb enough to be suckered into buying this junk, then so be it. They made their bed, now they should lay [sic] in it.

Wow, I guess this worked. Now after twenty-five minutes of writing this and watching people with rock-hard abs do more exercises than are humanly necessary, I think I'm finally getting sleepy. I guess that sometimes what we learn in school, although usually boring and dumb, sometimes has purpose. I'm not going to be one of those idiots suckered into buying a worthless product I don't need or fooled into believing something that goes against my value system. But that can wait until later. Time for bed . . . again.

Signing off,

Chester Funderburk

The Late Show with Chester Funderburk: Oatmeal Raisin Crisp Lie Exposed

8:17 A.M.—Chester is feverishly writing during First Block Spanish class, simultaneously tuning out his teacher, Mrs. Guadalupe.

<Audience applause sign frantically flashes>

CHESTER: Welcome back, gang! Our next guest is a man who needs no introduction . . . wait . . . too late, I already started introducing him.

<Audience applause sign flashes>

CHESTER: Anyhow. Ladies and gentlemen, here is your friend and mine, Mr. Wilfred Brimley!

<Applause sign looks as if it will explode>

<Wilfred and Chester shake hands. Wilfred sits down across from Chester.>

CHESTER: It's good to see you!

WILFRED: It's good to be seen.

<Studio audience laughs>

CHESTER: *<smiling>* Willy, old boy. I have a bone to pick with you.

WILFRED: *<somewhat surprised>* Really now? Well, what's that?

CHESTER: Why are you currently on the cover of my favorite cereal box?

WILFRED: Oh. *<laughs>* Well . . . I'm a big fan of Oatmeal Raisin Crisp cereal and they called and said they'd like me to be their primary celebrity sponsor . . . so it all worked out.

CHESTER: *<smile now vanished>* Did it? Did it really work out, Wilfred? See, I heard different. I heard that you have nothing whatsoever to do with the product but the company wants to appeal to older folks who need to have more frequent bowel movements. Wilfred, how often do you defecate?

WILFRED: Just a minute here! What the heck are you trying to pull?

CHESTER: Oh no, my friend. You are the one who is pulling the wool over everyone's eyes! Isn't it true you never even tasted one spoonful of Oatmeal Raisin Crisp cereal before the company paid you to do so?

WILFRED: Well . . . yes . . . that is true.

<Studio audience gasps and makes disapproving sounds>

CHESTER: And isn't it also true that during the commercial you state, "I grew up on this cereal and look where I am today?"

WILFRED: Yes, alright? Are you happy? Any of you would have done the same thing! I don't get any residual checks from my days on the popular and family values-centered television show *Our House.* Work is tough. I got that bit in the film *The Firm,* starring Tom Cruise, Gene Hackman, Holly Hunter, and Hal Halbrook, but it didn't pay much.

CHESTER: Selling your soul for cereal checks. It makes my skin crawl. I like the taste, Will, I do. But now with your crusty mug on the box I can't bring myself to eat it. I hope you're happy.

<Wilfred Brimley breaks down>

CHESTER: Stay tuned, folks! We'll be right back with Carrot Top!

<Studio audience applauds wildy>

As Clear as Mud

10:45 A.M.—Fifth Block All-School Assembly

Note: Three-star General James B. Gilgood is speaking at MacArthur High School for a Veterans Day celebration. The problem: The general has spent too many years briefing the media on frontline news and is not making the transition to youngsters very well.

"Thank you all for coming today. First off, I'd like to thank Superintendent Jackson Smithers and Principal Gary Proctor for allowing me to speak here today on behalf of the United States Army. Now, I'd like to address the current situation, as I understand it, in Afghanistan. I feel this is relevant because this is the most recent development our country has entered in and if I talked about World War II or Vietnam—well, I may lose some interest from you out there.

"We are faring well thus far in the fight against the evil-doers. Our troops have trained hard, doing countless front-leaning rest exercises in anticipation of a fight. Air support in classified areas of Afghanistan is servicing targets as I speak. I know that all of you have seen pictures on television of ground zero here in the States, and let me assure you that our troops have those same images embedded in their minds as they prepare to do their jobs. I know they worry about your safety here in the United States, and I, for one, am not worried about a large, potentially disruptive reentry system or any inhalation hazard. Of course, in times as uncertain as these, collateral damage can happen, but we do our best to prevent that. The risk of a preemptive counterattack is minimal, so ease your minds. Our resolve is strong and we shall prevail. Thank you all and God bless."

<The general exits the stage as students and faculty passionately applaud— clueless about the meaning of most of what he just finished talking about.> Chester happens to hear Ms. Osborn, who teaches history, say to Mr. Koonce, "That was amazing. Clearly, it was the best example of doublespeak I have ever heard. How sad for these kids."

<Suddenly, the wheels in Chester's head start turning. The connection to school and the "real" has just taken place.>

Is There Truly a Party in Every Can? Inquiring Minds Want to Know!

Chester's living room—4:10 P.M.

<commercial on TV>: "It's a party in every can! Once you pop, you can't, you can't, you can't stop!"

CHESTER'S FRIEND GABE: What a bunch of garbage.

CHESTER: Huh?

GABE: What in the heck did that Pringles commercial have to do with chips?

CHESTER: Well . . . nothing.

GABE: Exactly! So why do that? I mean, why make a commercial as corny and dumb as that for chips?

CHESTER: That's the beauty of it, dude. If you see a can of Pringles in a store you think, "Wow, If I buy that, I'm gonna have fun."

GABE: Uh, are you smoking crack? I don't think that when I buy food.

CHESTER: Look, you probably don't say it aloud or even realize you're thinking it, but your brain remembers the connection.

GABE: I dunno, dude. Maybe I just buy the dumb can of chips because I like how they taste.

CHESTER: True. But maybe that company doesn't want to count on taste being the only factor. I mean hey, when you think about it, there are hundreds of kinds of chips, and don't they all pretty much taste the same?

GABE: Well, no. Cheetos taste different than BBQ Lays. Duh, dude. Duh.

CHESTER: *<laughing>* OK, yeah. But don't the chips of the same flavor taste about the same regardless of the brand?

GABE: Yeah, pretty close anyway.

CHESTER: Exactly. So what I'm saying is maybe the Pringles company needs one gimmick or even two. Heck, they have their chips associated with fun and partying and they're in a can, for crying out loud!

GABE: Dang, dude. That's whacked. I never thought about that before. Pringles must have hired some M.I.T. grads to come up with that idea.

CHESTER: Man, you had better start thinking more deeply about stuff. You're gonna get suckered into whatever the government wants you to think. You'll be a conformist and won't even know it—a damn zombie.

GABE: Whatever, dummy. All I know is, I'm going on strike against Pringles. I ain't eatin' them no more because they are tricky. Let's go outside and shoot some hoops. My brain is full.

CHESTER: *<Rolls eyes and turns off the TV>*

Works Cited

Bushman, John H. *Teaching the English Language,* 2nd ed. Springfield, IL: Charles C Thomas, 2000.

Bushman, John H. "Honesty in Language: Is This the Way to Achieve Power?" *English Journal* (March 2001): 17–19.

Goodson, F. Todd. *Doublespeak, Lies, and Videotape.* The Writing Conference, Inc., 1994.

Lutz, William. "Fourteen Years of Doublespeak." *English Journal* (March 1988): 40–42.

Romano, Tom. *Blending Genre, Altering Style: Writing Multigenre Papers.* Portsmouth, NH: Boynton/Cook Publishers, Inc., 2000.

Multi-Genre Biography Project & Persuasive Speech

Goal: In the next several weeks, you will <u>select and research</u> a person who has set out on a "hero's journey" to obtain new skills and knowledge. You will then <u>write a biography using several literary forms and voices</u> to illuminate the individual's call, trials, and triumphs (see samples) <u>and give a persuasive speech</u> convincing us that the subject of your multi-genre biography project (MGB) is a hero.

Your biography will be made up of <u>a "grabber lead" or introduction and five different pieces of writing</u> (i.e., interviews, poetry, letters, confessionals, dramatic monologues—see attached list) that arise from your research and imagination and work together to give the reader an <u>in-depth</u> sense of the person/hero being explored. Your biography will also contain a <u>bibliography</u> and a <u>notes page</u> acknowledging sources.

Process—tentative scoring: 200 pts

1. Generate ideas in your log, then share on butcher paper around the room.   10 pts
2. Select a hero to explore.   5 pts
3. Begin research in the library (in class at school <u>and evenings</u>).
4. Compile at least 10 pages of log notes based on your research.   100 pts
5. Begin experimenting with different genres—in other words, begin writing!

6. Finish five rough drafts or five different
   pieces of writing, and select images if any.   25 pts
7. Get peer response on all five drafts.   25 pts
8. Revise drafts.
9. Write a "grabber lead" and compile
   bibliography and notes page.   20 pts
10. Compile complete revision.
11. Peer edit.   15 pts
12. Turn in final MGB for product evaluation.
13. Give persuasive speech about your
    hero (more on this later).

Product—tentative scoring: 150 pts

1. *Idea Development:* Focuses deeply on one character
   with details that show rather than tell.   20 pts
2. *Idea Development:* Gives comprehensive (broad)
   picture of a multifaceted human being.   20 pts
3. *Idea Development:* Developed with a variety of
   authentic voices.   10 pts
4. *Idea Development:* Developed with a variety of
   appropriate genres.   10 pts
5. *Oraganization:* Each genre, as well as the MGB
   as a whole, has a strong sense of direction
   and balance. The reader does not need to stop
   periodically to find his own way.   10 pts
6. *Voice:* The writer's energy and passion (yours)
   for the subject drive the genres, making the
   text lively, expressive, and engaging.   10 pts
7. *Word Choice:* Precise, vivid, natural language
   paints a strong, clear, and complete picture
   in the reader's mind.   10 pts
8. *Sentence Fluency:* An easy flow and sentence
   sense make the MGB a delight to read aloud.   10 pts
9. *Conventions:* Shows excellent control over
   grammar, spelling, punctuation, and capitalization. 10 pts
10. *Conventions:* Note page and bibliography are
    accurate and polished.   20 pts
11. *Artistry:* Each genre is a masterpiece; imagination
    has built on extensive research.   20 pts

Appendix B

RESOURCES FOR CREATING AND ASSESSING PORTFOLIOS

Figure B–1 Portfolio cover assignment

An important part of any portfolio program is the goal setting that students do. Over the course of the portfolio year, students assess themselves periodically and then set goals for the next period. In this case, students complete Goal Setting Sheets for each of the four quarters of the school year.

Figure B–2 Four quarters writing goals

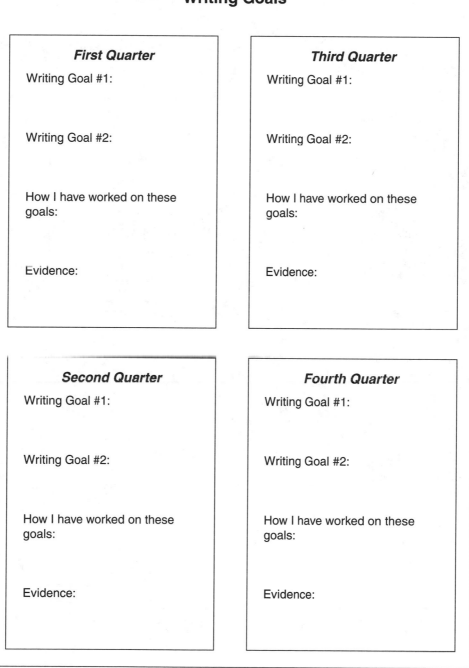

Writing Goals

First Quarter

Writing Goal #1:

Writing Goal #2:

How I have worked on these goals:

Evidence:

Third Quarter

Writing Goal #1:

Writing Goal #2:

How I have worked on these goals:

Evidence:

Second Quarter

Writing Goal #1:

Writing Goal #2:

How I have worked on these goals:

Evidence:

Fourth Quarter

Writing Goal #1:

Writing Goal #2:

How I have worked on these goals:

Evidence:

Six Trait Track Record

_____	1	2	3	4	5
Ideas and Content					
Organization					
Voice					
Word Choice					
Sentence Fluency					
Writing Conventions					

_____	1	2	3	4	5
Ideas and Content					
Organization					
Voice					
Word Choice					
Sentence Fluency					
Writing Conventions					

_____	1	2	3	4	5
Ideas and Content					
Organization					
Voice					
Word Choice					
Sentence Fluency					
Writing Conventions					

_____	1	2	3	4	5
Ideas and Content					
Organization					
Voice					
Word Choice					
Sentence Fluency					
Writing Conventions					

_____	1	2	3	4	5
Ideas and Content					
Organization					
Voice					
Word Choice					
Sentence Fluency					
Writing Conventions					

_____	1	2	3	4	5
Ideas and Content					
Organization					
Voice					
Word Choice					
Sentence Fluency					
Writing Conventions					

_____	1	2	3	4	5
Ideas and Content					
Organization					
Voice					
Word Choice					
Sentence Fluency					
Writing Conventions					

_____	1	2	3	4	5
Ideas and Content					
Organization					
Voice					
Word Choice					
Sentence Fluency					
Writing Conventions					

Figure B–4 General writing rubric

	5	3	1
Organization	• I know where I am going • I love my beginning • My ending is COOL! • Follow me! • I see how all the parts fit together	• I am starting to see a pattern here • My beginning and ending is OK • My paper is pretty easy to follow • Maybe I need to move things around	• How do I begin? • What should I tell first? • What comes next • My reader would feel lost • I don't know where I am headed
Voice	• It's ME! • This is what I think • It might make you laugh or cry • I love this topic • I want my reader to feel what I feel	• I hear a little of me in the writing • The topic is OK • I am starting to have fun	• I don't care • I don't hear myself in this paper • This topic is boring • SNORE!
Words	• My reader will love the words I choose • My words paint a picture • My words make the message clear	• I like some of these words • I need more imagination • There is probably a better way to say it	• My reader might wonder what I meant • These words are not my favorites • I used the first words that came to my mind
Sentence Fluency	• My sentences make sense • My paper is easy to read out loud • Some sentences are long and some short • My sentences begin in several different ways	• A lot of my sentences being the same way • I wish my paper sounded a little smoother • My paper is PRETTY easy to read out loud, if you take your time	• Some of my sentences do not make sense • My paper is hard to read out loud • I'm not happy with it yet
Ideas	• I love the sound of this paper • It all makes sense • My reader will learn a lot • There are good, juicy details	• I need to add some details • I'm still working on it • My reader might have some questions • There might be some questions • There might be more to tell	• My reader won't understand this yet • I'm not sure what to say • I don't really have a topic yet • I need some more time to think
Conventions	• You have to look hard to find mistakes • My word has been edited and proofread; it is easy to read • I checked my spelling and end punctuation	• I am not sure I spelled all the words right • I might have left out some end punctuation • I have more editing tools	• My reader would notice lots of mistakes • I haven't edited most of my work yet • I need to correct some things before I publish this

Figure B–5 Essay six-traits scoring model

Essay Six Traits Scoring Model

	5	4	3	2	1
Ideas and Content	• the paper is focused on the topic • there are supporting details for each main idea • the writer received information from a variety of sources • the supporting details (facts, examples and quotes) explain the main idea		• the writer provides some basic information • there is some support of the main ideas • more details could be added		• the paper wanders through ideas • the writer doesn't have enough information to help the reader understand the topic • the details included are too vague or are missing
Organization	• the introduction grabs the reader's attention and shows where the paper is headed • there is a strong structure that gives direction to key points • placement of details, facts, and examples seems well thought out • purposeful transitions guide the reader from point to point • the reader's understanding of the topic grows throughout the paper • the conclusion shows the reader how everything ties together		• the structure of the piece moves the reader through without confusion • the intro offers a small clue about what is coming • details, examples, and facts are linked to the main idea but may be in illogical spots • transitions are attempted • the conclusion wraps up the discussion but leaves some loose ends		• the structure needs a stronger sense of direction • the paper just starts in and doesn't have an introduction • ideas and supporting details are randomly ordered • stronger transitions are needed to link ideas • the reader may miss the whole point or have difficulty following what the writer is trying to say • the conclusion doesn't wrap up the piece effectively
Voice	• the writer's tone is lively, engaging, and appropriate for the topic • the writer is enthusiastic for the topic and holds the reader's attention • Hear me roar! I love this topic!		• you hear a little of me in this topic • the writer's voice seems sincere • enthusiasm for the topic appears at times • moments of spontaneity enliven the piece at times		• the writer seems too indifferent to either the topic or audience • the writer seems bored, distracted, or just anxious to be done with it • moments of excitement just aren't there

Essay Six Traits Scoring Model (continued)

	5	4	3	2	1
Word Choice	• well chosen words convey the writers message clearly and precisely • words suit the writer, subject, and audience • the writer consistently uses vivid words and phrases		• words are reasonably accurate and make the message clear • there is probably a better way to say it		• the writer struggles with a limited vocabulary that restricts what is conveyed • the language does not deliver a clear message
Sentence Fluency	• there is an easy flow to the piece • the reader can almost hear the piece's rhythm • sentences vary in structure and length making the reading pleasant and natural, never motionless		• the text hums along with a steady beat • there is some variation in length and structure		• there are run-on sentences • there are numerous short, choppy details that bump the reader through the text • repetitive sentence patterns put the reader to sleep • transitional phrases are either missing or overdone so that it is distracting
Conventions	• the writer demonstrates a good grasp of conventions • only light editing errors would be required to prepare this for publication		• errors in conventions often enough to become somewhat distracting • moderate editing needed to prepare this for publication		• there are numerous errors that make the text difficult to read • there are numerous mistakes that need correcting • extensive editing is needed to prepare this text for publication

Figure B–6 Six traits research scoring model

Six Traits Research Scoring Model

	5	4	3	2	1
Ideas and Content	• the paper is focused on the topic • there are supporting details for each main idea • the writer received information from a variety of sources • the supporting details (facts, examples, and quotes) explain the main idea		• the writer provides some basic information • there is some support of the main ideas • sometimes there seems to be information missing • more investigation is needed due to lack of details		• the paper wanders through ideas • the writer doesn't have enough information to help the reader understand the topic • the details included are too vague or are missing
Organization	• the introduction grabs the reader's attention and shows where they are headed • there is a strong structure that gives direction to key points • placement of details, facts and examples seem well thought out • purposeful transitions guide the reader from point to point • the reader's understanding of the topic grows throughout the paper • the conclusion shows the reader how everything ties together		• the structure of the piece moves the reader through without confusion • the intro offers a small clue about what is coming • details, examples, and facts are linked to the main idea but may be in illogical spots • transitions are attempted • the conclusion wraps up the discussion but leaves some loose ends		• the structure needs a stronger sense of direction • the paper just starts in and doesn't have an introduction • ideas and supporting details are randomly ordered • stronger transitions are needed to link ideas • the reader may miss the whole point or have difficulty following what the writer is trying to say • the conclusion doesn't wrap up the piece effectively
Voice	• the writer's tone is lively, engaging, and appropriate for the topic • the writer is enthusiastic for the topic • the writer holds the reader's attention		• the writer's voice seems sincere • enthusiasm for the topic appears at times • moments of spontaneity enliven the piece at times		• the writer seems too indifferent to either the topic or audience • the writer seems bored, distracted, or just anxious to be done with it • moments of excitement just aren't there

Six Traits Research Scoring Model (continued)

	5	4	3	2	1
Word Choice	• well chosen words convey the writers message clearly and precisely • words suit the writer, subject, and audience • the writer consistently uses vivid words and phrases		• words are reasonably accurate and make the message clear • sometimes the language is too difficult or technical		• the writer struggles with a limited vocabulary that restricts what is conveyed • technical or specialized vocabulary is overused • the language lacks the ability to convey a clear message
Sentence Fluency	• there is an easy flow to the piece • the reader can almost hear the piece's rhythm • sentences vary in structure and length making the reading pleasant and natural, never motionless		• the text hums along with a steady beat • there is some variation in length and structure		• there are run-on sentences • there are numerous short, choppy details that bump the reader through the text • repetitive sentence patterns put the reader to sleep • transitional phrases are either missing or overdone that is it distracting
Conventions	• the writer demonstrates a good grasp of conventions (including source citations if needed) • the bibliography (if needed) is formatted and punctuated correctly • only light editing errors would be required to prepare this for publication		• errors in conventions often enough to become somewhat distracting • the bibliography (if needed) is present but requires some more editing • moderate editing would be required to prepare this for publication		• there are numerous errors that distract the reader and make the text difficult to read • the bibliography (if needed) is perhaps not created, or there are numerous mistakes that need correcting • extensive editing would be required to prepare this text for publication

Portfolio Checklist

Summer is almost here, which means the school year is coming to a close. Thus, our seventh grade team writing portfolio is nearing completion. There are a few things we need to do to get it ready to go on to eighth grade. Listed below is a checklist of items to complete for your portfolio reflection and evaluation. Take your time with your reflections; it's vitally important to sit back and actually think through your accomplishments this year.

Organize your class journal and folder.

Portfolio completion:

      Portrait of Myself as a Writer
      Writer's Reflections
      Goal Setting/evaluation sheets for each quarter
      Eighth Grade Writing Goals
      Student and Parent Portfolio Responses
      Six Trait Track Record
      Two Most Satisfying Pieces from English
      Unsatisfying Piece from English
      Free Pick Writing Piece from any core class
      Three free picks from other team writing activities
      Most satisfying science writing piece
      Most satisfying geography writing piece
      Most satisfying math writing piece
      The Best of the Six Traits
      How I Have Changed as a Writer: A Final Reflection

Make sure each piece is clearly labeled and has either an introduction or reflection tag attached to it.

Once everything is put into a logical order, create a Table of Contents to put into the front of the portfolio.

Next, assess yourself on the provided rubic. I will assess it after you have. We will then conference on your completed portfolio.

Figure B–8 The best of the six traits

The Best of the Six Traits

Ideas and Content: _____

Explanation:

Organization: _____

Explanation:

Word Choice: _____

Explanation:

Sentence fluency: _____

Explanation:

Voice: _____

Explanation:

Writing Conventions: _____

Explanation:

Items You Can Select the Free Bees from in English Class:

Gratitude journal entries

Story starters

Writer's Circle
- Downriver Diary
- Personal Essay
- March Madness report
- The Giver essay/story
- Narrative
- Poetry
- Journal entries or activities
- Essay Final

- Other ideas? See me!

- Previously graded

Figure B–10 Peer portfolio evaluation

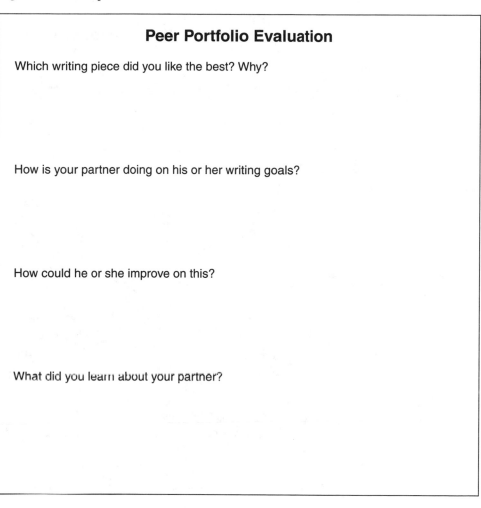

Peer Portfolio Evaluation

Which writing piece did you like the best? Why?

How is your partner doing on his or her writing goals?

How could he or she improve on this?

What did you learn about your partner?

Figure B–11 Student portfolio response

Student Portfolio Response

I am most proud of . . .

I'm currently working on . . .

I have learned . . .

I'm challenging myself on . . .

Date: _____

Figure B–12 Parent portfolio response

Parent Portfolio Response

What were your favorite parts of my team writing portfolio?

What did you learn about me?

What suggestions do you have for me?

Parent Signature: _____

Date: _____

Eighth Grade Writing Goals

Writing Goal #1:
Reasoning:

Writing Goal #2:
Reasoning:

Writing Goal #3:
Reasoning:

Writing Goal #4:
Reasoning:

Writing Goal #5:
Reasoning:

Figure B–14 Rubric for team writing portfolio

Rubric for Team Writing Portfolio

	1	2	3	4	5
Presentation/ Organization	Organization needs work; no creative effort put forth		Some organization evident, a little creative effort displayed		Well organized! Creative effort is shown off!
Assessment/ Reflections	Assessed a few pieces of writing; missing numerous intros/ reflections		Assessed many of the pieces; many intros/ reflections completed		Each piece is assessed and all intros/reflections are done
Personal Growth	Set some goals but little or no effort put forth to work on them; Intro/ Conclusion missing		Goals set but not actively worked on; Intro/ Conclusion present but still in progress		Goals set and actively worked on; Intro and Conclusion in presentation form
Materials Includes	Less than half of materials included from checklist		Majority of selected materials from checklist are included		All of the chosen materials from the checklist are present

Total Points: /20

Reflection on Score:

Figure B–15 Writing survey

WRITING SURVEY

NAME _____ **DATE** _____

1. Are you a writer? _____
   (If your answer is YES, answer question 2a. If your answer is NO, answer 2b.)
2a. How did you learn to write?

2b. How do people learn to write?

3. Why do people write? List as many reasons as you can think of.

4. What does someone have to do or know in order to write well?

5. What kinds of writing do you like to write?

6. How do you decide what you'll write about? Where do your ideas come from?

7. What kinds of response helps you most as a writer?

8. How often do you write at home?

9. In general, how do you feel about what you write?

Figure B–16 Reading survey

READING SURVEY

NAME _____ DATE _____

1. If you had to guess . . .
   How many books would you say you owned? _____
   How many books would you say there are in your house? _____
   How many books would you say you've read in the past year? _____

2. How did you learn to read?

3. Why do people read? List as many reasons as you can think of.

4. What does someone have to do or know in order to be a good reader?

5. What kinds of books do you like to read?

6. How do you decide which books you'll read?

7. Who are your favorite authors? (List as many as you'd like.)

8. Have you ever reread a book? _____ If so, can you name it/them here?

Writing Self-Evaluation: First Semester

1. How many pieces of writing did you finish? _____

2. Which piece of writing did you consider your most effective? _____

   _____

3. What new things did you try as a writer?

4. What did you learn as a writer this quarter?

5. What are your goals for the next quarter? Set at least five specific goals. Use the goal worksheet to record them.

Figure B–18 Peer evaluation form

Peer Writing Conference Record

Writer's Name _____ **Date** _____

Responder _____ **Title/Topic** _____

Writer, before you conference, your job is to consider what you want help with: ideas, language, images, organization, coherence, a part of the piece, a sense of the whole? Tell the responder what you want a response to:

Responder, when you agree to confer with a writer, your job is to help the writer think and make decisions about the writing:

- Ask what he or she needs help with.
- If there are parts that confuse you, you don't understand, or you'd like to know more about, ask the writer about them. It will help you—and the writer—if you jot down your questions during and after the reading in the space below.
- Ask the writer what he or she plans to do next.
- Give this record of the conference to the writer

Writer, jot down your plans before you forget them. What did you learn from your conference? What is your plan of attack to improve this piece of writing?

Six-Trait Writing Scale

Higher Order Concerns

_____ *Ideas and Content*

     _____ 5 The paper is clear and holds the reader's attention all the way through.

     _____ 4

     _____ 3 The reader can figure out what the writer is trying to say, but the paper may not hold the reader's attention all the way through.

     _____ 2

     _____ 1 The paper is unclear and seems to have no purpose.

_____ *Organization and Movement*

     _____ 5 Ideas, details, and examples are presented in an order that makes sense. The paper is very easy to follow.

     _____ 4

     _____ 3 The writer has tried to present ideas and details in a way that makes sense, but the order may be unclear or may not work well.

     _____ 2

     _____ 1 Ideas seem tossed together, and the paper is hard to follow.

_____ $\times$ 5 = _____

Middle Order Concerns

_____ *Voice*

     _____ 5 The writer is very sincere, individual, and honest. This paper stands out from the others.

     _____ 4

     _____ 3 The writer tries to deal with the topic but does not seem to get very involved.

     _____ 2

     _____ 1 The writer seems to make no effort to deal seriously with the topic.

_____ *Word Choice*

     _____ 5 The writer carefully selects words to make the message clear.

     _____ 4

     _____ 3 The writer chooses words that get the message across but only in a very ordinary way.

     _____ 2

     _____ 1 The writer struggles with a limited vocabulary and has a hard time finding the right words to get the meaning across.

_____ $\times$ 3 = _____

Six-Trait Writing Scale (continued)

Lower Order Concerns

_____ *Sentence Fluency*

     _____ 5 The paper is easy to read and understand. It flows smoothly from one idea to the next.

     _____ 4

     _____ 3 Most sentences are understandable but not very smooth or graceful.

     _____ 2

     _____ 1 Sentence flaws make this paper hard to read and understand.

_____ *Writing Conventions* (grammar, capitalization, punctuation, spelling, paragraphing)

     _____ 5 There are no glaring errors in writing conventions, and the paper is easy to read and understand.

     _____ 4

     _____ 3 The reader can follow what is being said. However, there are enough mistakes that the reader sometimes has difficulty concentrating on what the writer is saying.

     _____ 2

     _____ 1 There are so many errors in conventions that the reader has a very hard time just getting through the paper. Some parts may be impossible to follow or understand.

_____ × 2 = _____   Total (HOC + MOC + LOC) = _____   (NEXT PAGE)

Writing Goals Worksheet

Below list your five goals you have for the next quarter, and develop a plan of achievement for each goal. Be sure to use complete sentences in writing each.

After you write your goal and plan for achievement, review each with your parents and record the following:

Parent Response to Goals:

Parent Signature _____

• *Goal #1:*

   Plan of Achievement:

   Evidence of Achievement

• *Goal # 2:*

   Plan of Achievement:

   Evidence of Achievement

Figure B–21 Writing the final reflection and self-assessment: Questions to ponder

Writing the Final Reflection & Self-Assessment: Questions to Ponder

- When I am assigned a writing task, I . . .
- By looking at this collection of my work, you will be able to tell . . .
- I'm getting much better at _____ as can be seen in the piece

  _____ .
- When I look at _____ , I know I have grown because

  _____ .
- In _____ , I struggled with _____ , but I solved it by

  _____ .
- I'm getting much better at . . .
- I can help others by . . .
- I'm proud of the way I . . .
- I need to work harder on . . .
- I'm still not sure how to . . .
- I need to get help with . . .
- I wish I were better at . . .
- The part I found the most difficult was . . .
- Last year I thought _____ , but this year I think . . .
- I surprise myself when I . . .
- Before you read the work in this portfolio, you need to know . . .
- What problems did you encounter?
- What makes your most effective piece different from your least effective piece?
- Prior to this class, how did you get ideas for your writing?
- What goals did you set for yourself?
- How well did you accomplish them?
- What are you able to do as a writer that you couldn't do before?
- What has helped you the most with your writing during this semester?
- What are your writing goals for the next grading period?
- As a teacher what could I have done differently to help you?
- How do you think your writing has changed?
- What do you know now that you didn't know before about writing?

Continued

Figure B–21 *(Continued)*

Writing the Final Reflection &
Self-Assessment: Questions to Ponder (continued)

Reading Questions:

- What frustrations did you have with reading earlier in the year and how has that changed?
- What currently frustrates you as a reader?
- Prior to this class, how did you choose what you would read?
- How do you choose now?
- What did you do at the beginning of the year to help you understand your reading?
- What helps you understand your reading now?
- What made your favorite piece of reading different from other books you have read?
- Are there any other observations you would like to share with us?

Figure B–22 Growth graph for first semester

GROWTH GRAPH FIRST SEMESTER

WEEK 2 3 4 5 6 7 8 9 10 11 12 13 14 15 16 17 18

Figure B–23 Portfolio requirements: First quarter

Portfolio Requirements
First Quarter

Introductory Materials:
- Table of Contents
- Letter of Introduction
- Writing Survey
- Reading Survey

Writing Pieces from First Quarter:
- Introduction to Best Piece
- Best Piece
- Introduction to Piece #2
- Piece #2
- Introduction to Piece #3
- Piece #3
- Best Short Piece from the Quarter
- Free Pick

Reading from First Quarter:
- Introduction to Best Book Project
- Sample of Best Book Project
- Sample from Book Project #2
- Sample from Book Project #3

Evaluation Forms:
- Writing Self-Evaluation (Be sure goal section is thoroughly filled out)
- Reading Self-Evaluation
- Growth Chart

Misc. Materials:
- Peer Evaluation Forms
- Teacher Conference Forms
- Rough Drafts
- Any additional writing you have done
- Notes/Handouts

Figure B–24 Portfolio rubric: First quarter completeness of portfolio

Portfolio Rubric
First Quarter Completeness of Portfolio

Student _____ Date _____

Points	Category	Area for Improvement 0–3	Basic Skill Level 4–6	Proficient 6–8	Exemplary 8–10
Total Points ____ × 3	Writing Samples from the Quarter	• One major polished piece of writing missing. • If more than one piece is missing, you will receive no points for this section.	• All major polished pieces are included. • Both short pieces and timed writing are missing.	• All major polished pieces are included in the portfolio. • Half of the shorter pieces are included.	• All required polished writings and short pieces can be found in your portfolio.
Total Points ____	Reading Samples from the Quarter	• If more than one reading project sample is missing, you will receive a "0" on this section.	• One reading project sample is missing.	• All reading project samples are present, but the reflection is missing.	• All reading project samples and reflections are present in portfolio.
Total Points ____ × 2	Writing Reflections	• One or more of the reflections are missing.	• All reflections are present. • Reflections are limited in length and insight.	• All reflections are present. • Reflections serve merely as introductions to the works, or limited insight is offered.	• All reflections are present. • Reflections serve as an introduction to the work. • Reflections offer insight into the writing process and functions as a learning guide.
Total Points for Page #1					

Continued

Figure B–24 *(Continued)*

Portfolio Rubric (continued)
First Quarter Completeness of Portfolio

Student _____ Date _____

Points	Category	Area for Improvement 0–3	Basic Skill Level 4–6	Proficient 6–8	Exemplary 8–10
Total Points _____	Introductory Materials	• If the intro letter or the writing and reading surveys are missing, you will receive a score in this range.	• Rough introduction letter present. • Contains Writing and Reading Survey. • Table of Contents is missing.	• Introduction letter present, yet it could be rewritten. • Contains Writing and Reading Survey. • Table of Contents included.	• Introduction letter present and well written. • Writing Survey present. • Reading Survey present. • Table of Contents included.
Total Points _____	Organization	• There is no sem-blance of order, and the reader gets a headache trying to decipher the meaning of your portfolio.	• Items in correct order. • Notebook is neat.	• Items in correct order. • A three-ring binder is used. • Notebook is neat.	• Items in correct order. • Dividers are used to organize the sections. • A three-ring binder is used. • Notebook is neat.
Total Points _____ × 2	Self-Evaluations	• No signed parent evaluation is included.	• Writing and Reading Evaluations are haphazardly completed. • Signed Parent Evaluation included.	• Writing and Reading Evaluations are completed using short, succinct responses that leave the reader wanting more information. • Signed Parent Evaluation included.	• Writing and Reading Evaluations are thoroughly completed. • Signed Parent Evaluation included.
Total Points for Page #2			Page #1 Total _____ Page #2 Total _____	⎯⎯/100	**Total Percent** ⬭

200

Figure B–25 Portfolio requirements: Final showcase portfolio

Portfolio Requirements
Final Showcase Portfolio

Introductory Materials:
- Table of Contents
- Letter of Introduction
- Writing Survey
- Reading Survey

Writing Pieces:
- Introduction to Best Piece
- Best Piece
- Introduction to Most Unsatisfying Piece
- Most Unsatisfying Piece
- Introduction to Free Piece
- Free Pick
- Introduction to Best Short Piece
- Best Short Piece
- Introduction to Best Timed Writing
- Introduction to Best Piece from Fourth Quarter
- Best Piece from Fourth Quarter

Reading Projects:
- Introduction to Best Book Project
- Sample of Best Book Project
- Best Book Project from Fourth Quarter
- Book Project #2 from Fourth Quarter
- Book Project #3 from Fourth Quarter

Evaluation Forms for End of the Year:
- Final Reading & Writing Reflection (2–3 pages)
- Growth Chart
- Final Visual Growth Chart
- Final Parent Reflection

Misc. Materials:
- Polished Writing from Previous Quarters
- Book Projects from Previous Quarters
- Peer Evaluation Forms
- Teacher Conference Forms
- Any additional writing you have done
- Notes/Handouts

Figure B–26 Portfolio rubric: First semester progress

Portfolio Rubric
First Semester Progress

Student _____ Date _____

Points	Category	Lacking Expected Progress 0–3	Writer Needs to Stretch for More Progress 4–6	Evidence of Progress 6–8	Strong Evidence of Progress 8–10	
Total Points ____ × 6 = ____	Evidence of Goal Setting and Achievement (The portfolio and the writing evaluation should convey evidence.)	The portfolio contains little evidence that the writer set or achieved significant goals. The writer's goal-setting process needs to be improved.	• The writer set three or more goals. • The writer developed a plan to achieve each of those goals. • The writer can cite examples to show that at least three of the goals were obtained.	• The writer set four or more goals. • The writer developed a plan to achieve each of those goals. • The writer can cite examples or evidence to show that at least four of the goals were obtained.	• The writer set five or more goals. • The writer developed a plan to achieve those goals. • The writer can cite examples or forms of evidence to show that goals were obtained.	
Total Points ____ × 2 = ____	Range of Writing	The portfolio shows us that writer only achieves one of the following: • The writer attempts to write in different genres. • The writer writes for a variety of purposes. • The writer writes for a variety of audiences. • The writer creates more material than expected.	The portfolio shows us that the writer achieves two of the following: • The writer attempts to write in different genres. • The writer writes for a variety of purposes. • The writer writes for a variety of audiences. • The writer creates more material than expected.	The portfolio shows us that the writer achieves three of the following: • The writer attempts to write in different genres. • The writer writes for a variety of purposes. • The writer writes for a variety of audiences. • The writer creates more material than expected.	The portfolio show us that the writer achieves all of the following: • The writer attempts to write in different genres. • The writer writes for a variety of purposes. • The writer writes for a variety of audiences. • The writer creates more material than expected.	
Page #1 Total						

Points	Category	Lacking Expected Progress 0–3	Writer Needs to Stretch for More Progress 4–6	Evidence of Progress 6–8	Strong Evidence of Progress 8–10
	Writing Process	Your portfolio shows us that as a writer you have done two of the following to create your polished works: • You are able to create and develop topics independently. • You have obvious purposes for writing; you write about your interests and background. • You revise your work and work from multiple drafts. • You are effective at self-assessing your work. • You seek out readers for your work.	Your portfolio shows us that as a writer you have done three of the following to create your polished works: • You are able to create and develop topics independently. • You have obvious purposes for writing; you write about your interests and background. • You revise your work and work from multiple drafts. • You are effective at self-assessing your work. • You seek out readers for your work.	Your portfolio shows us that as a writer you have done four of the following to create your polished works: • You are able to create and develop topics independently. • You have obvious purposes for writing; you write about your interests and background. • You revise your work and work from multiple drafts. • You are effective at self-assessing your work. • You seek out readers for your work.	Your portfolio shows us that as a writer you have done all of the following to create your polished works: • You are able to create and develop topics independently. • You have obvious purposes for writing; you write about your interests and background. • You revise your work and work from multiple drafts. • You are effective at self-assessing your work. • You seek out readers for your work.
Total Points _____ × 2 = _____ Page #1 Total Points _____			Total Points = _____ /100	Final Percent	

203

Appendix C

SAMPLE HIGH SCHOOL PAPERS
AND RATING RATIONALES

Ideas

The following sample papers are examples of student work.

IDEAS

"I Am Not a Nugget: The Tragedy of Owen Hart"

Rating: 5 (Ideas)

"This paper is clear and focused. It holds the reader's attention. Relevant anecdotes and details enrich the central theme" (Northwest Regional Educational Laboratory, 2003).[1]

"I am not a nugget!" Owen Hart would yell, but the crowd would just scream it louder. No matter what Owen Hart did in the World Wrestling Federation, the crowd always was against him. He'd triumphantly say, "Whoooo!" but the people didn't respond. Perhaps the only time Owen got a standing ovation was on Monday night. The only problem was that Owen was not around to enjoy it. The night before, Owen Hart died in a freak accident at Kemper Arena. It is a horrible irony that a man who was so dearly loved by his family and friends would never get to witness the respect finally shown to him by the fans.

Owen Hart was the loving father of two children. He was an honorable husband to his wife. He was a friend to many of the WWF superstars who pretended to be his enemies in the ring. Owen was a true professional. As shown by their tribute to him on Monday night's television show, Owen was always willing to try and cheer someone up who was having a bad day. He would do whatever it took to make people feel better.

He was willing to do whatever was asked of him regardless of the negative reaction of the fans. He was always willing to entertain. That desire to entertain was what led to his extremely untimely demise. He was going to pull off a stunt, that had been done many times before, of flying down to the ring from the ceiling, only this time something went wrong. As Owen was beginning his descent, the cable which held his life in its hands let go, snapping and sending Owen Hart to the floor from 50 feet in the air.

During his 13-year career in the WWF Owen held just about every championship belt there was. He held the tag team belt numerous times and most recently with his partner, Jeff Jarrett. Twice in his career he won the Intercontinental Championship and had extended runs as champion, taking on all comers and shying away from no challengers. He was also the recipient of a "Slammy," which is an award for the best professional wrestler of the year. Owen's brother Bret "The Hitman" Hart was the five-time WWF champion, so being a champion was in his blood.

[1]From *6 + 1 Trait ™ Writing Assessment Scoring Guide,* by Northwest Regional Educational Laboratory, 2003, Portland, Oregon: Northwest Regional Educational Laboratory, retrieved January 7, 2004 from **http://www.nwrel.org/assessment/ pdfRubrics/6plus1traits.PDF.**

Owen Hart will be missed not only by friends and family but also by the millions of people who tune in every week to be entertained. One of the most spirited and talented performers will be gone, and there will definitely be a major void. Anyone who considers himself a fan of professional wrestling would have been saddened at this loss of human life. And anyone who was a true die-hard fan of Owen Hart's would have felt like they lost a family member.

Rationale for 5 Rating in Ideas

The topic of this paper is crystal clear: Only after accidental death in the ring did professional wrestler (and professional villain) Owen Hart finally receive the fan recognition he deserved. That's definitely a fresh idea. The writer's details are relevant and gripping. He tells us that Owen Hart was taunted by ringside fans who nicknamed him the "Nugget" and that Hart and his partner, Jeff Jarrett, won the Intercontinental Tag Team Championship. The most riveting detail is the writer's description of Hart's 50-foot fall from the arena ceiling that resulted in his death. The writer anticipates the reader's questions with insightful details that explain the irony; contrary to the character he portrayed in the ring, Owen Hart was actually a "loving father of two children, and an honorable husband." The writer's insight steps outside the carnival theatrics of pro wrestling and examines the reality: "It is a horrible irony that a man who was loved so dearly by his family and friends would never get to witness the respect finally shown him by the fans."

"Sleep"

Rating: 3 (Ideas)

"The writer is still beginning to define the topic, even though development is still basic or general" (NWREL, 2003).

Have you ever woke up in morning & you're just as tired as when you went to bed? Perhaps your cycles of sleep were interrupted, this is called sleep deprivation.

When your head hits that pillow when you go to sleep your brain goes to work. It restores all the chemicals that were used that day. Your breathing & heart rate increase & your eyes move around in the sockets, which is called rapid eye movement (REM). But aside from all this your body becomes paralyzed, so you cannot harm yourself if you have a bad dream.

While you're asleep you go through four cycles of sleep. The first cycle is tight sleep, you are sleeping but you can still hear noises around you. The second & third cycles you are a little more deeply in sleep. During these two cycles rapid eye movement (REM) & dreams occur. The fourth cycle is deep sleep. This is the cycle when you get the best sleep. Each cycle lasts about 90 min.

There have been studies that show when you are deprived of REM sleep you do make it up, but you are short tempered & distractable. If you are deprived of deep sleep you do make it up, but you feel depressed. So this is why you might feel as tired as you were before you went to sleep.

When you fall asleep your body does not shut down. Your brain is busy at work producing dreams so that you can have a good nights rest. But sleep deprivation does occur often & that's why people are short tempered & distractable & sometimes even depressed.

Rationale for 3 Rating in Ideas

The broad topic of this paper is restricted only to the general topic of sleep, leaving the focus fuzzy. The opening, "Have you ever woke up in morning and you're just as tired as when you went to sleep?" is a reference to sleep deprivation, and the reader might expect the following paragraphs to support that idea with specific information; instead, the paper moves on to other ideas: the physiological, biochemical aspects of sleep and the parameters of sleep cycles. Finally, the writer comes back to sleep deprivation in the last two paragraphs. The writer could improve the paper by giving a more detailed answer to the opening question and making that the focus of the whole paper. One well-developed idea would be better than several underdeveloped ones.

"Psychology in Everyday Life"

Rating: 1 (Ideas)

"As yet, the paper has no clear sense of purpose or central theme. To extract meaning from the text, the reader must make inference based on sketchy or missing details" (NWREL, 2003).

Psychology is the scientific study of human and animal behavior. There can be many causes for a particular behavior. For example, people can be violent if they come from a family in which they have learned that arguments are dealt with by beating each other up. But there are also cases in which a person suddenly goes into a rage for no apparent reason. there is a part of the brain that, when touched causes a person to become extremely violent.

Psychology is everyday life is everywhere, to think is to do. You can do whatever you want whenever you want.

The brain allows you to think through things it helps you to do what you want.

The brain goes free and helps you think through things At the best you can be.

Rationale for 1 Rating in Ideas

Although the title identifies "psychology in everyday life" as the topic of this paper, the paper itself does not inform the reader about psychology, the study of the mind and behavior, "in everyday life." Although the second and third sentences explain that environmental conditioning can influence behavior, the rest of the paper rambles. We learn that some behavior can not be explained and that behavior originates in the brain. After the introductory paragraph there really isn't any more information. Three one-sentence paragraphs fail to state, support, or develop any other ideas. After the first two sentences the remainder of the paper has no hierarchy of important points and sub-points. It is a string of vague, random, unconnected thoughts.

Ideas

ORGANIZATION

"I Need a New Pair of Shoes"

Rating 5: (Organization)

"The organization enhances and showcases the central idea or theme. The order, structure, or presentation of information is compelling and moves the reader through the text" (NWREL, 2003).

"I need a new pair of shoes." "I need to get more sleep." "I need people to listen to me more." As human beings, we all have certain needs. Some needs are more basic than others. Nevertheless, if these needs are not fulfilled, we feel a void that nags at us. As humans, we have five basic sets of needs. These needs are described in Maslow's Hierarchy of Needs. Maslow's Hierarchy of Needs must be fulfilled in every human being in order for them to succeed.

The first need of Maslow's Hierarchy is physiological needs. These needs include hunger, thirst, etc. The second need is safety needs. These needs include feeling safe and having protection and shelter. The third need is belongingness. This includes having meaningful friendships and feeling close with others. The fourth need is self-esteem. This means feeling good about yourself, no matter what others say about you. The feeling of being important. The fifth need, which Maslow says only 5% of the world reaches, is self-actualization. This means realizing who your true self is and actively putting it into practice. Maslow says that if any one of these needs are missing, then that need is the one focused on.

Looking at humans in general, one can see how this theory of needs is applied. As parents, fulfilling all the needs is essential. Children that do not get certain needs met, tend to obsess over the missing needs. For example, if a parent does not make a child feel that they are in a safe environment, then the child will become paranoid and conscious of everyone. They may not trust easily. Therefore, this leads them to shy away from others because they are wary of them. The belongingness need then suffers because no one is there to support them or recognize their accomplishment. Clearly, if one need is not met, the rest suffer, all because one of the building blocks is missing. This can also be seen at school. If c child is teased by their peers, they will have no self-esteem.

Therefore, their need to belong will not be fulfilled because they have no friends. This leads to a feeling of not being safe. The child always has to be aware of their environment and potential harassment. It does not matter where, in the pyramid of needs, the need is missing. I will always effect those needs around it. Although the person may only recognize that their need to belong or feel safe is missing, the others do suffer, whether the person is conscious of it or not. If needs are not met a person can either turn inward with their feelings or explode on others and demand or force, sometimes violently, that those needs be met.

Each person knows what it is like to lack a need. However, what happens if all of the four needs are successfully met? The next stage is self-actualization. Examples of people who have reached this point would be people like Mother Theresa, Martin Luther King, Jr., and Ghandi. Each one of those people realized they were created for a purpose. Who they were had value and merit. They knew they had specific gifts that were worth putting into practice. Most people never reach this stage because they are stuck at a different stage. A certain need is not being fulfilled and that breaks the ladder to success. Certain rungs of the ladder are missing, so it is impossible for one to climb to the top. In order for all of us to reach this point, we must try and fill needs of others, such as belongingness, so that success will follow.

As humans we have a definite set of needs that must be met in order for us to fully succeed. Five is not a big number, but yet that is how many needs must be met in order for us to be fully successful. Each rung must be there or the ladder of success is broken. Some things we say we need are obviously more important than others; however, even if the simplest need is missing, life cannot be truly successful.

Rationale for 5 Rating in Organization

This paper has an interesting lead-in. From that opening, the writer describes the premise that the rest of the paper will develop. The introduction creates a degree of tension, or anticipation, and promises to relieve it as the writer explains how and why "human beings feel a void that nags at us." Ideas follow a logical progression and have smooth transitions between them. After explaining each of the levels of need, the writer uses the example of parents carefully fulfilling the needs of a child. The author uses a specific need and explains the consequences of fulfilling or failing to fulfill that need. It is an effective example. The pacing of this paper is constant with no sudden jumps or voids. The pattern is easy to follow: idea, explanation, elaboration, and example. The ending of this paper comes back to the original premise and tension (which has been relieved in the papers' body) and draws a satisfying conclusion. The reader feels a sense of resolution with this topic of fulfilling human needs.

"Florida"

Rating: 3 (Organization)

"The organizational structure is strong enough to move the reader through the text without too much confusion" (NWREL, 2003).

Spring and summer are the biggest vacation times of the year people migrate to the sunny beaches for big vacations. The bad thing about some

Organization

of these places is there is the beach and only the lonly beach. However if people go to Florida you will not run into problems like these. I should know I have seen everything there is to see in Florida.

To start off, Florida is a great place to go for vacation because of its spectacular weather. The lowest it will get is about 40 and that's in the winter so you don't have to worry that messing up your summer plans. Instead of snow, there is lots of rain which is easier to drive in than snow. The most important thing is there is lots of sunshine that is why Florida is called the sunshine state.

Next, there is always something to do in Florida. If people are sick of the beach there are several amusement parks they can adventure through. One of the most outstanding amusment parks in Florida is Bush Gardens which has some of the most exciting roller coasters and a large number of beautiful wildlife to look at. Sea World is great too if you like marine life. The most commonly known park is Disney World in Orlando. Its most popular for kids to go and see their favorite cartoon characters.

Finally, If you run out of amusment parks to go to then there is always some type of sporting event going on. In the spring Florida hosts half of the Major League baseball teams for spring training. In the fall there are three outstanding college football teams, Florida State, Florida, Miami. There are good pro football teams as well in Jacksonville, Tamps Bay, and Miami. When those two sports aren't around there two hockey and to basketball teams as well.

Florida is one of the best places to go for a vacation. The sky is the limit when it comes to things to do down in Florida. The people have shown their opinions of Florida already by making Florida one of the most popular tourist attraction places in the world.

Rationale for 3 Rating in Organization

A little revision would easily earn this paper a 5 rating. Although it has a recognizable introduction, the controlling idea of the paper is unclear in the first paragraph. Is it about beach vacations versus other kinds of vacations? Is it about the variety of recreation in Florida? Is it about Florida's superiority over other states as a vacation spot? The second paragraph begins with a transition and seems to hold the theme: "To start off, Florida is a great place to go on vacation because of its spectacular weather." The rest of the paper continues to elaborate on Florida as a vacation spot and the conclusion clearly states "Florida is one of the best places to go for a vacation." Each paragraph develops a different part of that theme. Although the paragraph about weather digresses momentarily into a comparison of driving in rain and driving in snow, mostly the paragraphs state and develop easily followed ideas about the virtues of a Florida vacation.

"The Diary of A Young Girl"

Rating: 1 (Organization)

"The writing lacks a clear sense of direction. Ideas, details, or events seem strung together in a loose or random fashion; there is no identifiable internal structure" (NWREL, 2003).

Anne Frank, a German-Jewish girl, wrote a graphic, remarkable diary, while hiding from the Nazis during World War II. Anne was born on June 12, 1912 in Frankfurt, Germany. Anne Frank wrote in her diary every day while hiding in the attic from the Nazis. It was her only way of being free from the anxioty of the Nazis' persecution.

Anne didn't care much for socializing with the others in the attic, not even her mother. She was Daddie's girl.

Anne Frank wrote about the horrors of war and the persecution of the Jews. She was a very detailed writer and never failed to keep my attention.

After living in the cramped attic for six months, she was the only person who still held her spirit. She was a great leader and motivator for those who were ill-hearted and who had lost all hope.

Even though they had not idea when their lived could end, she kept that behind her. She knew she and the others would soon be found.

Frank said that she wanted to live on even after her death. Even though she never got to feel the fame that would soon live on her name, she will always have a place in each persons mind who has had to undergo persecution.

Rationale for 1 Rating in Organization

Although the introduction does give background information about the paper's topic, the writer does not clearly state a controlling idea. None of the statements made in the first paragraph are developed as a theme. Connections are not made between paragraphs, and it is unclear if there is any relationship between the ideas from one paragraph to the next. Even within paragraphs there is a lack of cohesion. The third paragraph, for example, has only two sentences in total; the first one tells that *The Diary of Anne Frank* is about "the horrors of war and the persecution of the Jews." The second and final sentence of that paragraph advises that the book "failed to keep" the writers attention. The relationship between these ideas is unclear. Pacing is awkward because the writer jumps back and forth between global and specific ideas without giving development to them.

VOICE

"The Feeling of Music"

Rating: 5 (Voice)

"The writer speaks directly to the reader in a way that is individual, compelling and engaging. The writer 'aches with caring,' yet is aware and respectful of the audience and the purpose for writing" (NWREL, 2003).

As my hand slides back and forth on the neck, and my calloused fingers hit each string, I feel the biggest wave of energy sweep over me. No thought is involved. It's action, reaction, chord after chord, note after note. No greater feeling. The only thing that eases my mind. Music.

To some, religion is God. To others, experience is knowledge. But to me music is the powerful and purest thing in the world. Music is God, religion, experience and knowledge all wrapped up. It is energy and as Newton's theory goes "Energy can not be created or destroyed." Music (energy) touches everything and keeps going. It echoes into deepest corners of the galaxy, to the bottomless ocean. Without it, the world would not be complete. I would not be complete. I first completely realized this power when I began to play the guitar.

When I first started, I was terrible. I couldn't play one chord. But there was something inside of me that kept pushing. I had never taken lessons so it was very hard to get started. I remember watching MTV and recording rock videos so later I could pause when there was a close-up of the guitar. But finally I began to learn easy riffs that consisted of 2–3 chords (all power chords). After about two months I started to stop playing other band's stuff and just fool around. That's when everything came out, and for once I stopped thinking. I just played. It was such, and still is, a huge high. Every day now, I fantasize about being on the road starving and having to live at strangers' houses or in the back of the van covered in sweat to wake up and do it all over again. Only for the pure passion. Fame is not part of my dream. It's the only thing that depurifies it. To headline a show for 500 people is all I want. Being on stage is the greatest thing I've ever experienced in my life.

The amp hums in your ear as the people in the crowd are full of anticipation. They're all crowded up like cattle, and finally the once monotone amp releases a painting of notes and chords come flying in your ear. Screaming and yelling with all of your heart as the drums behind you crack like shotguns and the only thing that keeps the music semi-sane is the bass guitar. Song to song, high to low, you finally crack. With your body throwing itself on the ground uncontrollably, still playing the guitar, you shout and writhe with no conception of what you are doing. I have this theory about why this happens. I believe there is this line between what is music and what is you. As the show keeps progressing and the energy builds. You and the music keep getting closer and closer until you are one. You finally become what you are playing. It is the most intense, insane, draining and beautiful thing I've ever experienced. Someone said that "Jimi Hendrix was a thin wire with too much current running." That's the only thing I can think of that describes how I feel. With music, a portion of that gets released. Like I said before, without music, the world would not be complete.

Whether it makes you cry, laugh, angry, or energized, it's all the same. I've never seen another thing that can rip your innermost thoughts and feelings out of you and put them right in front of your face so that you feel something. But music, all over the world, all over the galaxy, is happening. To the deepest corners of the galaxy, to the bottomless ocean. It's there.

Rationale for 5 Rating in Voice

The writer/guitar player has definitely taken "a risk by revealing who he is. . . what he thinks" and how he feels. This is from the heart when he says, "No greater feeling. The only thing that eases my mind. Music." Parts of this work read especially well out loud, such as: "It echoes into the deepest corners of the galaxy, to the bottomless ocean. Without it, the world would not be complete. I would not be complete." The reader can not help but think about/react to the writer's point of view about playing the guitar. "The person behind the words" is evident. The "flavor and texture" of the writing fit the passion this writer feels for music

"Twiggy"

Rating: 3 (Voice)

"The writer seems sincere, but not fully engaged or involved. The result is pleasant or even person able, but not compelling"(NWREL, 2003).

Insecurity is a very big problem throughout young girls in America. Twiggy was a model/trend setter in the 1960's. She was extremely thin, tall, with a very narrow uncurvy figure. Twiggy set the trend to be skinny, which caused girls all over to feel inadequate and insecure.

In magazines, young girls would no longer just see Twiggy, they saw numerous perfect thin bodies. This gave them the idea that something was wrong with them. Teenagers strived to be thin just like the media was telling them. "It's glamorous to be skinny." There's some news for you, not everyone is skinny.

The media caused the youth to be insecure with there bodies. Women feel they can't live up to the models they see on television or in magazines. Some argue that they try to be thin and wear tons of make-up not because of the influence media has on them, but because they want to look good. Why would being as fake as possible make you look good?

Natural beauty is what each woman needs to find in themselves and rise above all the media. No one can set a definition for what is beautiful,

Voice

especially not the media. People feeling comfortable with their natural beauty will solve the insecurity problem the media caused.

Insecurity continues to be a serious problem throughout the youth of America. The media sets standards for them that they can't live up to.

Rationale for 3 Rating in Voice

"Sincere, but not passionate" fits this writer. Moments do happen when the writer emerges strongly such as: "Here's some news for you, not everyone is skinny." Most of the time, however, she sticks to stating fairly "safe generalities" about the media-created image of the super-thin female glamour stars such as Twiggy, the British supermodel from the 1960s. Describing Twiggy as "a very narrow, uncurvy figure" is accurate but not passionate; "anorexic" or "concentration camp figure" would more deeply express a writer's disenchantment with the image of femininity forced on young girls. The writer loses the potential for really grabbing the reader at times by using "vague generalities." She tells us that girls got the idea that something was wrong with them and they tried to be thin, but more specifically she might have described the specific psychological problems whose rise was documented during this period, such as suicide, anorexia, and bulemia. The writing is "pleasant .... but not compelling."

"Why the Young Kill"

Rating: 1

"The writer seems indifferent, uninvolved, or distanced from the topic and/or the audience" (NWREL, 2003).

I agree w/ this article when it says that there isn't just one cause or explanation to why America's youth is killing one another. Violence in today's youth is caused by everything that has made them angry, acess to guns, problems at home, and so on. This also says that traumatic experiences when a young child will effect a person's development for the rest of their life. This article give's many interesting facts and conclusions. I agree with a lot of it and other stuff not necessarily, however that doesn't mean that this article didn't keep my attention.

Rationale for 1 Rating in voice

This paper has the look of one that was hurriedly done to hand in by the deadline and not really given much thought. The writer hasn't really expressed a point of view and takes no risk whatsoever: "This article gives many interesting facts and conclusions. I agree with a lot of it and other stuff not necessarily." What does the reader know about the writer after reading those sentences? Not much. The writer has quickly summarized the article but not truly reacted to it in the paper. The writer's rhetoric is noncommittal: "however that doesn't mean this article didn't keep my attention." Did the article keep her attention, and if so, specifically how? The writer gives no sense of herself in her writing.

WORD CHOICE

"Drawing vs. Computer Graphics"

Rating: 5 *(Word Choice)*

"Words convey the intended message in a precise, interesting, and natural way. The words are powerful and engaging"(NWREL, 2003).

As a person who likes to draw I can honestly say that drawing by hand on paper is infinitely better than drawing on a computer. With a pencil, you are able to have better control of what you wish to draw. It takes practice and technique, but is more authentic. With your hand, you get a better view (as well as others) of what your drawing from you hand, which is a very satisfying feeling.

Take a pencil, for example; it has incredible maneuverability and never lies. With a pencil, your drawings are controlled (no matter how good an artist you are), unique and authentic. The lead has better shading abilities, and is able to make the hardest pictures look easy. No matter how you put it, the pencil is the best utensil to utilize for a drawing or sketching situation.

Graphics from a computer are cool looking and are sometimes (not always) easy to resurrect. They are fun to mess with and very precise, but they lack any labor. Labor on your eyes maybe, and patience, but not the actual skipping of a pen or pencil. When I see computer art, I see something that looks very neat and very well processed, but at the same time I see something created from a digitized perspective. Something which was "magically" (electronically) transported from a monitor to a printer.

Once again, computer art is neat and pleasing to the eye, but it's not real. It's a computer, artificially creating art depicted from the perspective of an almost artificially intelligent machine. An almost complete fraud of an actual drawing, created through electronic impulses. I close with this: Drawing is just drawing, no matter how you do it. But drawing from a pencil and drawing with a mouse are like two totally different worlds. And no matter how you manufacture your thought into art, all that matters is that you are pleased with your work.

Rationale for 5 Rating in Word Choice

While the writer's language feels natural, it is still striking. For example, he tells us that a pencil has "incredible maneuverability and never lies." His word choice is accurate. He describes pencil drawings as more "authentic" than computer graphics and graphic art as "easy to resurrect" and coming from "a digitalized perspective." Another accurate and striking word choice is his choice of "fraud" to describe art done by "artificial intelligent." The writer has "put just the right word or phrase in just the right spot," as in the paper's very first sentence which is easy to understand, individual, and effective. In this sentence he has chosen

Word Choice

to add words beyond what is required and the effect is engaging. His choice of "As a person who likes to draw" is more effective than a more minimal choice (As an artist) would be. "I can honestly say" might seem unnecessary but it adds to the effect, as does his choice to say "drawing by hand on paper" rather than just "drawing." The redundancy here is purposeful.

"Teen Jobs"

Rating: 3 (Word Choice)

"The language is functional, even if it lacks much energy. It is easy to figure out the writer's meaning on a general level" (NWREL, 2003).

Word Choice

Flipping burgers, waiting tables, and changing diapers. These are all some of the jobs teens occupy, but are they being treated fairly? Teens today in the workplace are getting the bad end of the deal.

Teens these days occupy many different jobs, weather it be at McDonalds, Applebee's, Bagel and Bagel or just a babysitting job. All these jobs also are occupied by adults at the same time. Teens in the work force is becoming more popular, with single parents & unemployed parents. Teens are forced to make there own money to give themselves the luxeries they want & usually deserve.

At many of these jobs teens are treated very unfairly, they are given the crappy shifts, the grunt work, and they have to do it all with a smile. Managers feel they can tell teens to do something & automatically we do it, and if we don't they threaten your job. Should they be aloud to do this. I don't think so, they don't do it to the adults so why to us? They do it simply because we have no voice or say in anything, they know we have to have money so we need the job & we'll do anything to keep it. When it comes to the pay for teens we are again cheated. They feel since we are kids we don't need money, so they think paying us minimum wage is OK. We get payed half as much as the adult employees, sure adults have more responsibility, but we have some too, like college tuition, car insurance, our clothes & our entertainment. How are we suppose to do anything making $5.50 and hour flipping burgers or serving food. We begin to think that its going to be like that forever & have no sense of hope.

Teen jobs are important to the teen & the employer, but what employers don't realize is that if they don't start giving fair treatment, they are going to lose them & then have no one. So if you are an employer please realize that teens have needs & financial responsibility & also we do have self dignity, so please stop treating us unfairly & give us an equal shot.

Rationale for 3 Rating in Word Choice

Although the word choice in the very first sentence (fragment) is engaging, choices after that are generic. The reader can understand the writer's meaning but the words lack flair, originality, precision, and effect. Phrases like "the bad end of the deal," "many different jobs," and "tell teens to do something" are adequate but not interesting, detailed, or effective. Precise word choice might substitute "equitable scheduling" for "treated fairly." Other words that are adequate but not as effective as they could be include "important," "these days," "popular," and "many." Active voice and action verbs should replace passive voice and state-of-being verbs when they are used as main verbs.

"Relationship"

Rating: 1 (Word Choice)

"The writer struggles with a limited vocabulary, searching for words to convey meaning"(NWREL, 2003).

Love . . . Is that the main key? Love has to be in every relationship, whether it's your friend, a family member, or even a boyfriend, a family member, or even a boyfriend or girlfriend. You may not think you do, but that's what it is, and it ends up helping you in the end.

Friendships, and boyfriend and girlfriend relationships are very important to have in your life. If you think about what you would do without friends, there really isn't much to say. Relationships, however, are good no matter which way you look at it.

Having friends is how everything starts off. Whether it's with a boy or a girl. The good thing is, that they are the people who are there for you during the good times, and even the rough times. Everybody needs at least one of those in their lifetime. I'm telling you, you can't get very far without them.

Switching to a different point of view. Boyfriend and girlfriend relationships. This is all about learning to grow up and falling in love with somebody. If you look around more people are happy when they have this kind of relationship. It makes them feel good about themselves. At least it does for me. That's a good thing though.

No matter what people think about relationships, they are definitly for the better. Even if they don't plan to work out, it helps you grow, and learn to love people.

Rationale for 1 Rating in Word Choice

The vague quality of the language in this paper limits the message. Words like "important," "good," and phrases like "rough times," "good times," "helping you in the end," "learning to grow up" don't carry much meaning. Additional phrases are cliché, such as "what you would do without friends," "you can't get very far without" friends, "love has to be in every relationship," "people who are there for you," and people must "feel good about themselves." Redundancy weakens the writing, as in "ends up helping you in the end." The word "good" is used five times. Concrete words are uncommon in this paper and abstract words, words that do not refer to a tangible specific, take their places.

SENTENCE FLUENCY

"Gram"

Rating: 5 *(Sentence Fluency)*

"The writing has an easy flow, rhythm and cadence. Sentences are well built, with strong and varied structure that invites expressive oral reading" (NWREL, 2003).

"There is always someone in a person's life that makes footprints in their heart and music in their soul." Be it a friend, sibling, parent, grandparent or complete stranger, everyone has that certain person who is their epitome of joy. My source of happiness is my grandmother, more affectionately known as Gram. She has been there for me as a loving and gentle friend, role model and guide.

The earliest memories of my childhood, those inadvertent flashbacks you sometimes have at random moments, are with Gram. Since I was born, she has lived in Somewhere, South Dakota. Somewhere is quite a small town, easy to drive through and forget, but not if Gram is there. She would play Annie-Annie-Over, an innovative, incessantly fun game, repeatedly with my cousin Joy, my sister Barbara, and me. When Joy and Barbara would leave me out of their games, Gram always had a warm smile and a gentle word.

Anyone in Somewhere will tell you that Gram's kindness is never ending and unbelievable. She has never said a mean word to anyone. The best compliment I have ever received is that I have her personality. Her ability to make everyone feel special is incredible. She is outgoing and bubbly and I strive daily to possess her strength and compassion for other people.

Whenever I need anything, I turn to Gram. I know that she has been watching over me since January of last year, and although at times it is difficult, I count my blessings that I have such a wonderful guardian angel. Whenever I am in a situation where I question my capability to do something, I feel her hand on my shoulder and cherish her embrace in my heart. She has never failed to help me make the right decision.

There is not a day that goes by that I don't miss my Gram. Her love is exemplified in all she left behind. I frequently speak with my grandpa, her best friend and husband of 56 years. I can not imagine a lifetime without her, and I feel an overwhelming advantage that I had her in reach for 15 years. I know that I will see her again someday in a more tangible sense, but until then I bask in her remembrance and live to be more like her.

Rationale for 5 Rating in Sentence Fluency

This paper reads well out loud, especially the fourth paragraph. The phrases and clauses fit together smoothly to create a graceful cadence. The lengths and patterns of sentence structure are varied, and long and short sentences are used purposefully. For example, a short sentence might make a point, and then a long sentence follows to elaborate: "Whenever I need anything, I turn to Gram. I know that she has been watching over me since January of last year, and although at times it is difficult, I count my blessings that I have such a wonderful guardian angel." Subordination within sentences enhances meaning: "Somewhere is quite a small town, easy to drive through and forget, but not if Gram is there."

"In the Future"

Rating: 3 (Sentence Fluency)

"The text hums along with a steady beat, but tends to be more pleasant or businesslike than musical, more mechanical than fluid" (NWREL, 2003).

In the future, the world will have seen a lot of changes from the early man to advanced man. Each century, there are dramatic changes in technology, in each century the changes are more dramatic. The future holds changes in travel, space, and communication. Technology recently has advanced so much, but the future holds many more opportunities of improvements.

Communication has gone from the "pony express" to now the telephone. The telephone is a direct form of communication where you can speak with the person there and now. We are beginning to see the video phone and by 2005 I believe that video phones, where you not only speak to the person but also see them, will become more widely used.

In space, we have learned so much and gotten so far. We will go farther and learn even more. Scientists have advanced space travel and we will see even more. We will search other planets in other galaxies and might even find life. One of the most amazing things is that just maybe, there are others just the same as us living somewhere out in the distance.

Travel has also been revolutionized. From Henry Ford's Model T we now see cars that can reach up to two and three hundred miles and hour. It is amazing, but that also will change. We will have cars that fly and boundaries and speeds that are unknown. It will be very interesting to see what will happen.

Technology recently has advanced so much, but the future does indeed hold so many more opportunities of improvement. Scientists have made many scientific advances and advanced technology pushes out in to the open. It will be made public and the advances will be made for all of us. The future looks bright in the face of technology.

Rationale for 3 Rating in Sentence Fluency

The sentences in this paper "get the job done in a routine fashion" with a reasonable variety of sentence beginnings and sentence patterns, but not to the

Sentence Fluency

point of fluidity. Some of the paper reads well out loud, but much of it is a little stiff or ungainly. Phrases and clauses are correctly but not always gracefully joined. Oral reading requires a little effort to figure out how the writer meant the emphasis to be placed. The paper could be improved if the writer would use more signposts to the reader like subordinating and coordinating conjunctions, and conjunctive adverbs.

"Call of the Wild #1"

Rating: 1 (Sentence Fluency)

"The reader has to practice quite a bit to give this paper a fair interpretive reading" (NWREL, 2003).

Call of the Wild is a really good book. "You might wrap up the good befor you deliver them." That's what they said when they stole Buck. It's about a dog name Buck who one of the greatest dog vere lived. Erey person want to buy him. The aurthor Jack London give Buck humen personality. In Call of the Wild, the characters are Buck, Spit, John Thornto & his friend Pete, Indians name Yeehats, Mercedes, Hall, Charles, and the bad guy Black Barton. The basic storyline is that a dog can do anything a person can do. Theme is great man & dog are one of the best friend your ever going to find.

There are gradual changes that happen to Buck. A normal dog can become a wild dog but, what stand between hem is John Thornton "God you can all but speak" John Thornton tells Buck but that he can do everthing but not talk to him because he is a dog. That tell that the love each other and John want Buck to speaks.

Buck find a gril wolf.Buck is a hughe St Bernard who find a wolf. Buck should have been killed by the wolf like did to the other dog but know they know he is a great one or when he pull 1,000 pound over a football field. This come to show the he is strong.

He save John when John falls into the river Buck swam to save him but did not untill they tie a rope "Pete tie it" and try again. Save him that time.

Everyone want to buy Buck from John but John is the only one that Buck has gotton close to. Buck want to go to the wild but the only thing that is stoping Buck is John. Buck gose off to the wild once Butt when John called him he came back to John so there's something in between.

He goes under a big change when he take over the team of dog slide because to take it over he had to kill Spit aother dog that was the leader of the pack. He learn a lot of Spit. How to keep warm at night. How to eat any thing and still ge the best out of it. After that none of the dog mest with him/

When John Thornton die Buck became a wolf. Befor that he was a house pet pleyed with kid went to go hunting with them. He was normal but the wild

Sentence Fluency

was calling him and the only thin stoping him was John. The love that they had was the only thing. John was the only thing that Buck had.

Rationale for 1 Rating in Sentence Fluency

Sentences in this paper tend to repeat the same pattern; there is little variety in sentence length or structure. In the first three paragraphs the sentences are short and choppy. Omitted words, omitted word endings, misspellings, and punctuation mistakes make reading out loud difficult; for example, "It's about a dog name Buck who one of the greatest dog vere lived." Awkward phrasing also makes reading clumsy, as in "Before that he was a house pet pleyed with kid who went hunting." The phrasing does not sound natural.

Sentence Fluency

CONVENTIONS

"IQ #1"

Rating: 5 *(Conventions)*

"The writer demonstrates a good grasp of standard writing conventions (e.g., spelling, punctuation, capitalization, grammar, usage, paragraphing) and uses conventions effectively to enhance readability. Errors tend to be so few that just minor touch-ups would get this piece ready to publish" (NWREL, 2003).

The definition for intelligence quotient is a measure of brightness obtained by comparing mental age with physical age. There are some problems with how someone's IQ is measured, however. An IQ test can not predict things such as how well a person actually does a certain task in the real world. Also, mistakes can be made during an IQ test.

So an IQ test may answer the question how smart are you? But it does not answer how are you smart? That is why I don't think a person's IQ should be made public. People are such complex creatures that one test can tell you very little about the actual person. I know some very intelligent people who would definitely do well on an IQ test but to me they seem to have difficulty relating to other people. It's as though their intelligence is a barrier to the relationships they form in the real world.

The person with the average IQ might fall through the cracks. He or she might be dismissed simply because they are average. This would be sad because IQ does not measure a person's emotional intelligence, or EQ, which I think plays as great a role in whether a person succeeds or not.

To base a person's character around one test reminds me of the ideals of fascism. If an IQ test shows that you are really brilliant, and this information is made public, then certain biases may be made. The same could be said for someone whose IQ is lower than average. People might point you toward certain jobs because they think that these are the best-suited jobs for your IQ. This would really be unfortunate because even if you are really good at science, this does not mean that you couldn't be, say, an actress.

An IQ score made public may also ruin a person's feelings of self-worth. If someone's IQ is slightly less than average or just average, this person may feel inferior and give up on life instead of thinking that they can rise above the test. Because right now a person's IQ is not made public, most people feel that with hard work, they can accomplish anything.

I've taken an IQ test, and I think my score was average, I think that it would be nice if had a really high IQ, but I don't, and maybe that's a good thing. I'm not faced with certain pressures and expectations that come along with having a great IQ. So, really, I am what I am, and right now I'm happy with that.

Conventions

Rationale for 5 Rating in Conventions

Conventions are generally correct in this paper, and the writer's use of them enhances the paper. The writer has attempted an advanced construction by placing two rhetorical questions within a statement: "So an IQ test may answer the question how smart are you? But it does not answer how are you smart?" The punctuation is incorrect, but the writer should be credited with attempting an advanced construction to make the paper interesting. One sentence has a spelling and punctuation error: "I know some very intelligent people who would *definitly* (definitely) do well on an IQ test (*comma missing*) but to me they seem to have difficulty relating to other people." Other than that, the paper is relatively free of error. Grammar, usage, and paragraphing are all correctly and effectively used.

"IQ #2"

Rating: 3

"The writer shows reasonable control over a limited range of standard writing conventions. Conventions are sometimes handled well and enhance readability; at other times, errors are distracting and impair readability" (NWREL, 2003).

Would it be good or bad to have everyone's IQ as public knowledge? Having your IQ known could be a good thing or a bad thing It really just depends on how you look at it.

Your IQ is personal it shouldn't really be anyone elses business. Also people really shouldn't be labeled by there IQ. If there IQ is low it doesn't necessarily mean that they are stupid. They might have another talent that is really good, but can't be measured on the IQ scale.

If your IQ was posted or it was publically known everyone would be in their approiate class depending on their IQ. Also for jobs the emplyees can just look at the IQ test to see if the person is qualified.

My honest opion is that I wouldn't like my IQ test posted because I don't believe people should be judged by a test. Also you can't tell how smart a person is in other areas by just an IQ test.

Rationale for 3 Rating in Conventions

Although spelling and punctuation are mostly correct, the writer does make some mistakes: "If there (*their*) IQ is low (*comma missing*) it doesn't neccisarily (*necessarily*) mean that they are stupid." Another missing punctuation mark in the opening sentence of the second paragraph makes reading it a little confusing at first: "Your IQ is personal (*omitted period*) it shouldn't really be anyone elses business." Paragraphing is attempted, but ideas could be more separated and developed individually. Moderate editing needs to be done to this paper before it would be ready for publishing.

Conventions

"Call of the Wild #2"

Rating: 1 (Conventions)

"Errors in spelling, punctuation, capitalization, usage and grammar and/or paragraphing repeatedly distract the reader and make text difficult to read" (NWREL, 2003).

in the book the Call of The Wild buck who was the Main charcter changed form good to bad. Thoughot the book you can see him change. There are also symbols about him changing.

in the begging of the book buck was a gentel dog. he loved to play with the grand children. every one lovd buck until the men came.

when the men came and took buck buck was frightened. he was not used to this kind of treatment. buck was confused and grew a little angry on the men.

When the man droppd him at he saw a man in the red sweater. buck tried to attack that man but the man hit buck in the nose with a club. This happens several times until buck lernd to obey the man. this time buck grew more angry

buck was starting to turn into a feroscious dog. on the runs he saw a sertan wolf and grew in love with her. Buck also met a nice man named Johm Thornton. John loved buck and without John buck would run with the wolves.

in the book john Thornton dies. buck was Johns frien because Buck was fierce he could protect John form people and other dogs and wolfs. now that Joh was dead no one could bring buck back to civilization. buck was now a wolf.

as you can see buck changed in this book This is an example of what can happen is some one is treata bad are not cared for. buck was from good to one wolf. this book was good.

Rationale for 1 Rating in Conventions

The writer misspells many words in this paper, even ones that are not commonly misspelled: charcter/character, begging/beginning, gentel/gentle, lerned/learned. Often sentences do not begin with capital letters, and some sentences do not have ending punctuation. Some proper nouns do not have capitals. The reader has to decode some sentences first and then ascertain the meaning, such as "in the begging of the book buck was a gentel dog." The writer's use of conventions distracts the reader.

Conventions

Appendix D

SAMPLE MIDDLE SCHOOL/JUNIOR HIGH SCHOOL PAPERS AND RATING RATIONALES

IDEAS

"Planet of the Apes"

Rating: 5/4 (Ideas)

"This paper is clear and focused. It holds the reader's attention. Relevant anecdotes and details enrich the central theme" (Northwest Regional Educational Laboratory, 2003).[1]

Talking Apes? Well, that caught my curiosity right off the bat! The original *Planet of the Apes* was actually a trilogy; it was quite good, too! But now they've gone and produced a new *Planet of the Apes*, which in my opinion was almost the same.

The original *Planet of the Apes* (POTA) was superbly done for that time era. The acting was good, the special effects were good, and the sound was ok. But what really made the movie was the ending. IN the original POTA, the main character is walking along the beach when he sees a hand, and it turns out that it's actually the Statue of Liberty sunken in the Earth. Also the most famous line in the movie was when the main character yells, "Take your hands of me, you d**** dirty ape! And then he is knocked unconscious.

The 2001 version of POTA is pretty good. The acting could stand some help, but the special effects and sound are excellent. But what made this version weird was that the actor who played the main character in the original movie is now an ape, the lead ape, no less. In the original he was captain of the humans. The ending was also weird. The new main character lands on Earth and is instantly surrounded by apes who are civilized like humans. The ending takes place some time in this universe and in Washington, D.C. It is quite weird and mind-boggling. But as for the famous line, the old main character, who is now the head ape, says "those d**** dirty humans" and then dies.

So as you've noticed there are a couple changes. There are also some similarities. The character development is the same, and the plot is virtually the same. Human falls into ape territory, ape falls in love with human, human saves mankind, ape is killed and so on. The makeup of the characters is also the same , and so are the personalities along with the layout of Apeville.

I've told you most of the similarities and couple of differences. But now, I think you should see the three originals and then watch the new version. It's actually kind of cool how they've recreated it. So go see and form your own original opinion of the movies. I guarantee the ending will still be a topic of controversy.

[1]From *6 + 1 Trait ™ Writing Assessment Scoring Guide,* by Northwest Regional Educational Laboratory, 2003, Portland, Oregon: Northwest Regional Educational Laboratory, retrieved January 7, 2004 from **http://www.nwrel.org/assessment/ pdfRubrics/6plus1traits.PDF**.

Rationale for 5 Rating in Ideas

The topic of this paper is crystal clear and remains in focus: This young person compared the original with the remake and preferred the original. The writer's details contain quotations from both movies and descriptions of crucial scenes. Development is accomplished as the writer anticipates the reader's questions and attempts to answer them by covering all aspect of the movie review/comparison, such as acting special effects and overall quality for the time.

"Skateboard Trucks"

Rating: 3/4 (Ideas)

"The writer is still beginning to define the topic, even though development is still basic or general" (NWREL, 2003).

In this SA III compare and contrast two skateboard truck makers that I used this summer: Independent trucks and the new Krux III's. I'm still using the Krux III's but I've skated them long enough to compare. In this SA I will tell you about the similarities and differences of these skateboard trucks.

The Independent trucks are by far the heaviest trucks I've ever skated However, they are one of the strongest trucks made. They are known a lot about, they make the most clothes and every poser wears them.

The Krux III's are nice trucks. They are some of the lightest and most durable trucks out there. The trucks I am comparing are the mirrored truck black base. These trucks are like trucks soaked in wax because they slide fast with or without wax. Also these trucks don't fast, which means that I'll have them alot longer.

One of the things these trucks have in common which is a disadvantage is they arnet for giant gaps and hard falls because the kingpins will break. Another similarity is there durability. They both are strong beside the kingpins, but those can be changed.

In concluttion I would take the Krux III's over the Independents because the Krux's are lighter and grind better.

Rationale for 3/4 Rating in Ideas

The highly technical nature of this paper requires that the writer anticipate the reader's questions, especially about terminology and skateboarding in general. Who is the audience? Other skateboarders might understand, but some definitions, explanations, and illustrating examples are needed for most of the writer's classmates. This paper could easily be revised into a solid 5 by adding those elements.

Ideas

"Swordfish vs. Planet of the Apes"

Rating: 1 (Ideas)

"As yet, the paper has no clear sense of purpose or central theme. To extract meaning from the text, the reader must make inference based on sketchy or missing details" (NWREL, 2003).

Over the summer I saw *Swordfish* and *Planet of the Apes*. Both movies were pretty good. So I'm going to compare and contrast them.

In the movie *Swordfish* it was very technical. You had to watch every bit of the movie to understand it. Hally Berrey who is in the movie made it a little better.

The Planet of the Apes was alright. The movie wasn't like a movie that someone would want to know what was going to happen. It was predictable.

They were alike in a few was because I saw them both, I liked them and both had pretty good cast.

Now there compared and contrasted so maybe you'll see both movies.

Rationale for 1 Rating in Ideas

The writer has not given the reader enough "interesting details" or even much information at all, other than that Halle Berry is in the movie. Too many unanswered questions are left, such as what are the two movies about, who else is in them, what is good and/or bad about them. This writer needs to go back and do some prewriting, such as listing everything that stood out about each movie and then lining them up, detail for detail.

ORGANIZATION

"Disappointed"

Rating: 5 (Organization)

"The organization enhances and showcases the central idea or theme. The order, structure, or presentation of information is compelling and moves the reader through the text" (NWREL, 2003).

Dear Principal Jones,

I was disappointed to hear that the school incentive program has been cancelled. I know that I really enjoyed the trips this year. I feel that cancelling the program is bad idea. There are several reasons why the incentive program is helpful in our school.

There are students who probably would not do as much homework or study as much if the incentive was not around. The incentive trips give students a reason to work hard in school. They also give the students something to look forward to. I think that the incentive program is a good way to keep student on track throughout the school year.

The incentive program also disaplines behavior in the class room. The program keeps talkative students quiet because they want to go on the trips. The quiet atmosphere helps other students work and concentrate. This in turn earns them better grades.

The incentive program is a good way to teach responsibility. Students have to keep track of the cards all week. This teaches students how to organize thore belongings and assignments so that nothing gets lost. This skill helps student all the way through college.

I belive that cancelling the incentive program is a bad idea. I feel that some students will not try as hard in school without a reason to work. I also think that the class rooms will become much less displined without cards. This could make it hard for other students to work, resulting in low comprehension of the subject. This could have serious effects in the future. Please do not cancel the incentive program.

Sincerely,

Rationale for 5 Rating in Organization

This paper has an attention-grabbing opener: "I was disappointed to hear." Even before stating its main ideas, the paper draws in the reader. Once the main idea, canceling the incentive program is a bad idea for many reasons, is out, the writer follows a logical sequence by detailing each consequence, illustrating, and justifying. The transitions are smooth from problem to solution, from cause to effect. The whole piece comes back full circle and has a definite note of finality when the writer asks the principal, "Please do not cancel the incentive program."

"Siblings"

Rating: 3 (Organization)

"The organizational structure is strong enough to move the reader through the text without too much confusion" (NWREL, 2003).

My sister Virginia and my brother Bob are very different. They hardly have any similarities. The thing they don't have in common is that Virginia is very tall and Bob is still a little short. Though they have differences, they are alike in some ways.

Virginia is fun to hang out with. She doesn't realy get annoying. She has a lot of patience with other people. Something Virginia does is also different from what Bob does is she won't change her mind if she has decided on something.

Bob is very annoying. He talks non-stop. He plays football. Bob loves all of the attention he gets, whether it is positive or negative.

Both Virginia and Bob are generally good people. Both of them play sports. Bob and Virginia love to be social. They hate anything strenuous. When asked what they are going to do after school, they would reply either going with my friends or some kind of athletic practice.

Even thought they are both my siblings, I can only be around one of them for a short time. Both Virginia and Bob have friends who are fun to talk to. I am lucky to have two siblings who I don't argue with all the time, but with Bob I sometimes come close.

Rationale for 3 Rating in Organization

This paper would benefit from a little imagination. The details are there, but the structure is too obvious. The point of the paper is stated in the very first paragraph rather than waiting until the reader has been hooked with an attention-grabber. After that, the paper reads more like a brainstormed list of how the siblings are the same, followed by how they are different. The concluding paragraph does not provide a satisfying ending but rather opens new ideas and ends in a detail rather than a conclusion.

"Ninth (Homework) Hour"

Rating: 1 (Organization)

"The writing lacks a clear sense of direction. Ideas, details, or events seem strung together in a loose or random fashion; there is no identifiable internal structure" (NWREL, 2003).

Organization

> Dear Principal Jones,
>
> 9th hour was a big sucsess and a huge help for me, because I found that I got a lot of work done. I think the 6th graders should have to have 9th hours next year. I also found that when I got home I had barely any homework, and lots of time to play or study for a test.
>
> When you are involved in a sport, it is hard to get your homework done, so that is why 9th hours is successful. I definetly would not mind having 9th hour again. 9th hour keeps you organized and in your sorts. We have agendas that we have to have filled in each day, and it has to be signed as well.
>
> I had _____ for my 9th hour teacher, and he was always late, and always forgot about 9th hour.
>
> I think that the kids next year should have 9th hours. So keep 9th hours so the kids next year, won't have as much homework, it was a help for me, and should be a help for them.
>
> From,
>
> _____

Rationale for 1 Rating in Organization

This paper doesn't seem to have any preconceived structural plan. The points the writer makes are not in any discernible order. Indentations suggest paragraphs, but after the opening sentence of each paragraph, the writer wanders away from the apparent topic sentence. This writer needs to take the information here, plan an order for it that includes main points in a meaningful sequence, and then develop it with illustrations. An inviting opening and an ending that feels final would also help.

VOICE

"The Highlight of the Year"

Rating: 4/5 (Voice)

"The writer speaks directly to the reader in a way that is individual, compelling and engaging. The writer "aches with caring," yet is aware and respectful of the audience and the purpose for writing" (NWREL, 2003).

Dear Principal Jones,

The highlight of every Junior Higher's school year are the incentive trips. These trips to different places in the state of _____ are a good way to reward the kids who have done good in class. From the information that I have heard, the incentive trips have been canceled for next year; we need to keep them.

There are many reasons why I think that the incentive trips should be kept. The first reason is that if you keep the cards and trips, then the teachers won't have such a hard time disciplining rowdy kids. If the trips are canceled and you keep the card punches, then the kids won't be affected if their card is punched. Most of the kids in my class hated it when their cards got punched because it took away their chances of going on the trips. So you see, if you take away half of the program, such as the trips, then the system will not work at all. If that program doesn't work then the students would get detentions. As you can see, we need to keep this incentive system otherwise there would be crazy teachers always yelling at students and bringing down their self-esteem.

If the school is not able to keep the program going to other places then we should come up with inspirations on what to do here at school. One option that I thought might work if finances fail, is to have movie days here at school. I got this idea from the one day that had this year. I had a lot of fun doing that and it would be a great incentive "trip" for us.

I believe that we should keep the incentive program going even if we don't go somewhere exotic. My class and I personally liked it and would be crushed if it stopped. I think that it is a great reward for kids who do well in school

Sincerely,

_____

Rationale for 5 Rating in Voice

This writer is committed to getting that incentive program back, and if the principal doesn't know how, that's okay because this young person already has a plan, and it's an inspired one! The writer goes out on a limb when describing the potential for "crazy teachers always yelling at students and bringing down their self-esteem." The writer also takes a risk and reveals something of him/herself by explaining just how bad it would be to lose this program (the writer and friends "would be crushed") and just how much of a sacrifice they're willing to make to keep the program (movie days at school rather than expensive trips).

"With Great Appreciation"

Rating: 2/3 (Voice)

"The writer seems sincere, but not fully engaged or involved. The result is pleasant or even personable, but not compelling" (NWREL, 2003).

Dear Principal Jones,

I am writing to you saying you keep 9th hour for next year's 7th graders. I think that 9th hours is an oppertunity to get homework done. You should also make it about 5 minutes longer. I like have 9th hour from September to October. I think that next year's 7th graders will thank you for giving them ninth hour. The 9th hour teachers must be a little more strict on kids. You will be greatly appreciated for keeping the 9th hour. I think that if you had no work in 9th hour, the teachers would still give you something to do. Ninth hour should be around for years to come. I like 9th hours. I got a lot of my homework done in 9th hour when it lasted and so will next year's 7th graders.

Sincerly,

_____

Rationale for 2/3 Rating in Voice

This writer doesn't have the passion or commitment of the previous one. The lukewarm tone of words and phrases like "opportunity" and "should be around" indicate that this writer doesn't care all that much about the topic. The writer "like(s) 9th hours" and that's as far as it goes. The writer attempts only a weak connection with the reader and no major call to action. The author seems sincere but doesn't express any heartfelt emotion or personal investment in the topic.

Voice

"Older Sister vs. Younger Sister"

Rating: 1/2

"The writer seems indifferent, uninvolved, or distanced from the topic and/or the audience" (NWREL, 2003).

There are many differences between my older sister and my younger sister besides their age. Such as where they live, where they work and how they look.

My younger sister, Susan, lives in the town of _____. My older sister, Lisa, lives in the state of _____ in her own house. Susan lives with her parents and one sibling, While Lisa lives with her husband.

Susan doesn't have a real job, since she's only 11. Although she does make a profit by selling "Retro Rings" at Barney's Store with a neighborhood friend. Lisa has a real job, after attending college, at a company which makes and sells parts for the Toyota car company.

Both my sisters do not look alike. Susan has short, blond curly hair with blue eyes and freckles. Lisa has shoulder length, brown, straight hair, with brown eyes and now freckles. The only the thing they share in looks is that they are both shorter. But my younger sister has the potennial to be taller than expected.

So as you can see my younger sister and older sister have very little in common. Yet like most people they have a few interests and traits in common.

Rationale for 1 Rating in Voice

This paper may be accurate, but it doesn't seem to have struck the writer's fancy. It has the feel of a topic that was not one the writer really chose unless it was the lesser of evils. At one point, the paper starts to get interesting (Susan must be quite the little entrepreneur), but the writer chooses not to develop the point, especially not in comparing and contrasting the two sisters. The writer has given a bare minimum of details, which makes it hard to get a feel for the person behind the words. What does the writer think and feel personally about these two?

WORD CHOICE

"Best Friends for Life"

Rating: 5 (Word Choice)

"Words convey the intended message in a precise, interesting, and natural way. The words are powerful and engaging" (NWREL, 2003).

Melissa and I have been best friends since we were two years old. We almost everything together, but we have very different personalities.

Melissa loves punk music, skate boarding and Chinese food. She doesn't like police dramas or television or going to church. Melissa is about 5'3" tall. She wears baggy jeans and T-shirts with her favorite bands' logo on them. Melissa also often dies her hair wild colors, like pink or blue.

I love country music, 4-H, and Taco Bell. I love all television, especially "Darmah and Gregg." I am 5'9" tall. I wear cowboy boots, Levi's 505 jeans, a big belt, and a T-shirt. I love going to Nashville, TN, and seeing where my favorite stars love to be.

Although Melissa and I are very different, we still have some similarities. We both love going to festivals to see our favorite bands. We both love walking on the lake trail. We both like the television show "Family Guy. But most of all we like each other.

Melissa and I are best friends. We probably always will be. We have even planned to go to college together. Melissa and I fight sometimes, but through it all we know that we will always be friends.

Rationale for 5 Rating in Word Choice

The word choice here sounds natural for a teenager as she talks about her friend, and it also contains a wealth of precise information. The author isn't just tall; she is 5'9" tall. She doesn't just wear jeans; she wears Levi's 505 jeans. This author uses concrete descriptions, appeals to the senses (Can you smell Taco Bell?), and chooses specifics (proper nouns, even) such as "Darmah and Gregg" when explaining her entertainment preferences. Although we may get a somewhat more detailed and precise picture of the writer than of Melissa, we can definitely see the two of them—Melissa with pink hair and the author towering over her in cowboy boots—as they rock out at a music festival.

"Two Wild Animals"

Rating: 3/4 (Word Choice)

"The language is functional, even if it lacks much energy. It is easy to figure out the writer's meaning on a general level" (NWREL, 2003).

When you have two wild animals in your house, it's hard to get things done or do thing peacefully. The name of these two wild animals is Bill and Doris. They are my little brother and sister. Though they are both alike, they are also very different.

Bill is in the 7th grade and has hasle eyes, blondish darkish hair, and is on the skinny side. Doris is in the 4th grade and has brown eyes, brown hair, is tall and slim. They both are athletic but life different sports. Bill likes to play soccer and he loves to roller blade. Doris likes soccer, capture the flag, basketball, football, and loves to ride bikes. As you can see, the physical features and what sports they like are different.

Their personalities are very different. Bill doesn't play outside much. He likes to play indoors, go on the computer, watch TV, and go places with friends. He also isn't that loud but, he is a very picky eater. You can count on two hands what he likes to eat. There are no other exceptions.

Doris absolutely loves to play outside. She always playing outside with neighbors outside playing games. She also likes to fish. She also likes to go see movies at the theatre with my parents. Doris is very loud and obnoxious sometimes. If she doesn't get her way she complains a lot and becomes difficult.

As you read my brother and sister area alike and different in many ways. Sometimes for better, other times for worse. I just have to go with the flow.

Rationale for 3/4 Rating in Word Choice

This piece gets off to a good start with "wild animals" describing the author's two siblings, but it turns a little timid after that as word choice becomes generic. Specifics would help, such as replacing "tall and slim" with 5'8" and 110 pounds, or "ride bikes" with "crash her titanium mountain bike down Goblins Gulch." Other places where revision for more specific, concrete, sensory-appealing word choice would help include "play indoors," "outside playing games," "movies," and "go places." Verb choice is too often a form of "be" used as the main verb rather than an action verb, and phantom subjects ("There are no other exceptions"—with a subject that serves no purpose) rob the language of interest.

"Video Games vs. School"

Rating: 1 (Word Choice)

"The writer struggles with a limited vocabulary, searching for words to convey meaning" (NWREL, 2003).

This is my esay. It is going to be comparing and contrasting video games and school.

The difference between video games and school is that you can play it for how long you want. Video games you can choose what game you want to play. You can play video games at home or at someone's house. Video games are better than homework.

School is different from video games because there are more your friends with you. You are always walking around in the halls or in a class room. You don't watch the T.V. all day. Your always doing the same thing. In school you get homework.

School and video games are alike in some ways. When you play video games you sit down and in school you sit down. You can eat during school or during playing video games. They both can be fun. You can learn from both of them.

These two things are alike in some ways and different in others. These things can be boring and fun at different times. This is the difference Between them.

Rationale for 1 Rating in Word Choice

This paper would benefit from a word hunt to find and replace tired, overused words, including "fun," "you," "it," "there," "want," and more. If the writer participated in an activity to generate ideas, much better words might have been elicited—for example, what are the names of the video games? Car Jacker II? Space Invaders? And what classes is the writer really thinking of when using the words "class room"? Beginning algebra? The history of Mesopotamia? Thinking of point of view would also help the author to come up with better word choice—in other words, tell this as a narrative in which the writer relates actual experiences. That approach would elicit concrete nouns and precise adjectives and perhaps get rid of forms of "be" as main verbs and replace them with action verbs.

Word Choice

SENTENCE FLUENCY

"The Problems of Ninth Hour"

Rating: 5 *(Sentence Fluency)*

"The writing has an easy flow, rhythm and cadence. Sentences are well built, with strong and varied structure that invites expressive oral reading" (NWREL, 2003).

Dear Principal Jones,

On the first day of school it seemed like I would never get to leave. After a grulling day of listening to rules and lectures, all I wanted to do was leave and relax at home. Instead, I had to stay one more hour. I did not have any assignments, so all I did was sit and wait. On the days that we did have assignments, I did not want to get everything out and set up for ten minutes just to have to put it away again. You had to have all your books packed up by the time the bell rang because the buses only waited four minutes.

Some of the 9th hour teachers would not let you leave the room. This ment that if you had to ask a teacher a specific question about homework, you had to wait and see them after 9th hour. The same thing happened if you wanted to use the computer lab. You had to sign up after 9th hour to use it. These problems made it nearly impossible to work during 9th hour.

I think that 9th hours is good for some student who have truble getting motivated or are distracted at home. I think that students who are getting poor grades in class should have to stay after for extra help. Other students could choose to stay after. I feel that this plan would bennifet all students.

Sincerely,

_____

Rationale for 5 Rating in Sentence Fluency

This paper would be especially effective if the principal had to hear it out loud. The writer has used the structure of the sentences purposefully to make points. For example, a short sentence opens the second paragraph and states the problem. Then a longer sentence explains, followed by another short sentence to drive home the point. The sentence types, lengths, and openers have variety, and that variety keeps the message from getting cold and boring. Not only is the order of the sentences graceful, but the order of words (the phrasing) within the sentences is also pleasing (even though the tone is complaining).

"Don't Deprive Next Year's Students"

Rating: 3 (Sentence Fluency)

"The text hums along with a steady beat, but tends to be more pleasant or businesslike than musical, more mechanical than fluid" (NWREL, 2003).

Dear Principal Jones,

I am now aware that the next year's incentive program has been taken away as an effect of the referendum. I think it is a big mistake to deprive next year's students of this program. It helps a lot.

The incentive program keeps the students in line as far as homework and behavior at school go. By using the incentive cards the students only have 4 chances per week to mess up. If they go over five, they start to get detentions, and if they lose two of the cards, they stay back from the trips. Therefore this keeps the students out of trouble.

An idea I have recently thought of to lower prices of trips is to have more at-school activities as trips. So the bus prices will greatly lower. Another idea would be to have only 2 out of school trips; this was 1/2 of the money. Our trips' costs will be deducted. I know the school lunch administrator said that we could not turn on the soda machines during the day, but I think if we would, we could go on at least one big bus trip with the earnings.

I think it is a big mistake to deprive next year's students of the incentive program. It keeps the students in line as far as schoolwork and behavior goes in school. I belive that if you can at least consider this paper and the other students' in my class also, maybe it will work.

Sincerely,

_____

Rationale for 3 Rating in Sentence Fluency

Although this piece has a variety of sentence lengths, types, and openings, the sentences themselves are sometimes awkward. The paper would benefit from an oral reading by someone other than the writer so that the writer can hear where the reader stumbles or doesn't give the appropriate intonation in a first reading. Phrases and clauses are correctly but not always gracefully joined. The very first sentences in the first and third paragraphs are good examples. This paper could easily become a 5 with a little revision.

Sentence Fluency

"Earning the Privilege"

Rating: 1/2 (Sentence Fluency)

"The reader has to practice quite a bit to give this paper a fair interpretive reading" (NWREL, 2003).

Dear Principal Jones,

I am writing to you to tell you that I, along with many other students, agree that we should keep the incentive program. Students have to earn the privilege of going, and as for the students that have a horrible attitude, poor behavior, and don't do there homework should not be privileged of going. Students should relize that being great in class can lead to great results. So all of the students that are willing, to try should have the chances of going and having a fantastic time. Thank you, have a super day.

Sincerely,

_____

Rationale for 1/2 Rating in Sentence Fluency

This paper does not suffer from simplicity of sentence construction as many new writers' papers do but rather from attempting some sophisticated constructions over which the writer did not have complete command. The first two sentences should be broken into their individual phrases and clauses and then some experimenting should be done to see what sounds best (or at least more clear).

Sentence Fluency

CONVENTIONS

"An Excellent Reward"

Rating: 5 (Conventions)

"The writer demonstrates a good grasp of standard writing conventions (e.g., spelling, punctuation, capitalization, grammar, usage, paragraphing) and uses conventions effectively to enhance readability. Errors tend to be so few that just minor touch-ups would get this piece ready to publish" (NWREL, 2003).

Dear Principal Jones,

I understand that the Incentive Program has been canceled due to lack of money in the school. I think that is terrible.

The Incentive Program motivates kids to behave well in class. Without the Incentive Program teacher will probably be giving out detentions rather than punching cards. Most kids would rather take ten detentions rather than not go on an Incentive trip.

The Incentive Program is an excellent way to reward students for their good behavior. This year if a student didn't get out in 2 cards or more, that student would get to go on the trip. We went to Devil's Lake, The Petit Ice Center, Sunburst, the bowling alley and Six Flags. All of these places are excellent reasons for students to be good.

There are many ways of keeping the Incentive Program while saving money. We could have in-school activities like a game day, a movie day, an athletic day and a bunch more. We could also have the Lock-in or Six Flags trip with some in-school trips that cost little or no money. For the Lock-in or Six Flags we could organize fundraisers to raise money for these events.

The Incentive Program needs to be saved. There are so many ways we could save it if we work together. It does so much good, and I think if is something the school needs.

Sincerely,

_____

Rationale for 5 Rating in Conventions

A 5 rating does not require a perfect paper, but no mistakes in conventions are readily apparent in this one. One possibility, however, is the use of the numeral *2* instead of the word "2." Although different style manuals may set the upper limit at different places (ten is most common for spelling out numerals), "two" as a word, not a number, is fairly universal. Students should not be penalized for attempting constructions that are beyond their grade level, although corrections should be made during the editing phase of the writing process.

Conventions

"Anything but School!"

Rating: 3/4 (Conventions)

"The writer shows reasonable control over a limited range of standard writing conventions. Conventions are sometimes handled well and enhance readability; at other times, errors are distracting and impair readability" (NWREL, 2003).

Dear Principal Jones,

I think it is bad that they got rid of the incentive program. Us kids are good for a long time to be able to go on these trips. Now that this is gone not all of us are going to be good any more. Incentive trips are a great way to get a break from school.

We don't need alot of money to have a good incentive trip. It could be as simple as a movie day, just anything that doesn't involve school.

Teachers are going to get even more bad students than they already have. This could really effect our school's reputation.

We must keep the incentive program, Even if it means having an all gym day or movie day. It doesn't matter if it is cheap or expensive, as long as it's anything but school!

Sincerely,

_____

Rationale for 3/4 Rating in Conventions

The most glaring error in this paper is a grammar/usage one ("Us kids") that could be considered by some grammar scholars to be a status marker, a mistake that readers interpret as a sign of the writer's lack of formal education. Other errors are not of great significance, such as "alot," a common error for all ages, and the capitalization mistake in the next-to-the-last sentence ("Even" following a comma), which is likely a proofreading mistake. This paper could become a 5 with 5 minutes of editing.

Conventions

"Please, Only One Week"

Rating: 1 (Conventions)

"Errors in spelling, punctuation, capitalization, usage and grammar and/or paragraphing repeatedly distract the reader and make text difficult to read" (NWREL, 2003).

Dear Principal Jones,

This is John Ellis. I'm conserned about next years 7th Graders. I thought you should send a form to the elementry asking if the would want 9th hour. Explain it to them in the form, because I remember wanting to come to seventh grade because you get out early compared to the other school. Admit to them to do work outside, so they get some fresh air. My expierence wasn't the best. I think if they have to nith hour they should hire out food and drink in classroom because you are starving. Principal Jones, one deffinate thing is make sure that if they make them have ninth hour, make all the rooms big and open because alot of times. My old 9th hour teacher got mad because we were standing up because she couldn't see our hand. Please at least only have it a week . . .

Sincerely,

_____

Rationale for 1/2 Rating in Conventions

The writer misspells "conserned," "elementry," "compaired," and "deffinate," all of which are likely to be words the writer does not commonly write since the mistakes don't look like proofreading errors (although "nith" obviously is since it is spelled correctly elsewhere, and "expierence" may be a typographical error). These mistakes, along with some punctuation errors (comma preceding "because") distract the reader from the paper's message.

Conventions

Index